threads
SEW
SMARTER, BETTER & FASTER

threads

SEW

SMARTER, BETTER & FASTER

894 SEWING TIPS, FITTING FIXES, *and* HANDY TECHNIQUES

Editors, Contributors & Readers of *Threads*

The Taunton Press

The Taunton Press
Inspiration for hands-on living®

The Taunton Press, Inc.,
63 South Main Street,
PO Box 5506,
Newtown, CT 06470-5506
e-mail: tp@taunton.com

Editor: Renee Iwaszkiewicz Neiger
Developmental editors: Francine LaSala and Sarah Rutledge Gorman
Copy editor: Betty Christiansen
Indexer: Cathy Goddard
Cover and Interior design: carol singer | notice design
Layout: carol singer | notice design

The following names/manufacturers appearing in *Threads Sew Smarter, Better & Faster* are trademarks: Bestine®, Bounce®, Burda®, ChapStick®, Clover Mini Iron™, Crayola®, Dritz® Jean-a-ma-jig™, Dylon®, Easy-Knit®, Fiebing's®, Formica®, Fray Block™, Fray Check™, Fuse-A-Shade™, Gingher®, Glad® Press'n Seal®, Grabbit®, Hump Jumper®, iPod®, Jones Tones 400-Plexi Glue™, June Tailor®, Krylon®, Liquid Paper®, Microsoft®, Mylar®, New-Skin®, Nexcare™, Parowax™, Pellon®, Pigma® Micron®, Ping-Pong®, Plasti-Tak®, Plexiglas®, Polarfleece®, Post-it® Notes, Q-tip®, Rit®, Rubbermaid®, Schmetz Needles®, Scotch® Magic™ Tape, Seams Great™, Sharpie®, Snuggle®, Sobo®, Static Guard®, Steam-a-Seam®, Stitch Witchery®, Sulky® Solvy™, Sulky® Sticky+™, Synthrapol®, Teflon®, Thread Heaven®, 3M™ Command™, 3M™ Micropore™, Tiger Tape™, Tintex™, Tulip®, Ultrasuede®, Vaseline®, Velcro®, Vilene®, Warm Window®, Wash Away™ Wonder Tape, Wonder-Under®, X-Acto®

Library of Congress Cataloging-in-Publication Data in progress

ISBN 978-1-62113-797-9

Printed in the United States of America
10 9 8 7 6 5 4 3 2 1

ACKNOWLEDGMENTS

Special thanks to the readers, authors, editors, copy editors, and other staff members of *Threads* and The Taunton Press books department who contributed to the making of this book.

CONTENTS

INTRODUCTION

These pages are packed with sewing wisdom from knowledgeable sewing professionals, teachers, industry leaders, and home sewers.

At Threads magazine, we love to make new sewing discoveries and share them with our readers. We are also happy participants in a sewing conversation with the Threads community that now spans nearly three decades. It is our readers who push us to be our best, to test—and test again—new sewing techniques, tools, projects, and materials. And it is our readers who are responsible for the book you now hold.

Collected here for the first time are favorite tips, tricks, shortcuts, and sewing savvy from Threads' editors, contributors—and, most important, readers.

Need a quick alternative to basting? Try spray adhesive to keep fabric layers from shifting. Want to become an ace at straight seams and smooth corners? Practice sewing on gingham (it's symmetrical print is a great guide). Wish your invisible zipper would stay invisible? Serging the seam allowance edges first is the answer. Ever wish you had a third hand to help with a project? Use your sewing machine presser foot as a "sewing bird" to hold fabrics for easier ripping or hand sewing. In these pages, you will find a treasure of sewing tips like these—and much more.

These pages are packed with sewing wisdom from knowledgeable sewing professionals, teachers, industry leaders, and home sewers. Here is all the sewing know-how you may ever need, from a passionate community of people who love sewing. We hope you will enjoy each and every page!

PART ONE

MATERIALS

& more

FABRIC

BUYING FABRIC

Search for Swatch Sales

—PATRICIA C. ELKOVITCH,
SKANEATELES, NY

Looking for a great way to build a beautiful fabric collection? Check in with local designers, who will sometimes sell swatches of discontinued designer fabrics at very reasonable prices. Some designers and upholstery shops may even donate obsolete fabric samples and leftovers.

HOW TO BUY THE RIGHT AMOUNT OF FABRIC

Do you often end up with more fabric than required for a given project? Here's how to create a reusable vinyl template to help determine exactly how much fabric is needed for all possible fabric widths before shopping for the fabric. You may be surprised to see how much fabric you will save by knowing the exact amount you need to buy.

Make the Template

1 Purchase 6 yd. of 60-in.-wide fabric-backed vinyl, and cut the vinyl into two 3-yd. lengths, which will make it easier to work with. (When you need a longer piece, place them end to end.)

2 Using a long straightedge and permanent markers, draw four lines in different colors along the length of each piece—one line for each of the common fabric widths available: 30 in., 45 in., and 60 in.

3 Mark the lengthwise foldline location for each of the fabric widths, as if you were going to fold each fabric width in half, at 15 in., 22½ in., and 30 in. Use dotted lines to distinguish the foldlines from the full-width lines with the corresponding color.

4 Using a different marker color, mark the entire length of vinyl in ⅛-yd. increments. Store the vinyl on a roll to prevent fold marks.

Use the Template

1 Purchase patterns prior to buying the fabric, or use patterns from your stash.

2 Cut out the appropriate pattern pieces, alter them if necessary, and then press them flat.

3 Spread the vinyl on the floor or table and place the pattern pieces on the vinyl to determine exactly how much fabric is needed.

—LIV MANZER, VICTORIA, BRITISH COLUMBIA, CANADA

Collect Textile Souvenirs
—DIANNE BOATE,
SAN FRANCISCO, CA

Have traveling friends or family members? Give them some money to buy fabric from exotic locales they visit. They will benefit from the added adventure, and you'll receive some unusual and fascinating fabrics.

Create a Design File Card
—JEAN MARGOLIS,
SEBASTOPOL, CA

When planning a multifabric design, prepare a design file card to carry to fabric stores, including a sketch of the garment with a number assigned to each part for which you are planning a different fabric. Staple fabric samples you have on hand and add appropriate yardage notes and facts needed.

PREPPING FABRIC

Prewash Silky Fabrics
—KATHY WAGNER, SEATTLE, WA

Silk charmeuse and other silky fabrics are extremely slippery and sometimes difficult to sew. Prewashing the fabric with Synthrapol® (a product typically used as a prewash and afterwash when dyeing fabric) and adding liquid starch to the rinse water makes a friendlier fabric. It's best to hang the fabric to dry and press it lightly before sewing. The pins stay in the fabric better, and the fabric has a little friction to make sewing easier with minimal slipping. Although it's always best to test a swatch first, if you wash or dry-clean the fabric after sewing, it returns to normal.

Partially Preshrink Denim
—JULIETTE CURTIS,
LEEMING, WESTERN AUSTRALIA

Everybody knows that old jeans fit best: They have shrunk and stretched until they conform to curves. You can completely preshrink denim by washing and drying it three times, but if you make your own jeans, wash and dry the denim material just once. This lets the denim do most of its shrinking before you cut out the jeans, but it also allows it to shrink a little the first few times you wash the completed jeans. The jeans will not shrink radically—just enough to give that perfect-jeans fit. Denim shrinks mostly in length, so consider cutting the jeans an inch longer than the desired finished length.

Preshrink Seam Tape
—JANN JASPER, NEW YORK, NY

It's a good idea to preshrink seam tape, twill tape, and other such materials with your fabric. To avoid having to press it when it dries, wrap the damp tape around a large jar to dry.

Preshrink Muslin

—CAROLYN REHBAUM,
ALTAMONTE SPRINGS, FL

Looking for a quick way to preshrink muslin? Cut the amount of muslin you need, place it in a bowl, and pour near-boiling water over it (similar to preshrinking interfacing). Soak until the water is tepid, then wring it out. Place the wet muslin piece in a mixing bowl and dry it using a hair dryer. The bowl allows the hot air to circulate back into the fabric, which makes the drying time shorter.

Keep Fabric Untangled When Prewashing

—MARY JANE MCCLELLAND,
DIAMOND BAR, CA

Does fabric twist and tangle from prewashing, resulting in robust wrinkles that need serious pressing? Do the raw edges unravel into long threads that tie up the contents of the washing machine like some diabolically gift-wrapped package? It's easy to eliminate these issues with prewashing. Sew the two cut ends of the fabric together (right sides or wrong, it doesn't matter) with a ¼-in. seam allowance, which forms one big circular loop of fabric. This works with fabric lengths up to 5 yd.; the fabric loop comes out untwisted every time. Serging works best, because fraying is prevented and the seam allowance is a small ¼ in. However, straight stitching will also do the job, particularly if you zigzag the raw edge. When the fabric is removed from the dryer, clip the ¼-in. seam. Wrinkles and tangling are cut to a minimum, fraying is avoided, time is saved, and only ½ in. of the fabric is lost.

Sand-Wash Silk at Home

—SHEILA CARNEGIE,
VICTORIA, BRITISH COLUMBIA, CANADA

"Sand-wash" silk in the washing machine with great results, particularly with crepe-backed charmeuse and very lightweight silks. This process shrinks the fabric, so be sure to do it *before* cutting into it. Place the fabric and three or four heavy cotton towels in the washer. (For a more distressed look, use a few pairs of jeans instead of the towels.) Add a little mild detergent (no bleach), fill the machine with warm water, and set it to the longest washing cycle (6 to 12 minutes). Complete the wash cycle, but stop the washer before the water drains. Reset the machine to repeat this cycle, leaving the original water and detergent in the machine. Again, stop the machine before it drains, and repeat this start-stop process at least three and up to eight times. Add fabric softener to the final rinse, spin, and dry on medium heat along with four or five softener sheets and a towel. Sheer luxury!

Make Fabric Stiffer

—ANNMARIE WILSON, GARLAND, TX

Cotton-lace netting and other sheers straight from the bolt are never stiff enough to hold their shape. A concoction that stiffens even the limpest fabric is a mixture made from bits and pieces of water-soluble stabilizer. Dissolve a sandwich bag full of scraps with water till you get a thick, pudding-like mixture. (Proportions that work with Sulky® Solvy™ are 1 yd. of soluble to ⅔ cup water.) When the fabric is thoroughly soaked, gently squeeze out the excess moisture, safety-pin the fabric to a wire hanger, and hang it outside to dry. Check on the fabric often and straighten any wrinkles.

Control Fluff on Fleece

—SHERRY STOCKTON, KITCHENER, ONTARIO, CANADA

Prevent all those linty bits created when you cut fleece by reducing the amount of flying fleece before cutting. Mark the wrong side of each garment piece with a safety pin and put the pieces, along with a fabric-softener sheet, into the dryer on the fluff/air cycle. When you pull the pieces out, there won't be any more of that loose fluff.

Dry Fabric without Twisting

—LISHA VIDLER, CORDOVA, TN

To prevent a length of fabric coming out of the dryer as a twisted, skinny rope that is still damp, add two pairs of white athletic socks to the dryer, knotting each sock twice. The socks become solid balls that bounce around in the dryer with the fabric, which prevents the material from collapsing and twisting as it dries. The fabric will come out softer and drier, with minimum wrinkles or twists.

Help Fabric Keep Its Shape in the Dryer

—GRACE MALONEY, OAKVILLE, ONTARIO, CANADA

To dry a large piece of fabric without it losing its shape, try pinning it every 4 in. to 6 in., along the selvages on both sides, before putting it in the dryer. The fabric will come out of the dryer with no wrinkles. It will be slightly damp on the selvages under the pins, but not twisted out of shape, and it may only need a touch-up with your iron.

Dye Topstitched Fabric

—LINDA PRZYBYSZEWSKI, CHARLOTTESVILLE, VA

Topstitching often doesn't accept dye as the garment fabric does (especially in ready-to-wear clothing, since thread is usually synthetic and won't dye). To avoid unexpected and even ugly effects, think through what a garment will look like if the topstitching doesn't change color. Dyeing results are always slightly unpredictable, but this visualization exercise will increase the chance of a successful outcome.

Serge Fabric Ends before Preshrinking

—JANICE MORRILL,
WATERFORD, MI

Serge across the cut ends of fabric to prevent fraying while preshrinking it, especially when using the washing machine. This will help when searching for fabric; the serging will show which fabrics have been preshrunk and which haven't, which is very useful if the fabric has been stored for any length of time.

Prevent Frays on Tiny Edges

—M. PARFITT,
SACRAMENTO, CA

Sewing doll clothes can be frustrating because the tiny fabric pieces can quickly fray right to the seamline. Fray Check™, applied around the edges of all the tiny garment pieces before sewing them, makes finishing the garments easier, especially the threads holding each tiny snap, button, and bead.

Use Wallpaper to Prevent Unwanted Sticking

—CAROL STONER, DENVER, CO

Place a scrap of vinyl wallpaper on your worksurface when sealing the edges of fabric with Fray Check. The glue and fabric won't stick to it.

TESTING FABRIC

Check for Wool

—LAURA ZIEMER,
PORTLAND, OR

To determine if fabric is 100 percent wool, soak a small swatch of it in chlorine bleach for about eight hours. If the swatch dissolves completely, is significantly smaller, or has clearly disintegrated, it's all wool, not a blend. Some wool fabrics have finishes that inhibit the action of the bleach and may not disintegrate entirely. If in doubt, try washing a swatch thoroughly to remove any finishes, then perform the bleach test.

Test Interfacings for Smooth Collars

—FREDERIKA HAUSMAN,
NAPLES, FL

When testing interfacings for collars and other details that need to fold or roll smoothly, be sure to try out different directions for the interfacing grain. Even if the outer fabric is on the straight grain, you can get some of the benefits of bias by fusing a bias-cut interfacing to it. In the same vein, you can get some of the qualities of knit fabrics into your wovens by using knit interfacings either on the bias or cross- and straight-grain directions on straight-grain wovens. The different effect of each choice will be clearly noticeable.

Find Right and Wrong Sides
—ELEANOR BEARDEN, GRANITE BAY, CA

Here's a tip for determining the right from wrong side of fabrics: Rub the fabric across your nose and listen. The right side has a higher pitch than the wrong side.

Test "Dry Clean" Fabric for Washability
—SUSAN HERRMANN, DAMASCUS, OH

Cut a swatch of the fabric to be tested in half and measure each piece. Put one piece of the fabric in a bowl of cold, soapy water for three minutes. Rinse it in cold water, remove excess moisture with a towel, and let it dry—or press it dry if it's silk. Compare this piece with the unwashed half. Also test for water spotting by sprinkling some water on the swatch and letting it dry. To check the darker colors of prints for bleeding, fold a damp swatch in half and let it dry. To machine-wash, pin the measured swatch to a piece of stable fabric, and use the gentle cycle.

CARING FOR FABRIC

Soften Wool with Shampoo
—JO BOYD, FORT COLLINS, CO

To soften a wool sweater that is too harsh and scratchy, simply wash it with shampoo (inexpensive brands work fine) and give it an after-rinse with hair conditioner, following the directions on the bottle. The hair conditioner is the vital ingredient for softening the wool.

Clean Cashmere in the Wash
—LYNN ROOSEVELT, GREENVILLE, SC

Wash wool and cashmere knits in the washing machine if you can control some of the functions manually. Start the washer filling, add soap or wool detergent, and let mix well. Fold each garment into a neat bundle, like packing for a trip. Distribute these bundles evenly around the washer tub. Let the washer fill until the water level just covers the garments, and turn off the machine. Squish the bundles by hand a bit, then let soak a few minutes. After making sure the items are still in their bundles, set the control to drain the tub and let spin for 10 to 15 seconds. Follow the same procedure for the rinse, allowing the tub to spin just a little longer. Shape and dry flat as usual. There won't be any stretching or felting using this procedure, and it is far easier than regular hand washing.

Avoid Shrinking

—DIANNE HUSTON, MORTON, IL

Each time you cut out a new garment, immediately record the care information. On a small index card, describe the garment (red dress, navy skirt), list the fiber content and cleaning instructions, and attach a small swatch of the fabric. Be sure to post this in a handy place, like the laundry room, to avoid shrinking and otherwise ruining the clothes you make and love.

PREVENTING WRINKLES AND PRESSING

Use Silk Organza as a Press Cloth

—FRANCES COWAN, DECATUR, GA

Most press cloths are made of opaque fabrics, so you have to guess whether the fabric underneath is where it's supposed to be. Solve this problem by using silk organza as a press cloth. You can see through it, so you know the fabric being pressed is set up just the way you want. It can be used dry or dampened, and works on wool, silk, or synthetic settings. It won't scorch if pressed with a very hot iron (cotton or linen settings). For your own press cloth, cut a healthy-sized square of silk organza using pinking shears, so the edges won't ravel. That's it!

Ship Dresses with Balloons

—GINNY GROAT, WATKINSVILLE, GA

To keep dresses from wrinkling when they're shipped, try using balloons for packing material. Blow up a small balloon in each sleeve, a larger one in the bodice, and one or two in the skirt. You may even consider adding small balloons to fill in the empty spaces. Even taffeta dresses arrive without wrinkles, and all that "hot air" adds neither weight nor cost.

Press Flat Trims Fast

—TENLEY ALAIMO, BINGHAMTON, NY

To iron trims, tapes, flat cordings, ribbons, or strips of cloth quickly, place a hot iron on a cotton pad over the trim to be ironed. Then apply light pressure to the iron and pull the trims from the back of the iron. Most wrinkles will be removed easily.

Minimize Wrinkles in Linen

—ARIES SELWOOD, COLUMBIA, SC

After laundering small, embroidered linens such as handkerchiefs, tea towels, or lace, lay them out faceup and spread each wet, starched square out to dry on a Formica® countertop or enamel dryer surface. If the items need further pressing, steam-iron them facedown on a white terry cloth towel so as to not flatten the raised embroidery.

Remove Creases from Velvet
—SUSAN HERRMANN, DAMASCUS, OH

Remodeling garments made of velvet requires experimenting to remove the lines left by hem edges, seams, and topstitching. Wet the line with vinegar to soften the fibers and help them unkink. Gently raise the pile with a stiff toothbrush. Velvet can be steamed by pressing lightly on the back with a warm iron (hot iron if the fiber content allows). A blow dryer can be used on the right side to encourage the pile to lift. Steaming the surface of the fabric can be done by holding the iron over it no closer than 1 in. A scrap of cotton velvet can be used as a press cloth; press lightly, right sides together.

Use Snaps Instead of French Tacks
—ELISA J. DENABURG, AIKEN, SC

Do you need to press a lined garment from the wrong side? Pressing darts from the inside independent of the lining requires that the lining hang separately from the garment at the hem. So instead of using the customary French tacks at the side seams to keep the lining from twisting, strategically place a snap at the side and back seams. Simply unsnap the lining from the garment to press from the inside. Try this on any garment with a hanging lining, and see your pressing results improve.

WORKING WITH TRICKY FABRICS

Keep Slippery Fabric in Place
—CARLA LEINBACH, CHARLOTTE, NC

When working with slippery, hard-to-handle fabrics, cover your sewing table with Rubbermaid® rubber grip. It comes in rolls and is normally used to prevent plates and similar items from sliding around. It's inexpensive and leaves no residue (unlike flannel, which leaves fuzz). It's also easy to store when not in use.

Baste Slippery Fabrics
—LONNIE PIPOSZAR, PITTSBURGH, PA

Plain running stitch is sometimes not secure enough for slippery, stretchy fabrics, or for try-ons. Here's a strong alternative that goes in quickly and is easier to remove than backstitch: Hand-baste the entire seam with running stitch; at the end of the seam, turn around and make running stitches of the same size along the entire seam in the opposite direction, filling in the gaps between the stitches you made the first time. Try using lengths of tape laid against the seamline to provide a straightedge to guide hand stitches, which in turn provide a guide for accurate machine stitching. Before basting, be careful to pin at right angles to the seam to be stitched to avoid distortion while basting.

Gather Netting

—JUDITH R. SHAMP,
INDIANAPOLIS, IN

To gather large quantities of net, try using elastic thread. Set your machine to a large zigzag stitch (8 stitches to the inch), and zigzag over the elastic thread, pulling it tightly. The netting will gather up evenly and be ready for sewing where needed.

Make Net Edges Easier to See

—MARGARET C. STORY,
GOODRICH, MI

To make distinguishing the edges of net easier, mark the edge of each piece with a colored marking pen, using a different color for each piece. Cut off the lines with a serger knife so no unwanted marks remain.

Pin Silk

—VICTORIA VALDES-DAPENA-HILTEBEITEL,
COLLEGEVILLE, PA

People usually think of silk as a delicate fabric because of the special care it requires, but silk fiber is as strong as steel. For tightly woven silks, such as China or satin silk, it's sometimes impossible to pierce the fabric with the point of a pin, regardless of the quality of the pin used, and you never want to force the issue because silk will run. This trick for pinning such fabrics works like a charm. As you bring the point of the pin to the fabric, spin the pin between your fingers. It will slide in with little or no resistance.

Keep Miters Straight on Slippery Fabric

—MARGARET C. STORY,
GOODRICH, MI

Using a small piece of Wash Away™ double-sided tape works wonders for holding fabric in place when stitching mitered corners, especially on slippery fabric such as the satin binding on fleece blankets. It prevents the binding fabric from shifting as miters are stitched, but washes out completely when laundered.

Create Warmer Linings

—CORRIE CHORBA,
URBANA, IL

Warm Window® insulation can provide more insulation in winter wear. Its five layers include a metalized Mylar and a decorative cover fabric. Sew this material to a zip-out coat lining, and consider using scraps to line boots.

Machine Sewing Leather

—PATRICIA MORROW,
ERIE, PA

When sewing leather on a sewing machine, use an unthreaded leather needle to pierce stitching holes, usually six to the inch, on the seamlines on each piece. Then, making sure the holes are aligned in each layer, overlap the seam allowances and stitch through the holes with a size 16 needle threaded with button/craft (strong) thread.

Ultrasuede and Facile

—ALIDA MACOR,
MARTINSVILLE, NJ

Skipped stitches can be prevented on Ultrasuede® by using the Schmetz Stretch 75/11 needle (steel-blue color). Cut binding trim on the crosswise rather than the bias grain. To make sure strips are even, use masking tape on the wrong side as a guide. Consider combining two or more tape widths for odd sizes. It's easier if you cut only one section of a double-faced Ultrasuede belt accurately. Fuse it to a slightly larger piece of Ultrasuede, topstitch, and then trim off the excess.

For sewing with Facile, underline the major pieces by fusing Easy-Knit® right to them to provide a little more body. Be sure to preshrink the Easy-Knit in warm water, and dry it flat or hang. Voilà! Flow and fit with the same fabric.

Sewing Vinyl

—J. W. MONKO,
ST. LOUIS, MO

Since vinyl upholstery material is sticky and only sews reluctantly, try wiping a thin coat of Krylon® silicone on the flat area of your sewing machine. The silicone won't harm the vinyl or the machine and will allow the fabric to glide through the machine.

Sewing Foam Rubber

—SUZAN L. WIENER,
SPRING HILL, FL

When sewing fabric that has a foam rubber backing, backing side up, try placing a piece of plastic wrap between the sewing machine presser foot and the fabric. The fabric will move through the machine much easier.

HOW TO REINFORCE THE BRIM OF A FLOPPY HAT

Trying to sew a large-brimmed, floppy hat so it has a bit more drop to the brim? To get a heavier, more graceful fall of the brim, try Fuse-A-Shade™ or any iron-on product designed to make roller window shades from fabric. It's really just a glorified fusible interfacing and can be applied like one, but it's better than a regular interfacing in two ways: It's available in wider widths, and a single layer of Fuse-A-Shade has more weight than several layers of regular interfacing.

—JOHN MANGIAPANE, NAUGATUCK, CT

GRAINLINES

Pin-Pivot the Grainline

—CATHERINE BROMAN,
INVERNESS, FL

Here's a way to quickly align the grainline arrow on a pattern piece to the lengthwise grain of fabric. First, at one end of the grainline arrow, stick a straight pin vertically into the pattern tissue and measure the distance to the selvage. Then hold the pin secure to the cutting mat as you rotate your pattern around the pin, until the opposite end of the arrow is the same distance from the selvage.

ID "Grainline" on Knits

—HEIDI NORMANDIN,
MADISON, WI

Technically, knits don't have a grain as wovens do, but patterns should still be placed properly on the fabric. To find the correct "grainline," rely on a rib rather than the selvage. Lay out the fabric in a single layer, and place a pattern piece. Note the general area of the pattern grainline arrow by placing a finger on the fabric underneath the arrow and then removing the pattern. Take a 6-in. to 8-in. piece of blue painter's tape (or low-tack tape), and gently press it down along a rib, then reposition the pattern on the fabric by aligning the grainline arrow along one edge of the blue tape. For pattern pieces cut on the fold, cut out one half of the pattern and then flip the piece over to cut out the remaining half. Because all that is needed is to match the pattern edge to the edge of the blue tape, it's easy to flip.

Use Masking Tape to Straighten Grain

—MARJORIE DEBENEDICTIS,
TAMUNING, GUAM

Masking tape is a helpful tool when folding fabric selvage to selvage, and straightening the grain prior to cutting, especially with slippery fabrics. Start by placing a strip of masking tape on the fabric's cross-grain at one cut end. Next, tape one selvage to the long side of your cutting table. This enables you to fold the fabric in half lengthwise and align the opposite selvages without shifting. Once the fabric is folded, compare the cross-grain tape positions to determine how closely the fabric is on- or off-grain. If you need to make an adjustment by shifting the fabric, the tape is a helpful guide and makes it easy to straighten the grain.

INTERFACING

Baste with Spray Adhesive to Keep Layers from Shifting

—SUSAN TROUSDALE, HARTINGTON, ONTARIO, CANADA

To prevent layers from shifting when you work with sewn-in interfacing, use a temporary spray baste to secure the layers before stitching. Lay the fabric pieces to be interfaced on a piece of paper (to catch spray drift and to protect the table surface) and then spray them. Next, smooth the interfacing over the fabric piece. It works beautifully, and the two pieces can be treated as one while sewing without risk of shifting.

Make Flesh-Toned Interfacing

—TERESA HERING, TUKWILA, WA

Dye 100 percent cotton or silk fabric using Dylon® cold-water dye to cover shoulder pads or interface facings for any white garment. Both café au lait or cocoa brown shades work better than ecru, tan, or tea dye. They are dark and yet have a softness that fades into the background when the garment is worn. The dyes are permanent and easy to use. Dye a yard or two at a time and then use the fabric for facings or covering the pads. Try using dyed material to interface areas where a zipper goes in, or where fabrics are overlapped, like plackets or pockets. With a commercial interfacing, place the dyed interfacing between the wrong side of the fashion fabric and the commercial interfacing, baste the two together, and use them as one piece. The results are well worth the time taken: Facings, shoulder pads, or any other underlayers won't show on the finished garment.

Use Fusible Webbing with Flesh-Toned Interfacing

—SHARON WILSON, WAVELL HEIGHTS, QUEENSLAND, AUSTRALIA

Make flesh-toned interfacing also by using suitably colored lightweight fabric. Attach fusible webbing to the flesh-toned fabric and use as regular fusible interfacing. Both the Vilene® and Pellon® brands of fusible webbing work with equal success.

Try Cotton Cross-Stitch Canvas for Interfacing

—JULIE RHODES, CEDAR, MI

Cotton cross-stitch canvas is an easy-to-use, washable alternative for handbag and hat interfacing. It's firm but can be shaped, layered, trimmed, and sewn to fit. It's available in a variety of thread counts and can be found reasonably priced in craft and discount stores.

Interface with Sheer Fabrics

—EDITH FRANKEL, HANNAWA FALLS, NY

When using sewn-in interfacing on sheer fabrics, baste it to the top collar piece rather than the undercollar. The interfacing serves as a lining, hiding the seam allowance so it doesn't show through.

Secure Fusible Interfacing

—PATRICIA CLEMENTS, MADISON, TN

Since nonwoven interfacings tend to fuzz after repeated washings, use them only in enclosed areas. Fusible interfacing can also come loose, even after careful fusing. Here's how to prevent that. Place a sheet of tracing paper under the interfacing and use a tracing wheel to trace the seamline. Then cut the interfacing with pinking shears just outside the seamline. Fuse and sew as usual. The stitching just catches the pinked edges.

BUTTONHOLES

Create Buttonholes in Fleece

—JENNIFER ROBISON, RAVENNA, OH

When making buttonholes on fleece, place a piece of AquaFilm water-soluble stabilizer over the area to be stitched. It holds down the fleece and does not allow any fleece fuzz to show between the buttonhole stitches.

Make Buttonholes in Tweedy Fabrics

—KAREN WOLFF, LAGUNA HILLS, CA

Multicolored tweed fabrics often pose a challenge when it's time to make buttonholes. While there is often a variety of colors in the fabric that can be matched, selecting just one can create a buttonhole that calls attention to itself when it's preferred that the buttons or other details be the focal point. To help the buttonholes blend into the background more effectively, select a couple of complementary colors from the fabric, use a slightly larger needle and a somewhat less-dense buttonhole, and stitch the buttonholes with two colors of thread through the needle.

RIBBON

Use Ribbon as
Reinforcement

—SUSAN SWEET, RICHMOND, CA

Consider using a ¼-in.-wide ribbon in garment shoulder seams instead of twill tape. With knit and woven fabrics, it reinforces and prevents the seam from stretching. It's also cheaper than twill tape and comes in just about every color, so matching is never a problem.

Smooth Ribbon with a
Curling Iron

—TERESA MURDERS, SALEM, OR

Use a curling iron to "press" out wrinkles on ribbons, bias tape, and so forth. An automatic shutoff option is a plus as it can be left on constantly, instead of having to switch it off and on while sewing. Convenient and quick!

HOW TO USE RIBBON FOR BRIDAL LACE-UP

The zipper placket on my daughter's wedding gown did not lie as flat as I wanted. It had decorative, nonfunctional fabric-covered buttons on top of the zipper placket down its entire length. I added button loops to make the buttons appear functional while making the placket snug. Bridal elastic button looping is not available in my area, and it might have been too bulky to use without opening the zipper seam first, which I didn't want to do.

Remembering how snugly ice skates are tightened, I made a series of vertical tacks (wide zigzag stitches with zero stitch length) on the nonplacket side of the zipper directly over the zipper topstitching opposite every button— a total of 22 tacks. Using one long piece of ⅛-in.-wide ribbon, I pulled a loop through each tack using a small latch hook, forming approximately ⅜-in.-diameter loops that were ready to be buttoned. I anchored the top end of the ribbon just above the highest tack; the other end remained unattached until the day of the wedding.

After my daughter put the gown on and the zipper was closed, the loops were placed over the buttons from top to bottom, then pulled snug around each button, with the excess ribbon eased toward the waist. The ribbon was secured with small stitches at the base of the zipper just under the lowest tack, with the excess ribbon hidden in her skirt. The zipper placket remained flat and secure throughout the ceremony and the reception.

The bride was snipped out of the dress by cutting the ribbon. With the ribbon removed, the "fix" remains invisible. Now it's just a wonderful memory of a perfect January winter wedding.

—LAURIE NAUSS, SAUQUOIT, NY

THREAD

CONTROLLING THREAD

Double-Thread with Separate Threads

—ANGÉLIQUE SAROLEA,
VISTA, CA

To prevent knots from forming when hand sewing with a double strand of thread, never use a single strand folded in half. Because the two sides of the thread are running in opposite directions, they'll tangle and knot. Instead, cut two separate strands, keeping them in the same direction as they came off the spool, and thread them together through the needle.

HOW TO DEAL WITH THREAD NAP

Doing all hand stitching with the nap of the thread down from the needle will result in fewer tangles and knots, less untwisting and abrasion, and a better appearance because the thread nap will react uniformly to light rays. However, it's not always easy to figure out how the nap goes on some threads.

You can test wool for direction of nap by drawing the strand up and down between thumb and forefinger. The beginning of the smooth pass is the end that should go in the needle, with the waste knot at the other end.

Unfortunately, sense of touch doesn't work on all fibers. Filaments—man-made or silkworm-made—aren't a problem, because they are single continuous strands without nap, but other threads can be tricky. The best way to find the nap on these fibers is to compare two freshly cut ends of the thread. One end is always more rounded and more tightly twisted than the other, which tends to splay outward. If the difference isn't obvious, gently blow on the two ends. The rounded end is the top of the nap-down end and should enter the eye of the needle.

—BEE BORSSUCK, SCOTTSDALE, AZ

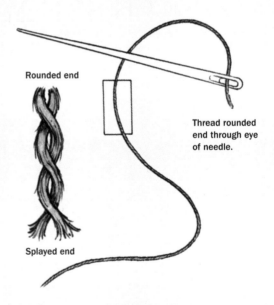

Rounded end

Splayed end

Thread rounded end through eye of needle.

Help Coned Thread Unwind
—LOIS CARROLL, PARMA, OH

When sewing with a large cone of thread, try placing it in an empty coffee can on the floor and thread the machine as usual. Since the thread is below the machine, it will unwind easily.

Get Perfect Tension
—APRIL MOHR, *THREADS* CONTRIBUTOR

Perfect your sewing machine tension by cutting a 6-in. to 8-in. square from the fabric and stitching a straight line diagonally from corner to corner across the square. Then, with a stitched corner in each hand, stretch the square along the stitching line until a thread breaks. If both the top and bobbin threads break in exactly the same place, the tension is perfect. If only one thread breaks (usually in two places), then that thread's tension is too tight, indicating it's time to either loosen the tension for that thread or tighten the opposite tension. Most of the time a very small adjustment does the trick.

Rein in Loose Thread
—ANNA VICTORIA REICH, ALBUQUERQUE, NM

Some spools of thread fit on the sewing machine spindle too loosely, which causes the thread to unwind too quickly. To help spools behave properly, place a small plastic faucet washer on the top of the spool of thread to restrain it.

HOW TO UNTANGLE TANGLED THREAD WITH VINYL STRIPS

Does your stored thread become a tangled mess of loose, unwound ends? Here's an easy, inexpensive alternative to the commercially packaged vinyl strips (one version is called Thread-Wrap) that keeps any size spool of sewing or serger thread tidy.

Buy a 1-yd. length of clear vinyl at the fabric store. Using a rotary cutter or scissors, cut the vinyl into 1-in. by 6-in. strips (for a custom fit, increase or decrease the dimensions of the strips to correspond to the height or circumference of the spools you frequently use). Simply wrap one strip around a spool and, as it clings to itself, the thread end is held in place. One yard of vinyl you cut into strips yourself will be inexpensive and will probably provide you with all the securing strips you'll ever need.

—CONNIE QUARRÉ, BELLEVUE, WA

Prevent Tangles When Hand Sewing
—SHERRI BROWN, BROOKSVILLE, FL

To keep thread from tangling when hand sewing with a single strand, knot the end that was last cut from the spool. For double thread, knot each end separately.

Use Fabric Softener Sheets to Curtail Knots
—SUZAN L. WIENER, SPRING HILL, FL

Polyester thread won't knot so badly when you're hand sewing if you first rub a sheet of fabric softener over the length of the thread.

Unkink Embroidery Floss with a Damp Sponge
—ANNA VICTORIA REICH, ALBUQUERQUE, NM

Keep a small damp sponge nearby when you're embroidering, and run the floss over the sponge to eliminate folds and creases.

MATCHING THREAD

Match Thread and Fabric
—SANDRA A. TEBBS, TREMONTON, UT

To get perfectly matched threads for hems and topstitching when sewing silks, unravel a few yards of weft from a torn straight edge and wind it onto an empty spool. Since raw silk is too nubby and silk taffetas and china silks tend to be fragile, some experimentation is necessary.

Cover Floss
—EVELYN BLAKE, ROANOKE, VA

Dental floss makes a nearly unbreakable thread for sewing on buttons and hooks, but it's pretty ugly. Unravel a few threads from the straight or cross grain of your fashion fabric and thread them on a needle to quickly cover up the white dental floss.

Create the Illusion of Matching Thread
—HEATHER LANGEMANN, LETHBRIDGE, ALBERTA, CANADA

What can you do if you lose a button and don't have matching thread on hand with which to sew it back on? Choose a thread a shade darker and one a shade lighter, put both colors together in the needle, and use the combination to sew the button back on. From about a foot away, the two colors will create the illusion of matching thread.

WORKING WITH TRICKY THREADS

Add Color with Embroidery Floss
—DONNA C. KORNFELD, DENVER, CO

When you need thread of an odd color for hand sewing, mending, or sewing on a button, try embroidery floss instead of standard spooled thread. It's relatively inexpensive and is available in an extensive array of colors, ranging from soft pastels to vibrant jewel tones. They also come in variegated, shimmery, and metallic colors as well as subtle tone-on-tone color variations. Embroidery floss is also available in mercerized cotton, satin, rayon, linen, and pearl cotton. Standard embroidery floss skeins include six strands of thread loosely twisted together in a piece approximately $8^7/_{10}$ yd. long. The threads are also easily divisible. The greatest benefit is that you can store the floss easily in a small area so you can keep many colors on hand without compromising much storage space.

Knot Invisible Thread
—DEBRA ARCH, KEWANEE, IL

When hand sewing with invisible thread, use a double strand and tie a knot at the end. To prevent the tiny knot from being pulled through the fabrics, anchor the knot at the starting point as follows: Insert the needle into the back of the fabric, and pull the double threads, stopping just before the knot reaches the fabric. Then push the needle to the back of the fabric $1/_{16}$ in. or more away from the original point of insertion. Next, push the tip of the needle between the knotted double strands, creating a locking stitch as you pull the threads snugly. This technique secures the knot so that it can't be pulled through the fabric and is especially helpful with loosely woven fabrics.

Keep Metallic Thread from Breaking
—MARY GIBBONS, OTTAWA, ONTARIO, CANADA

Do you find that when you sew with metallic gold thread, it often frays and breaks? To solve this problem, thread both the metallic thread and a yellow thread through the same needle. The dual threads give more definition to the stitch and work beautifully.

Use Invisible Thread with Metallic Thread
—KAREN SWEENEY, HARTWELL, GA

Here's a dependable and easy solution to metallic thread breakage: Use clear nylon invisible thread to accompany the metallic thread through the machine and needle, as if one thread. The clear thread provides support for the metallic thread while stressed and, because it's very fine, doesn't detract from the look of the embroidery. It is essential, though, to use a machine needle designed specifically for metallic thread.

Thread Woolly Nylon in Loopers

—NAN REBER, EL SEGUNDO, CA

To lessen the frustration of threading serger's loopers with woolly nylon, try tying approximately 4 in. of regular thread to the woolly nylon thread end, and thread a short hand-sewing needle with the free end. Use the needle to thread the looper "eyes," and pull the woolly nylon through each eye following the regular thread. Or, dab Fray Check or Fray Block™ on the woolly nylon end, and let it dry. Stiffening the woolly nylon in this way makes threading the loopers much easier.

Thread a Serger with Woolly Nylon

—JENNIFER PAKULA, CROYDON PARK, AUSTRALIA

Here's an easy way to thread the overlocker (serger) with woolly nylon. Make a loop of regular thread, lay the end of the woolly nylon through the loop, leaving a tail a few inches long, align the ends of the thread, and use tweezers to thread them as one through the needle or looper hole. Then pull the whole lot through together.

Make Invisible Thread Visible

—JUANITA DEAN, NASHVILLE, TN

Threading a needle with invisible thread can be a daunting task, but if you paint the end of the thread with a dark permanent marker, it's much easier to see it while inserting it into the eye of the needle. Placing a piece of white paper behind the needle also aids visibility.

THREADING A NEEDLE

Cut Thread Ends on a Slant

—MARY E. WEAVER, SAVANNAH, GA

To make threading needles much easier, follow these steps: Cut the thread on a slant. Hold the thread as close as possible to its cut end; hold the needle so that you easily see the eye (holding it up against a white background helps). Now push the eye of the needle over the thread, instead of pushing the thread into the eye. (If the thread is limp or frayed, try waxing where you cut.)

Use Hair Spray as a Threading Aid

—ANNA VICTORIA REICH, ALBUQUERQUE, NM

Before threading needles, apply some hair spray to your finger and then to the end of the thread. This will stiffen the thread, making it easier to guide through the needle's eye.

BOBBINS

Put Bobbin Thread to Good Use
—KAREN SWEENEY, HARTWELL, GA

Consider using one color of bobbin thread for all embroidery, no matter how many different colors the designs require. It will save time filling and organizing bobbins, and is less expensive. "Bobbin thread" is a fine polyester or nylon thread made for this purpose (available at most sewing stores). Since bobbin thread is fine, yet strong, it isn't necessary to change the tension on your machine to prevent the bobbin thread from showing on the right side. Try using bobbin thread with some regular sewing, unless an area of the garment will be seen from both sides. Keeping two colors of bobbin thread, a light neutral for light-colored fabrics and a darker neutral for darks, makes for speedy sewing.

Label Bobbin Thread
—PEGGY WHITE, SPRINGFIELD, MO

Use a permanent marker to label the type of thread wound on plastic bobbins. Write "poly" or "cot" on the side of each bobbin. With just one look, you'll instantly know the kind of thread you've picked up.

Wind Bobbins with Elastic Thread
–LIZ VIOLANTE, MARCO ISLAND, FL

Here's a quick, easy way to wind elastic thread onto a bobbin without stretching the thread: Slip the bobbin over the tapered end of an ordinary wooden chopstick, anchor the thread to the bobbin with a few turns, then roll the wide end of the chopstick with the palm of your hand over a book that's thicker than the bobbin is wide, winding the elastic off its spool. Keep the loose-rolling thread spool from falling off the table with barriers—perhaps other books—placed near the edge. If not using immediately, anchor the wound elastic with a piece of tape.

Prevent Tangled Bobbins
—BEVERLY C. STONE, ENCINITAS, CA

When winding thread onto a sewing machine bobbin, hold tightly to a 3-in. thread tail drawn through the hole in the top of the bobbin. If the thread doesn't break at the edge of the hole after a few revolutions, trim it and continue winding. This eliminates a loose tail to catch in the bobbin race as the bobbin unwinds.

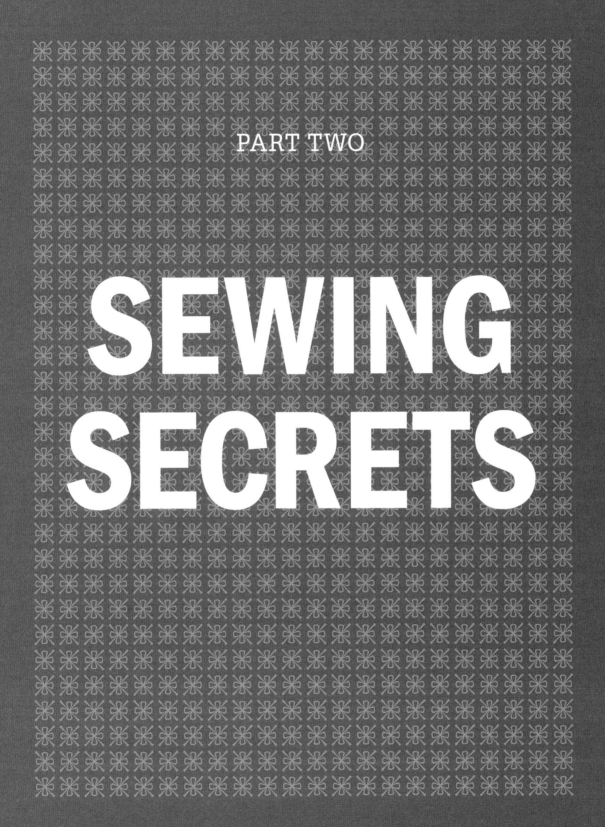

PART TWO

SEWING SECRETS

TECHNIQUES
& methods

SEWING MACHINE

Use Nail Polish to Premark Tension on Knobs

—SUSAN STRANGE, GLENCOE, IL

To avoid having to return serger tension knobs to zero each time you rethread your machine, mark the recommended tension settings required for standard size thread on each knob with red nail polish. After threading the serger, it will be quick and easy to return the knobs to their original tension settings by aligning the machine guides with the red marks. In addition, this will provide quick reference points for adjusting the tensions up or down to accommodate a special technique, such as a rolled hem, or nonstandard thread weights.

Pivot Garment to Alleviate Stretching the Needle Hole

—CECELIA SCHMEIDER, PELHAM, MA

Bulky, heavy projects can drag against the needle, bending it and stretching the needle hole, if you turn them with needle down, presser foot up. Next time, try pivoting the garment with the needle and the foot down, letting the fabric twist around the foot until the rest of the project is positioned where you want it. Lift the foot and complete the rearranging when there's no danger of the fabric shifting.

HOW TO MACHINE-SEW ON KNITTING

When machine stitching the armholes of my circular sweaters before cutting the center stitch for the opening, I used to have problems with the yarn catching in the feed dogs. I solved the problem by pinning a used fabric softener sheet on the wrong side of the sweater, directly below the area to be stitched. The sheet tears away easily after I've stitched down both sides of the armhole.

—SUSAN TERRY, NORFOLK, VA

Use Hook-and-Loop Rigging with Big Garments

—PATTY SMITH, MERION, PA

Here's a method that can save you from wrestling big, bulky garments (like long gowns) at your sewing machine.

Install a large hook in the ceiling over your machine, about 1 ft. to the left of the needle. Loop a strong cord about 4 ft. long over the hook and tie it at the appropriate height to hang a garment on a swivel hanger so you can sew around the hem and turn it. This system keeps the garment weight and bulk suspended and out of the way. This method also helps when sewing yards and yards of ruffle around the bottom of a slipcover.

STRIPES, PLAIDS, AND TRICKY FABRIC

Even Out Stripes

—GAYLA GARDNER,
HOUSTON, TX

To achieve a balanced appearance when working with uneven stripes, cut pairs of pieces (two fronts and two backs) with their hemlines in opposite orientation on the fabric, then align key stripes in the same position on each.

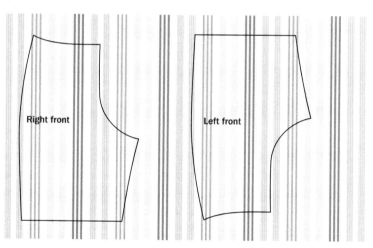

Cut Pieces One at a Time for Perfect Seams

—BRANDY ANDERS, BIGGS, CA

Some patterns instruct you to pin the lining piece to the fashion fabric piece after they've been cut and to treat the combination as one piece. Instead, try using the pattern to cut the fashion fabric and then lay the cut fabric over a large square of lining fabric. Next, carefully baste the fabric to the large, shapeless lining and trim the excess lining away when finished. You'll end up with nicely layered seams, perfectly matched pieces, and much less frustration.

USE A "FIRE-HOSE" TECHNIQUE TO MANAGE LONG FABRIC STRIPS

I was recently making yards and yards of corded welting for a slipcovering project, and I just about lost my mind trying to keep the very lengthy fabric strip I had made from twisting and tangling. Winding it onto a big spool didn't work very well.

Then I remembered how fire hoses are set up in emergency cabinets, ready to unwind as quickly as possible. Taking my cue from that idea, I purchased a dozen or so large, key-ring-type metal hoops. Then I threaded the end of the strip through all the rings. Grasping the first two rings, I stretched my arms out to create a length of fabric between them, which then hung nicely between the rings. I continued this with all the hoops, and then hung the rings from a rod where they couldn't fall off. When it came to sewing the cording into the fabric to make welting, the strip came off the rings without a hitch, saving me lots of time and aspirin.

—EVE NESS, SAXTONS RIVER, VT

Match Stripes or Plaids

—MARGUERITE F. CONNORS, DANVERS, MA

Lay the corresponding pieces right sides together. Then turn back the seam allowance on the top piece from ¼ to ⅝ in. Stitch on the turned-back seam allowance next to the fold (⅛ in. away for heavy fabrics). Adjust the fabrics as you sew to line up the stripe or plaid exactly. The seam will lie flat and open and won't pull out, since it is stitched through two layers of fabric. This method also works on curved seams and is always accurate because it involves matching right sides.

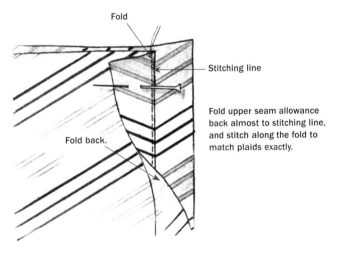

Fold

Stitching line

Fold upper seam allowance back almost to stitching line, and stitch along the fold to match plaids exactly.

Fold back.

KEEP STRIPES SYMMETRICAL

I recently made a garment that called for a bias collar. I realized that because I was using striped fabric, if I followed the pattern directions and made the collar in one piece, the stripes wouldn't be symmetrical at the front of the garment the way I wanted them. To prevent this problem, I added a seam and seam allowances to the center back and cut two separate half-collar pattern pieces. I placed each half on an identical section of the fabric's striped pattern (with one pattern piece upside down), and the resulting collar looks terrific.

—CATHY BENNETT, OKEMOS, MI

Match Fabric across Pockets
—MRS. GERALD TUBBS, PENN YAN, NY

To get patch-pocket fabric and garment fabric to line up, try this: Place the pocket pattern piece on the garment where the pocket is to be stitched and trace the printed fabric design on it. (To protect the pocket pattern or if more than one pocket is needed, trace the pattern onto tissue paper first.) Match the design traced on the pocket pattern piece with the fabric and cut out the pocket. If the garment is cut on the fold and you want two pockets opposite each other, fold the fabric like the garment. Place the pocket pattern on the fabric and cut both layers at once for perfectly matched pockets.

Sew Bulky Fabrics with Ease
—MARGARET C. STORY, GOODRICH, MI

Sewing over heavy seams such as those in denim jeans and jackets can be difficult when beginning or ending a seam. Cut three to four 1-in.-wide by 2-in.-long pieces from thin cardboard, and then simply tape them together into a stack. Place the stack under the back of the presser foot when you come to a heavy seam. The stack of cardboard levels the foot and allows for sewing without missed stitches or broken needles. A Hump Jumper® could also work nicely, but using cardboard permits adjusting it to the exact height needed.

Prevent Prewash Fraying

—NANCY SHERBA,
PITTSBURGH, PA

Before prewashing woven fabrics, especially fabric that's likely to fray, run a wide zigzag stitch along the cut ends. It helps to keep fraying to a minimum and prevents the frayed threads from getting tangled up with other items in the wash. To double the benefit, use old thread or thread from spools that are almost empty and, without any extra effort, effectively purge your thread stash at the same time.

PATTERNS

Preserve
Pattern Notches

—JOANNA WILSON,
DOVER, DE

How can you avoid having your serger cut off the notches needed for matching seams when finishing the raw edges of seam allowances? Simply fold the notch under and even with the raw edge of the fabric before it reaches the cutting blade. The notches will remain intact and visible in the seam when you need them. This works well for both lightweight and heavier-weight fabrics. To eliminate bulk, trim the notches after stitching the seam.

HOW TO SEW THE PATTERN NUMBER INTO THE SEAM

When I make a garment, I often forget the exact pattern I used in the months or years later, so I devised a way to remind myself. When I've finished the hand sewing required to complete a garment, I take an extra minute to embroider the pattern number, preceded by the first letter of the pattern maker, on an inside seam allowance. For instance, *Vogue* 4745 would be V4745; *Simplicity* 2184 would be S2184. This only takes a minute and works great for just about everything I make, with the exception of some sheers. There's one precaution: Make sure the thread is colorfast, so it won't bleed onto your garment.

—BERNADETTE PARRISH, COCKEYSVILLE, MD

BASTING

Baste Leather or Vinyl
—BETTY SAGER,
SPRING VALLEY, CA

When working with leather or vinyl, basting is difficult and pinning can be impossible. Try using staples in the seam allowance (the pliers-type of stapler is handier than the desktop version). After stitching, take out the staples with a small pair of needle-nose pliers or a staple remover.

Use Lightweight Nylon Thread to Baste Gathers
—MARTHA KELLY,
BROOKLYN, NY

Try using lightweight nylon thread in your bobbin when basting for gathers because it's easy to pull and never breaks. After stitching parallel rows, pull the two nylon threads from both ends. When the gathered piece is the right length, anchor the ends by wrapping the threads around a pin in a figure eight.

GATHERING

Zigzag-Stitch to Gather Fabric
—CORINNE ELWORTH,
ORRTANNA, PA

Lay a piece of heavy thread (buttonhole twist, crochet cotton) next to the seamline on the seam allowance side, and sew a narrow zigzag stitch over it. (Be careful not to catch the thread in the stitching.) Then pull the heavy thread to form gathers. The zigzag stitches make a channel, which allows the heavy thread to be pulled through easily without tugging or breaking threads. This method works especially well for gathering long ruffled curtains, but it is just as useful for short gathers, such as on sleeve caps. Simply keep zigzag stitches within the seam allowance, and no stitches will show when the garment is put together.

Gather with Nylon Thread
—ANNA VICTORIA REICH,
ALBUQUERQUE, NM

When you have a project that calls for gathering, use nylon thread in the bobbin. The gathers slide more smoothly over this thread than the typical cotton or polyester type.

Gather with a Guide

—MAE M. CONNER,
DAYTONA BEACH, FL

If you need to gather to a specific measurement, create a guide out of a strip of twill tape and a pull tab: Measure and cut a piece of cotton twill the length needed and attach it to a 1-in. by 2-in. pull tab with a few machine stitches. Fold the twill tape out of the way, and butt the side edge of the tab to the starting edge of the fabric to be gathered. Start the gathering stitches on the tab continuing onto the fabric. Be sure not to stitch into the twill tape. (The fabric will overlap the twill tape.) At the tab, tie off the top threads and pull the bobbin threads to gather the fabric to the length of the tape.

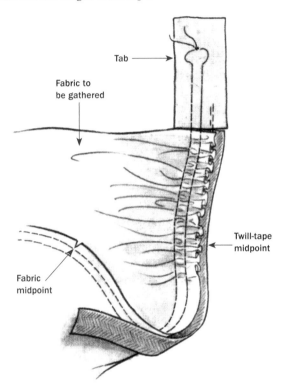

Tab

Fabric to
be gathered

Twill-tape
midpoint

Fabric
midpoint

SERGING

Replace the Serger Blade

—KAREN WOLFF,
LAGUNA HILLS, CA

When changing the cutting blade on your serger, first mark the blade level on your old blade. Then transfer the mark to your new blade by holding them side by side. This allows you to easily seat the new blade in your machine at the perfect level without difficulty or frustration.

HOW TO CREATE A SERGER TENSION GUIDE

It's sometimes difficult to determine what is causing tension problems with my serger because there are so many threads interlocking. I've found an extremely helpful aid that is best created when the serger is new or recently adjusted and the tension is perfect. I threaded each spool pin with the thread color that corresponds to the thread color used in my serger instructions—in my case, green, blue, yellow, and red. I made a sample serged stitch for each type of stitch my serger can create, and then I attached the sample to the instruction book on the appropriate page. Now when there's a problem, I just compare the sample to the work in progress and decide which thread needs to be tightened or loosened.

—GRACE MULLINS, PUTNAM VALLEY, NY

Serge to Remove Selvages
—ANTOINNETTE VALLA,
DIX HILLS, NY

To remove a selvage, use your serger to complete the task quickly and easily. Simply take all of the thread out of the serger, remove the needles, and use the serger's cutting blade to precisely remove the selvages. This method removes the selvage edge from yards of fabric quickly and accurately. You'll get such long strips of selvages, you can use them as "strings" for a variety of sewing and nonsewing purposes. The selvage of a sheer fabric looks like a ribbon, which can be used as embellishment on other projects.

Change Serger Threads
—KAREN ROTH WOLFF,
ALISO VIEJO, CA

Many serger users make thread changes by attaching the new thread to the old thread and easing it through the serger, but here's another efficient way to rethread a serger with new thread while it's still threaded with the old. Simply clip the serger thread you want to remove at the cone, put on the new cone, and guide the new thread by following the path of the old thread while it is still in place. Do this all the way to the eye of the looper or needle, remove the old thread, and finish. It can be easier than following the thread path illustrated on the machine's door/cover, and shows a lot about the serger in the process. It's always a good idea after rethreading the serger to do a test just to be sure the new thread is seated properly in the tension disks.

Serge with Water-Soluble Stabilizer

—LINDA LEE VIVIAN, LENNON, MI

To stabilize a silky fabric or prevent fabric from stretching while serging on bias edges, try using a water-soluble stabilizer like Solvy. Cut a 1-in.-wide strip of stabilizer a little longer than needed to complete the seam. Place the stabilizer under the serger foot with the end of the strip butted up to the cutting blade. Start stitching onto the stabilizer, allowing the blade to trim ¼ in. Now place the fabric on top of the stabilizer and under the serger foot and continue to stitch through the fabric and stabilizer. Trim excess stabilizer from the reverse of your fabric; the remainder will disappear with the first wash.

Remove Stabilizer Easily

—KAREN NOE, CEDAR RAPIDS, IA

To dissolve Sulky Solvy or a similar water-soluble stabilizer, "trace" the stitching lines with a Q-tip® soaked in cold water instead of soaking the entire project in cold water.

Prevent Serger Snarls

—SONYA JONES, BERWICK, NOVA SCOTIA, CANADA

When the thread cone on sergers is about to run out, the last of the thread frequently slips off the cone in a messy tangle. Turn the cone upside down before it reaches the end. The thread will not slip off in one lump but will ease off the way it's supposed to.

HOW TO TRIM TRICKY FABRICS WITH A SERGER

I frequently sew with fussy fabrics such as silk, chiffon, and burnout velvet. I love the look of French seams on these delicate fabrics, but I've always found it difficult to trim the seam allowances to a neat and even ⅛ in. after sewing the first row of stitching. I now call my serger into action, but not in the traditional way. I remove all of the threads and needles from the serger. I then run the garment seam through the serger, using the blades to trim the allowances. This results in a perfectly trimmed ⅛-in. seam allowance in short order. The technique also makes quick work of trimming allowances on fabric tubes before turning them right side out.

—PAMELA CROSBY, DATAW ISLAND, SC

THREAD

Use Capillary Action to Thread a Needle

—JACQUELYN JACOBI,
VICTORIA, BRITISH COLUMBIA, CANADA

If you wet the eye of the needle, instead of the thread, the capillary action of the moisture draws the thread through. This task becomes easier—even if you have good eyesight.

....

Help Short Thread Last

—E'ANNE FRYE,
TOPEKA, KS

Everyone has experienced the need to bury or knot a thread tail that is shorter than the needle. One easy solution is to position the tip of an unthreaded needle where you want the thread to disappear, and push it through the fabric, just up to the eye. Then thread the too-short thread through the eye and pull the needle and thread tail all the way through. An Easy Threading needle (the kind with a spring-closing slot at the top of the eye) makes it effortless—instead of pushing the thread tip through the eye, you snap the side of the thread through the slot.

....

Salvage Thread for Topstitching Repairs

—MARIANNE KANTOR,
BONDVILLE, VT

When you need to alter a garment with topstitching in a conspicuous spot and you can't find a good color match to replace the topstitching, look inside the garment for a three- or four-thread overlocked seam that matches the topstitching. Snip all the threads at both ends, then lift out the needle thread at intervals with a large, blunt needle that's short enough to allow it to slide out easily without breaking the looper threads. Snipping off the excess needle thread periodically lessens the resistance and prevents excessive rubbing against the looper threads. When the two looper threads are released, each one is about three times the length of the seam. Press them and wind them onto a bobbin, and you'll get perfectly matching topstitching. Don't forget to restitch the seam you snitched from.

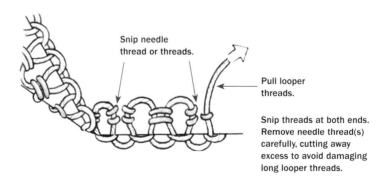

Snip needle thread or threads.

Pull looper threads.

Snip threads at both ends. Remove needle thread(s) carefully, cutting away excess to avoid damaging long looper threads.

Use Fusible Thread for Binding

—MICHELE BRAKEWOOD, VAN NUYS, CA

Use fusible thread for flawless binding applications. With the fabric right-side down, sew along one side of the binding. Align the unstitched edge of the binding to the garment edge and sew it right sides together to the garment. Then, fold the bias and turn it over the edge so the fusible is folded under next to the fabric on the wrong side of the garment. Press the edge of the bias tape to cover the previous stitching line. The fusible thread will hold the bias in place while the garment is flipped back to the right side. Then replace the bobbin with regular thread and topstitch through the binding edges.

Stitch Letters and Logos

—JEAN DUNNING, CROMWELL, CT

When satin-stitching complex solid shapes, like letters and logos, drawn outlines often aren't accurate enough guides. Here's a method that will provide more precise results: Cut out the desired shape in a fabric that is close to the color of the desired thread and attach it to the background with fusible web. It's easy to cover the cloth shape completely with neat rows of satin stitch, either finishing up with an outline row around the edge, stitching just off the shape (like appliqué), which gives a raised edge, or starting with the outline row and overlapping the interior ones, which gives the effect of a raised center.

STITCHING

Use a Honeycomb Stitch to Sew Decorative Lines

—JANE TUTTON, VERO BEACH, FL

Here's a trick for sewing solid three-thread decorative lines: Use the honeycomb stitch (most often used with wing needles for heirloom sewing or fagoting), and set the stitch width to zero to make a triple stitch.

Hide Topstitching on Ends

—MARY HARDENBROOK, HUNTINGTON BEACH, CA

To secure a line of topstitching, tie threads and weave the ends into the fabric instead of backstitching. Pull the top thread to the back and tie the threads. Leave thread tails long enough to thread into an embroidery needle. Weave the needle in between the layers of fabric for ½ in. and out again on the back. Pull gently to cause some tension and snip the thread at the fabric line, which will cause the thread to disappear between the layers.

Improve Topstitching at Corners

—KRISTINE DONOHUE, CARMICHAEL, CA

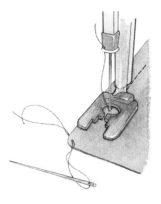

A nicely topstitched corner adds an instant professional look to a garment, but many sewers find topstitching around a bulky corner a challenge. To keep the layers of fabric from getting stuck under the needle, create a thread "handle," which allows you to literally pull the fabric and maneuver around the corner with even stitches. Thread a needle with a 12-in. doubled length of thread left unknotted. Take one stitch through the tip of the corner by hand, leaving the needle dangling. Pivot at the corner and make the turn, then slightly pull on the dangling threads, using gentle tension. This will guide the fabric smoothly under the needle and help keep stitches precisely spaced around the corner. Those days of uneven topstitching that signal "homemade" will be gone forever.

HOW TO CONVERT STITCHES PER INCH INTO METRIC STITCH LENGTHS

This list makes it easy to translate between metric stitch lengths and stitches per inch (spi) designations we see on older sewing machines:

20 spi = 1.3 mm

15 spi = 1.7 mm

12 spi = 2.1 mm

10 spi = 2.5 mm

8 spi = 3.1 mm

6 spi = 4.2 mm

5 spi = 5.1 mm

4 spi = 6.3 mm

—KAY LANCASTER, VIA *CREATIVE MACHINE NEWSLETTER*

HOW TO STITCH AND SLASH

I am intrigued with the stitch-and-slash fabric process, sometimes called chenille, and I especially love the shimmering texture and wonderful drape of the garments I've seen firsthand, made from several layers of rayon challis. However, those slippery rayon layers are difficult to keep lined up, especially when basted with straight pins.

My solution is to use a quilt-basting spray, a lightweight spray adhesive used for layering quilts (check quilt-supply stores or notions catalogs). When constructing the stitch-and-slash garment, spray each layer as they're put together, and press with an iron. Stitch the channels as usual, slash between rows of stitches, finish the garment, and wash it to make the slashed layers bloom. The spray, which washes out completely, eliminates the need for pins, which get in the way when sewing all those narrow channels.

By the way, if rayon challis seems too expensive for the many layers required for a vest or jacket, don't get discouraged. Check local thrift shops for gathered skirts of challis. Buy the skirts with the most yardage, wash them, and remove any elastic, buttons, or zippers. A single skirt usually provides enough fabric for one layer, but you can piece a layer with two different skirt fabrics of similar colors. There's no need to sew the pieces together. Just lay the sections in pieces, and stitch the layers in rows as usual.

I've made three beautiful jackets from thrift-shop skirts, a bargain compared with the cost of straight yardage. (A final hint: Always use cotton for the binding.)

—SYLVIA WHITESIDES, LAFAYETTE, IN

Try an Alternative to Backstitching
—PHYLLIS STILLWELL, EL CAJON, CA

Instead of backstitching, reduce the stitch length to 1 mm or less to secure the stitching at the start and end of a seam. Reducing the stitch length is no harder or slower, and there won't be loose threads to tie off. It's also a great, bulk-free way to end the stitching at the point of a dart.

Make a Presser Foot Like a "Third Hand"
—PARKER SMITH, CHICAGO, IL

Wrap a rubber band around the toes of a seldom-used presser foot. Then, when you need a third hand to hold on to your fabric for ripping out seams or braiding cords, just snap the foot onto your machine and drop it on the spot you want to hold, leaving your other two hands free to do the work.

Finish Tricky Inside Parts without Hand Stitching

—JANNAFORD JONES,
ALTADENA, CA

Here's a fast method for finishing the inside of a waistband, collar, or cuff without hand stitching. After stitching the seam, turn under the raw edge and pin it ⅛ in. below the seamline. Machine-sew on the right side of the fabric, in the "ditch" of the seam. While stitching, pull the fabric apart gently, on either side of the seam. The machine stitching will be virtually invisible on the right side of the garment, and the inside will have a clean, finished look.

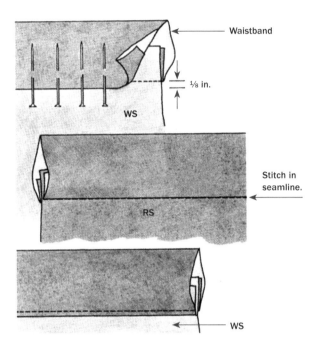

Waistband

⅛ in.

WS

Stitch in seamline.

RS

WS

Try Shorter Stitches

—BETTY BOLDEN,
BOLTON, CT

Shorten the stitch length a little at a curved section or a corner in a seam. The smaller stitches give added strength to the area and permit trimming closer to the stitching. Consider shortening your stitches at intersecting seams and at the beginnings and ends of seams to help prevent them from unraveling.

Use Machine-Stitch Guides for Hand Stitching

—JANICE ENGLE, AURORA, IL

Creating a rhythm when I hand-stitch helps me maintain equal stitch tension. I also find it helpful to use lightweight interfacing on both the fashion fabric and the facing wherever possible to provide extra body as I stitch. My greatest hand-sewing assistance, however, comes from my sewing machine. When I want to sew evenly spaced hand stitches, I machine-baste a line and use it as a stitch guide. I adjust the stitch length to the hand stitch I plan to use. I remove the machine stitches just before hand sewing and follow the stitch holes left behind. But if it's difficult to see the holes, I leave the stitches in place until after I finish my handwork. I can use the machine stitches as a guide for many different hand stitches—blanket stitch, topstitch, herringbone stitch, to name a few—and I always get perfect hand stitching. It takes some extra effort, but making a garment with details that rival very expensive designer clothing is a satisfying accomplishment that's well worth the time.

USE YOUR STITCH-IN-THE-DITCH FOOT

When sewing across the ends to create bound buttonholes, I've found my stitch-in-the-ditch foot to be extremely helpful. It makes it so easy to stitch the folded triangles close to the basting line (one of the early steps involved in making a bound buttonhole) and allows me to stitch around the buttonhole invisibly in the ditch. I often iron freezer paper templates to my fabric when sewing rounded corners on pockets or at the bottom edges of a jacket to ensure that both sides will have identical curves. Using the stitch-in-the-ditch foot, I can easily keep the blade of the foot right at the edge of the template, getting identical rounds every time without sewing into the template.

—KAY WAGNER, GOLDEN VALLEY, MN

MAKE A SAMPLER FOR A VISUAL INDEX

I recently purchased a new machine that sews a vast assortment of decorative stitches, and my first project was to sew a sampler of my favorite patterns. Initially, a sampler presents an opportunity to learn the machine and practice various stitches. But the most compelling reason to make one is to create a permanent visual index of your favorite patterns and record the settings you prefer. Plan to sew three to five versions before settling on the final assortment of stitches—you'll inevitably delete a few patterns that you expect to love, and add others that turn out better than you imagined.

Use dark thread on two layers of light-colored broadcloth or muslin (mine is 8 in. by 11 in.). Using marking chalk or a fabric pen with fading ink, draw three to five lines 1 in. apart. Select a few patterns and write their style numbers every 2 in. to 3 in. between the drawn lines with a fine-tip permanent marker. Sew 2-in.- to 3-in.-long patterns along each line, repeating this process until you've filled the sampler. Then study the stitches and determine which to keep, eliminate, or tweak: increase a width here, a length there.

I record custom settings on my final sampler so I can recreate them in the future. I find it useful to include one row dedicated to zigzag and satin stitches in a full range of lengths and widths. If you plan to use a machine's fonts, add another line devoted to lettering.

I pin my sampler to a bulletin board by my machine for easy reference, but you could hem it, or appliqué it to a sewing machine cover, or make it into a pillow. Wherever you store it, this tool will help you become a more creative sewer.

—SOPHIE P. ALLEN, CHARLOTTE, NC

Make a sampler of your favorite decorative stitches to record the machine settings you prefer.

SEAMS

Practice Seams on Gingham
—JAN GROVER, ST. PAUL, MN

There's much new sewers can learn by practicing basic sewing techniques such as curves and corners and simply stitching a straight line. Practicing on $\frac{1}{8}$-in. checked cotton gingham provides an instant seam guide to stitch in straight lines. Practice 90-degree turns with two oblique stitches across the corner to account for turn of cloth—it's much easier when the right angle is clearly visible.

Keep Seams Straight with Safety Pins
—MARGARET SMRKE-GLOVER, ETOBICOKE, ONTARIO, CANADA

When sewing fabric with similar right and wrong sides, determine which side is right, then pin a small brass safety pin to the right side of each pattern piece when it's cut out. Don't remove the pins until all seams are safely sewn. This will save hours of frustration and ripping!

Prevent Seam Jams in Delicate Fabrics
—AILEEN MARGULIS, JERICHO, NY

If your stitches get jammed at the beginning of a seam in delicate fabrics, try this: When beginning and ending the seam, place a 1-in. to 2-in. strip of scrap fabric under the presser foot and start stitching. At the end of the scrap, abut the seam to be sewn and continue. Clip off the scrap, then use it again at the end of the seam. Leave it under the presser foot, ready to start the next line of stitches. This technique is similar to chain piecing, when multiple seams are sewn without separating them by lifting the presser foot and snipping the threads. It really works to start seams faultlessly.

Manage Seam Allowances in Tricky Spots
—ELAINE RUTLEDGE, CHUNCHULA, AL

To keep seam allowances pressed open in places such as crotch curves, first sew the seam and press the allowances together. Fold and press one seam allowance back, lapping it over the seamline onto the other seam allowance by $\frac{1}{16}$ in. Stitch through both seam allowances on the edge of the fold. Then turn the garment right side out and press the seam open. In deep curves such as the crotch, trim the seam allowances to $\frac{1}{4}$ in.

Start and End Seams on Fabric Scraps
—KAREN MINTURN BROWN, LIVONIA, MI

Try starting seams on a scrap of fabric and continue sewing right onto the seam. At the end of the seam, run stitching onto another fabric scrap. Cut the scraps off and use them more than once. This method eliminates all those little threads around the sewing space and keeps thread from snarling under fabric at the start of stitching.

Eliminate Uneven Seams in Tricky Fabrics

—ANDREA MOORE,
SPOKANE, WA

Get rid of uneven seams in velvets, corduroys, and other napped and tricky fabrics by tacking both ends of the seam, exactly on the seamline, with three or four regular-length straight stitches. Next find the center of the seam, and tack again. Continue dividing the seam sections in half and tacking with a few stitches until the seam has been secured every few inches. If basting stitches are accurately placed on the seamline, don't remove them; simply stitch right over them for a flawless seam.

Make Neat Seams without Backstitching

—SUSAN LAFO,
SPRING VALLEY, CA

Begin and end machine-sewn seams using short machine stitches— such as 18 to 20 stitches per inch. Do this by either changing the stitch length on your machine for the first and last ½ in. of sewing, or by holding the fabric tightly in front of the needle for the first 5 stitches so the feed dogs can't pull the fabric while it sews. The result is a much smoother, neater seam than backstitching allows.

Follow Puncture Lines for Folding Seam Allowances

—JEANNE F. SCHIMMEL,
HOBE SOUND, FL

Here's a simple and certain way to mark hems and seam allowances, place trims, and fold and press under exact edges. When pressing under ¼ in. on an edge of a facing section, place a large needle (size 16 or 18) in the sewing machine, unthreaded. Run the fabric through at the ¼-in. mark, which makes a row of puncture marks, indicating the proper place for the fold. The pressing is more accurate, and you won't wonder if the edges are turned evenly.

Intersect Seams on Flowing Garments

—MARTHA MOSER,
EVANSTON, IL

When joining garment sections across a seam, don't stitch over the intersecting seam allowances, but rather stitch "under" them. At a seam junction, pull the seam allowances from the crossing seam toward you to prevent the seam allowance fabric from going under the foot; stitch just up to the seamline, and stop. Lock the thread with a few backstitches, and lift the presser foot. Shift the fabric, push the seam allowances away from you, and resume stitching just beyond the seamline on the other side of the seam. Stitching up to but not over seams creates a gap between stitches at the intersection, which provides wiggle room and allows the garment sections to respond independently to body movement.

Match Seams Perfectly in a Vest

—SONDRA FELDSTEIN,
BONDURANT, IA

When making a lined or faced vest, the garment armhole seams are typically sewn before the side seams. The side seams are completed in one step with the facing or lining side seams. No matter how carefully one matches and pins the seams before sewing, the fabric can shift during sewing or serging. This often results in an ever-so-slight mismatch at the point where the side meets the facing or lining.

Here's a way to eliminate this problem: Before completing the side seam, open the facing and use a single pin to very carefully match the front and back facing seams. Then sew across the seam beginning about $1/2$ in. from the join and continuing about $1/2$ in. beyond the join to ensure that the front and back facing seams line up properly. Now when the entire side seam is sewn (whether on a sewing machine or serger), there won't be any "fabric creep" at that juncture. This technique also works on pants or skirts with a facing in place of a waistband—as well as any other place where crossing seams need to match, such as in armholes or crotch seams, or when matching stripes or motifs in fabric.

Trim Sheer Seams with Ease

—PEGGY D. YACKEL,
PLYMOUTH, MN

Here's a way to easily and accurately trim seams with the help of double-sided adhesive basting tape on a sheer batiste gown. Use $1/4$-in.-wide tape that has a protective removable strip over the adhesive. Attach the tape along the edge of the seam without removing the protective strip. The strip's thickness provides a "wall" to cut against. This will help the seam to be trimmed without using a ruler or tape measure, and the result will be perfect every time.

Smooth Curved Seams

—LOIS PITCHER,
ITHACA, NY

Here's a tip to simplify sewing a convex curved piece to a concave curved piece. (If you look at a quarter moon, the moon's outer curve is convex, and the inside curve is concave.) It's helpful to run a machine-basting stitch just outside the seamline of the concave piece as a clipping guide. Then before sewing the pieces together, clip the edges of the concave pattern piece close to—but not through—the seamline. Stretch the concave edge until it's even with the convex piece as you stitch the two together. The seam will be easier to sew, and it's less likely there will be puckers.

Add Seam Allowances Quickly

—LYNN TEICHMAN,
LEWISBURG, PA

Here's an easy trick for adding seam allowances from patterns in books or magazines if they are not included. Make a pattern on paper. When tracing the pattern, make sure to include extra paper around the outside of all seamlines. When the pattern pieces are fully traced, stitch ⅝ in. (or whatever the seam allowance is) from the seamline using a wing needle and no thread. The wing needle not only accurately marks the cutting lines, but it will also neatly perforate the pattern paper as you sew, so there's no need to cut out the pattern pieces. Consider also using a standard sewing machine needle, though a wing needle does a better job of perforating the paper. Use a rubber band around the free arm of the machine or a piece of masking or painter's tape to mark the seam allowance width to the right of the presser foot. The band or tape is visible because the paper is somewhat transparent. It's a fast, easy, and accurate way of cutting out patterns and marking the cutting line at the same time!

Staystitch to Eliminate Seam Puckers

—DONNA KAYE CHILDRESS,
CARENCRO, LA

To help eliminate puckers on curved seams, staystitch from the widest to the narrowest part of the piece, and sew the final stitching in the same direction. For example, in a blouse with princess seams over the bustline, this usually means from top to bottom. In longer princess-seam garments in which the waist is more fitted, but the hemline is full, staystitch from the armhole (top) to the waistline and sew the bodice seamline in the same direction. Next, stitch the remaining seam from the hem to the waistline. In bell-bottom pants, where the hemline is wide, staystitch (if applicable) and stitch the seamline from the hem to top. It's important to press directionally as well.

TRIMS, EDGES, AND NOTIONS

Use Tape to Trim Pillows

—JAMIE DEMUMBRUM,
LOVELAND, OH

If fringed or tasseled trim gets in the way of seams when sewing the front and back of a pillow with right sides together, try taping the trim out of the way until the stitching is finished. Standard adhesive tape works well, but low-stick painter's tape also works. After machine basting the trim in place on the right side of the pillow front, use a long piece of tape to hold the fringe and tassels toward the center of the fabric. Pin the pillow back to the front, right sides together, and stitch, leaving a small area to turn the pillow right side out. Once the sewing is complete, and the pillow has been turned and stuffed, carefully remove the tape and hand-stitch the opening.

No-Sew Option for a Delicate Tulle Edge

—GAIL COOPER, TORONTO, CANADA

For her wedding, my daughter wanted a cathedral-length, silk tulle veil, roughly oval in shape, with a ribbon edge. This was a difficult project because even the narrowest ribbon refused to shape around the curved edges, and the silk tulle (sometimes called illusion) was too delicate to withstand machine or even hand stitching. But I devised a way to finish the cut edge. I hit on a no-sew solution by folding up a $\frac{1}{4}$-in. hem around the raw edge and steam-pressing it, and then folding up another $\frac{1}{4}$ in. and pressing again. My iron seemed to fuse the three layers of tulle together, creating the delicate, ribbon-like edge we wanted to achieve. I set the iron on low steam and low heat when pressing.

Create a Scallop Edge on Lingerie

—ELIZABETH RYDMAN-HARRIS, SANTA FE, NM

For an attractive scallop-edge finish on lingerie or lightweight garments, use the blind stitch on your machine. First, finish the raw edge by serging, or turn it under $\frac{1}{4}$ in.; then fold the seam hem allowance under and press. Do a test strip by setting the stitch width to the widest setting (4) and the stitch length in the middle (2). With the wrong side up, put the fabric under the presser foot with the edge to the left and the garment to the right of the needle. Feed the fabric through so that when the occasional zigzag stitch bites, it grabs just outside the finished edge. It is this zigzag stitch that forms the scalloped edge.

HAND-SEW BEADS WITHOUT SNAGS

I recently embellished a garment with hand-stitched beads and sequins, but my thread kept getting caught on the beads I had already attached. To prevent this, I now drape fabric (any type of lightweight fabric would be suitable) over my work. First, I pin one end of the fabric under the project. Then I fold it over the offending beads without covering the area I'm about to stitch. It is easy to move the fabric as my stitching progresses, and this simple solution allows me to easily hand-stitch and maneuver my thread without it getting snagged in my beading.

—CHERI DOWD, AIKEN, SC

Press Ribbon Using the Heat from a Lightbulb

—CAROL CURTIS, BELLFLOWER, IL

To press a length of ribbon, don't head for the iron and ironing board. The table lamp next to you may be all that's needed. Simply run the ribbon over any 60-watt to 100-watt lightbulb (turned on and warm-hot to the touch). Be certain the bulb is dust-free. This also works on narrow lace trim.

Create a Polished Piping

—GAIL COOPER, DON MILLS, TORONTO, CANADA

No matter how carefully piped edges are sewn, they often end up looking bulky (resulting from the six-layer fabric-and-piping sandwich) and stiff (the effect of the buildup of three rows of machine stitching). Here's a good remedy, which will also help create a polished, delicate piping for the finest of garments.

First, pinch-pin a scrap of the piping fabric around cording to find the measurement for the wraparound. For fine piping, this is usually ¼ in. Then add a ¾-in. seam allowance and cut the piping fabric into bias strips accordingly, in this case (and in most), 1 in. wide. Insert the cording off-center, with ¼ in. of fabric on one side and ½ in. on the other side, effectively grading the seams. Then hand-baste as close as possible to the cording. When stitching the piping to the garment, place the piping's wider raw edge ⅛ in. from the edge of the fabric, which allows the zipper foot to follow the cording precisely along the garment's ⅝-in. seamline. After joining the piping and garment, turn the piping to the outside of the garment.

Before attaching the facing to the garment, machine-stitch along the facing's ⅝-in. seamline, trim it to ⅜ in., and press under the seam allowance on the stitched line. Finally, slipstitch the facing along this fold to the machine-stitched line at the base of the piping. The result is a smooth, supple, piped edge with enclosed seam allowances, all perfectly graded.

Putting Together Quick Lace Designs

—BARBARA L. ANDERSON, URBANA, IL

To quickly combine lace tapes into wider strips to use as trims, use the faggot stitch on your zigzag sewing machine. Pin the lengths of lace about ⅛ in. apart on adding-machine paper tape (available in rolls in stationery stores), and sew the lace strips together. The paper stabilizes the lace as an interfacing would. Adjust sewing-machine settings as recommended by the manufacturer. Remove the paper carefully afterward.

Apply Lace

—ANDREA MOORE,
SPOKANE, WA

Here's an attractive and virtually invisible lace application that works equally well whether the lace will lie flat on the completed garment or will be an edge finish. If flat, place the lace on or adjacent to the placement line, wrong side up, and pointing in the opposite direction to its finished position. With the blind-hem setting on your machine, and with thread that matches the lace, stitch on the placement line next to the lace edge, just catching it with the swing stitch. A stitch length of 3 mm and a width of 1 mm works well, but experiment to find a good setting. Gently turn the lace down over the line of stitching (it pivots inside the tiny swing stitch), and press. For an edge finish, begin by placing the lace wrong side up with the lace band just above the hemline. Since this lace will be on the edge of the garment and may take more of a beating, use a shorter stitch length when you attach it. Press the lace down, turning the hem at the same time, and finish as desired.

....

Use a Manual Differential Feed to Bind Edges on Curves

—STEPHANIE CORINA GODDARD,
EASTON, MD

While a one-to-one ratio of binding to a garment edge may work fine on straight edges, some adjustment is required over curves to keep the work smooth and flat. The difference between the binding's wrapped edge and its sewn edge determines whether you need to ease or stretch the binding along the curve. Even on the narrowest bindings there is enough difference to warrant this compensation.

When the wrapped-edge curve is smaller than the stitched-edge curve (inside curve), stretch the binding along the stitched edge as you sew. Conversely, when the wrapped-edge curve is larger (outside curve), ease the binding when you sew it on.

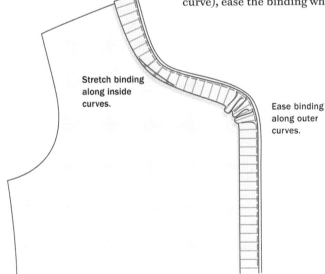

Stretch binding along inside curves.

Ease binding along outer curves.

HOW TO USE THE BLIND-HEM STITCH TO ATTACH BEADS

I discovered a good use for the blind-hem stitch found on most modern sewing machines when I was adding tiny, prestrung costume-jewelry pearls to a garment. I sewed the string on by blind hemming next to it so the straight stitches were alongside the string, and the sideways stitches caught it. When I used my adjustable zipper foot to get up close, it worked like a charm. After experimenting, I developed several ways to do it.

One way is to fold the material where you want the trim and then to run the fold with the right side up under the zipper foot so the sideways part of the blind-hem stitch falls off the edge. Hold the trim close to the fold, and it will be caught by the stitch. This creates a tuck where the fold is and works on straight lines only. The fold can be an edge or can occur in the middle of the fabric, but don't forget to allow for the material taken up by the tuck (not shown).

When you want the trim right on a curved edge, face the curve and turn the garment right side out. Then run the curved edge and trim under the foot, as described above.

In both cases, I usually use a thread that matches the fabric so it won't be seen, and I make the stitch width as narrow as possible. If you want to use a thread that matches the trim, not the fabric, or don't want the little tuck, leave the fabric flat as you stitch, and fold it at the trim later. The stitches will be on the inside of the fold only (top drawing). This will also work on faced edges. Stitch the trim onto the seamline of the garment piece, with the stitches in the seam allowance, before attaching the facing.

—DORIS GRAY, BLYTHEWOOD, SC

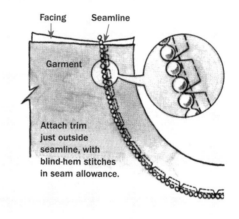

Attach trim just outside seamline, with blind-hem stitches in seam allowance.

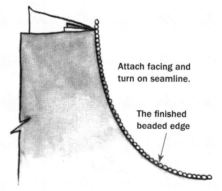

Attach facing and turn on seamline.

The finished beaded edge

ELASTIC

Reduce Bulk When Using Elastic

—BETH HAYES, RHINEBECK, NY

Most patterns advise overlapping the ends of an elastic waistband when sewing them together. To eliminate bulk, some sewers butt the ends together and sew through them and a piece of ribbon. Here's an easier method: Butt the ends of the elastic together and sew down the seam with a wide triple-zigzag stitch. Backstitch all the way back to the starting point. The seam will be virtually undetectable when the elastic is sewn into the casing.

Use Fabric to Forge an Elastic Joint

—TRUDY DIXON, PLATTE WOODS, MO

Here's a way to overlap the ends of a piece of elastic to form a ring. Butt the two elastic ends together over a thin piece of fabric (organza is best, but other fabrics will also work), and zigzag along the joint as well as on each side of the joint through the elastic and second fabric until the joint is stable. This makes a smooth connection, and there is no added bulk from overlapped elastic.

Attach Fold-Over Elastic Smoothly

—NANCY MCKENZIE, WAVERLEY, NOVA SCOTIA, CANADA

Love the look of ½-in. fold-over elastic on T-shirts and camisoles, but have trouble attaching it smoothly? Using the elastic effectively requires just the right amount of seam allowance to permit the elastic to fold flat over the fabric edge. This can be difficult to do, especially when using two very different layers on a curvy, uncooperative edge. To make it easier, place the elastic right side up on the wrong side of the garment before trimming the seam allowance. Match the fabric edge to the elastic edge and sew the inside elastic edge with a narrow zigzag stitch (2 mm wide and 2 mm long). The full width of the elastic and untrimmed fabric seam allowance help to keep everything in place while stitching. Next, trim the fabric just inside the elastic foldline. The elastic then folds easily to the right side of the garment. Use a narrow zigzag stitch to hold it in place along the elastic's inner edge on the right side.

Baste for Elastic Waistbands and Cuffs

—LISA WEATHERALL, BLOOMINGTON, IN

When making elastic waistbands or cuffs, baste down both edges of any seam allowances with the casing before you sew it closed. Pulling the elastic past these seams will be easier.

HOW TO FORM AN ELASTICIZED KEYHOLE

I recently finished a blouse for a client in a heavily embroidered cotton organza. She wanted a back keyhole opening with a button-and-loop closure. With the jewel neckline and firm fabric, I thought an elastic button loop would be more comfortable, as it has some give, but I preferred the look of a self-fabric loop. I cut a bias strip to cover the elastic but discovered that the thick embroidery made the fabric too bulky to make a neat loop. I tried again but first ripped out the bulkiest portions of embroidery from the bias strip. Then, I covered the elastic just as I would cover cording for a matching fabric button loop that stretches. This makes it easier to insert the button, and also more comfortable to wear so close to the neck.

—DAWN JARDINE, RED HOOK, NY

Try One-Step Elastic Pulling and Tube Turning

—TONI TOOMEY, WOODBURY, CT

Here's a quick way to turn a tube or casing and insert elastic at the same time. Use an Elastic Glide (sold at most notions counters) as the turning device because it's inexpensive and won't hurt the needle if you happen to hit it while tacking it down. Start by cutting the casing fabric at least 2 in. longer than its finished length. Next, machine-stitch both the Glide and one end of the elastic to the extra length on the right side of the unstitched casing using a wide, zero-length zigzag bar tack. After stitching the casing closed and trimming the seam allowances to ⅛ in., clip diagonally across the extra length just above the bar tack to reduce bulk and make turning easier. Now you can simply slip the fabric over the Glide, enclosing the elastic as you expose the Glide. Finally, trim away the excess casing and clip the bar tack so you can reuse the Glide. This method also works perfectly well when you're turning a tube; just leave out the elastic.

Bind Elastic without Bulk

—ANDREA MOORE,
SPOKANE, WA

To splice two pieces of elastic together without the bulk of an overlap, try this technique. Cut a piece of twill tape the same width as the elastic about 2 in. long and place it underneath one end of the elastic. Stitch the overlap, using a multistitch zigzag set to your machine's widest width, and a short stitch length. Butt the other piece of elastic to the end of the first piece and zigzag again. Secure the edges of the butted elastic with another zigzag between the first two. Trim off the remaining twill tape. The spliced elastic will slide beautifully within a casing.

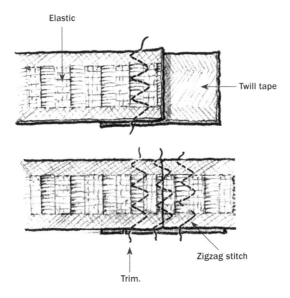

Elastic

Twill tape

Zigzag stitch

Trim.

Stitch Elastic at Center Back

—SARAH COLLEY JONES,
CARTHAGE, TX

When stitching around the casing for elastic-waist skirts or pants, try beginning and ending at the center back, overlapping the stitching for 3 in. to 4 in. Then thread a hand-stitching needle with about 10 in. of brightly colored pearl cotton or machine embroidery thread, and whipstitch over the double-stitched area, being careful not to let the stitches show on the right side. You can easily identify the center back visually or even feel it when dressing in the dark.

Insert Multiple Rows of Elastic

—MARSHA STEIN, WATERBURY, CT

When inserting multiple rows of elastic, at a waistline, for example, the trick is to work all the elastic strips through their respective casings at the same time. Try to work one through at a time, and the casing will be so scrunched up it won't be possible to get the second, third, and fourth pieces of elastic through it.

Cut the elastic strips to the required lengths to fit the waist, plus a ½-in. overlap. Attach a safety pin to one end of each elastic piece and a straight pin to the other, perpendicular to the length. Insert the elastic pieces one at a time, safety pin first, into their casings. The straight pin will keep the elastic from slipping into the casing as you work it through. Work ½ in. of each elastic strip into its casing at a time, thereby keeping the pieces nearly even and scrunching up all the casings at the same time.

Here's another hint: If one of the safety pins slips backward as you work the other elastic pieces through, put a straight pin into the casing between the two prongs of the safety pin, then up under one of them at an angle. Keep adjusting the positions of the straight pins as you push the elastic long. Once all the elastic strips are through their casings, overlap and pin the ends of each one with a safety pin. Try on the garment for size. Safety pins hold better than straight pins, and they won't stick you when you slip into the garment.

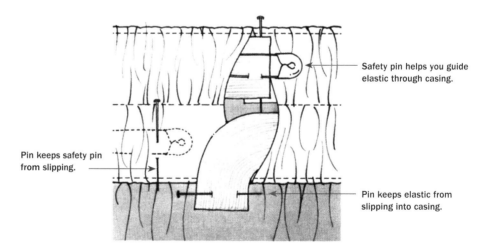

Pin keeps safety pin from slipping.

Safety pin helps you guide elastic through casing.

Pin keeps elastic from slipping into casing.

Cut Bias Strips Easily

—MARY E. WEAVER,
SAVANNAH, GA

Here is a way to cut bias strips that is less confusing and easier to remember than continuous-strip methods. Cut a square of fabric adequate for the bias strips you need. Fold it in half diagonally. Starting with the folded side, make folds toward the point. Stop folding 1 in. or 1½ in. from the point, and pin to hold the folds in place. Draw a perpendicular line from the point to the outside edge of the folds. Starting from this line, draw lines at intervals that equal the width of the strip desired. With knife-edged scissors or a rotary cutter, cut on the lines drawn, and the strips are ready to be joined. To estimate the total length of your joined bias strip, figure the total length you'd get from your square of fabric if the strips were cut on the straight grain. The result is a slightly shorter length when the strips are cut on the bias—almost 12 ft. of 1-in. strips from a square foot of fabric.

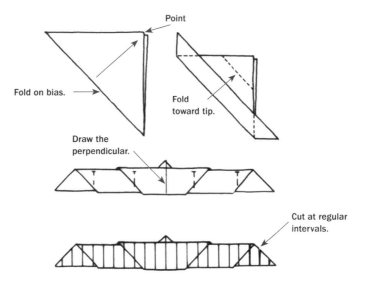

Prevent Sagging in Georgette-Lined Garments

—KAREN ROTH WOLFF,
ALISO VIEJO, CA

Using georgette is a nice way to line lightweight garments, thanks to the sheerness of the fabric and the wide variety of colors that are available. However, it sometimes, with time, sags below the finished garment hem even when the lining is tacked or sewn at the hem. To prevent this and to help keep it in position, align the fabric and lining over vertical darts and seams and stitch in the ditch for about ¼ in. to ½ in., close to the top of the dart or seam. It's a simple step that eliminates sagging.

HOW TO PREVENT RUNAWAY BEADS WITH STICKY-BACK PAPER

When I'm beading on fabric, I use sticky-back paper to keep my beads contained. I cut a piece of contact shelf liner, approximately 8 in. wide by 12 in. long (sticky-back stabilizer or any other adhesive-backed paper will also work), and remove the protective paper from the adhesive side. I then place the paper sticky-side up on a padded board or a piece of corrugated cardboard, and pin or tape it to each of the board's corners. When I spread the beads out on the sticky paper, they stay put. For added security, I sometimes place the board on a serving tray that has lips on four sides. The sticky paper allows me to sit in my favorite chair while I bead without worrying about beads spilling, and the beads don't roll away when I try to pick one up.

—GWENDOLYN LELACHEUR, HARSEN'S ISLAND, MI

Back Your Appliqués for Smooth Results

—JUDITH NEUKAM, *THREADS* EXECUTIVE EDITOR

Here's a way to apply appliqués easily with smooth results even around curves. First, stitch netting or organza to the appliqué with right sides together. Stitch along the design's outside seamline, overlapping the starting and ending stitches. Trim the seam allowance to about $\frac{1}{8}$ in., and clip the curves and corners as appropriate. Cut a slash in the backing fabric, and turn the appliqué right side out. Press the edges flat, and you're ready to attach the appliqué to your garment with ease.

Use Glue to Sew Beaded Fringe

—JANE TUTTON, VERO BEACH, FL

Beaded fringe can be tricky to sew into a seam by machine, because if the fringe moves, it's easy to sew through a bead and break the needle. To keep the fringe in place, try using a glue stick to secure the flange and painter's blue low-tack tape to secure the fringe out of the way. This ensures you won't have to wrestle with the fringe to keep from breaking beads or needles when stitching blindly through two layers with the beads sandwiched in between.

Make Your Own Piping

—BRENDA BLACKWOOD, BURLINGTON, ONTARIO, CANADA

Cut the bias strips, wrap the cord, and stitch it with a zipper foot. Next, unthread the serger and remove the needles. With the foot's left side against the stitching line, run the piping through the serger with the knife engaged. The knife trims the raw edges to a perfectly even width, ready to use.

Create Hanging Loops That Stay in Place

—SUSAN KHALJE,
THREADS CONTRIBUTING EDITOR,
GLENARM, MD

Ever made or bought skirts or slacks with hanging loops that slip to the outside and hang out at the waist? Here's how to prevent this: Pin the loop's midpoint at the side seam. Spread the loop out almost as far as it will reach (about 6 in. from end to end), then sew the ends in place by machine as you attach the waistband in a garment being made, or by hand in an already-completed or ready-to-wear garment. Unpin the midpoint. When wearing the garment, the loops will lie flat against the body and won't slip out. When hung, the garment is suspended from four points sewn at a distance from the side seams, so the waist doesn't droop.

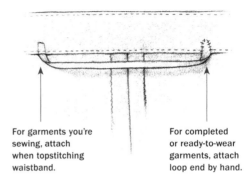

For garments you're sewing, attach when topstitching waistband.

For completed or ready-to-wear garments, attach loop end by hand.

HOW TO ATTACH TATTED LACE

I recently made a pillowcase using heirloom techniques on batiste. I tried to attach tatting to the very edge by machine with varied success. I knew there must be an easy way to attach the fine tatted header row (the straight edge that's typically attached to a garment or other item) without frustration and skipped stitches. Finally, I came up with a solution.

I lightly spray-starched and pressed the tatting flat, then I attached a clear foot and set a 2-mm-wide and 8-mm-long zigzag stitch using lightweight cotton thread (60/2) as the top and bobbin threads. Centering the tatting on top of a 2-in.-wide strip of very light tear-away stabilizer, I sewed it to the stabilizer, catching only the header cord. I placed the stabilizer edge under the pillowcase fabric, butting the fabric edge to the tatted header cord. Then, I zigzagged the tatting to the fabric using the same cotton thread, clear foot, and a 2-mm stitch length and width.

By using the red guide mark on my presser foot to follow the very edge of the header, I was able to sew it on quickly, effortlessly, and with no missed areas. The stabilizer provided an extra bonus at the beginning/ending join: It prevented the tatting from pulling into the throat-plate hole, and I was able to carefully match the two tatted ends to achieve a perfect join. After the stitching was complete, I was able to remove the stabilizer easily.

—SHELBY SMARTE, MIDWAY, KY

CLOSURES

Cover Buttons

—AMY T. YANAGI,
MILLERSVILLE, MD

Here's an improvement on the instructions that come with covered-button sets. It eliminates struggling to tuck the material around the pointed teeth of the metal button form.

Cut out circles of material to the size specified by the button manufacturer. Hand-sew a line of slightly longer-than-normal-length stitches around the circumference of the circle, about $1/16$ in. to $1/8$ in. from the edge. Leave the threads long enough to pull. If you're lining the button, attach the lining to the material with the same stitches.

Pull the threads to gather the circle of material loosely into a cap. Then insert the button form. Pull the threads until the material is wrapped tightly and evenly around the form. If there's a pattern on the material, position it as desired, and then tie off the threads and clip them short.

Gently push the material down into the center back of the button and around the teeth. Don't worry about hooking the material tightly over the teeth, because the material is already secure. Finish the button by snapping on the back plate.

Keep Buttons Secure

—ANN ESTEY,
BOULDER, CO

What's the secret to keeping buttons on? No knot! To begin sewing the button on, stitch the thread three or four times through the fabric where the center of the button will be. Don't tie a knot. Then sew on the button. If the button has no shank, put a pin on top of the button under the first thread sewn through it. Sew through the button's holes just three or four times. Remove the pin, and wrap the thread around the "shank" created between the garment and button. Catch the thread securely on the underside of the garment, clip it, and the button is on to stay.

Keep Buttons in Place with Glue When Machine Sewing

—MONTY S. LEITCH,
PILOT, VA

Attaching nonshank, sew-through buttons by machine is definitely the way to go. The buttons are securely attached, and it takes less time than hand sewing. But buttons, especially small ones, have a tendency to wiggle out from under the presser foot until the first few stitches are in place. To prevent the wiggle, touch each button to a glue stick before placing it on the fabric—just enough to keep it in place for sewing. The button stays firmly in place and makes the task quicker and much less frustrating.

HOW TO STITCH-MARK FOR FOOLPROOF BUTTON REATTACHMENT

Many buttons are too beautiful and too expensive to risk damaging by leaving them on a garment during dry cleaning. To avoid this, I attached special shank buttons with button pins (a ¾-in. safety pin with a hump that fits over the button shank).

But each time I repinned the buttons, I had to locate the correct position by trial and error, pinning and shifting the buttons until they were evenly spaced. I needed a way to simplify this process. I decided to "mark" the button positions by using my sewing machine's darning foot, dropping the feed dogs, and stitching a stippled circle (similar to a reinforced darned area), about ⅛ in. in diameter. Sometimes I match the thread color to the garment, but other times (when working with a busy print fabric, for instance) I use a contrasting color so I can better see the circle. The stippled area is so small that the button completely covers the stitching. Now when my garments come back from the dry cleaners, I can quickly and precisely reattach the buttons on these permanently stitched circles.

—EVELYN OWENS, ROANOKE, VA

Line Up Buttons

—DARLENE A. SUCHYTA,
DEARBORN, MI

Place a piece of double-faced basting tape under one side of a button to hold it in place while it is being sewn down. Be sure to place the tape out of the way of the sewing holes. Remove the tape when the button is sewn.

Hold Buttons in Place with Basting Tape

—EDNA ISAAC,
TULSA, OK

Here's a way to line up three or more nonshank buttons on a sleeve vent that produces perfect results. Place the buttons faceup on a flat surface appropriately spaced. Next, place a piece of transparent tape over the button faces, connecting them in the desired placement. Flip this unit over, so that the backs of the buttons are on top, and position the sticky side of ¼-in., double-sided tape over the strip of buttons. Remove the remaining protective paper from the other side of the tape and affix the buttons in place on the garment where they are to be stitched. The tape holds the buttons securely in place while you machine-sew right through the tape for perfect placement.

Attach Bulkless Buttons Worn below the Waist

—MARSHA M. KITT, TWO HILLS, ALBERTA, CANADA

Large, chunky shank buttons look great on blouses worn loose over trousers and skirts, but when the blouse is tucked in, the bottom button can create an unsightly and/or uncomfortable lump if it falls at or below the waistband. To eliminate this problem, attach the button with a button pin instead of sewing it on. The pin is similar to a regular safety pin, but one side includes a semicircular curve along its length that helps attach shank buttons without puckers. When the blouse is worn tucked in, just remove the pin-secured button for a smooth, more attractive look.

Matched "Lips" on Bound Buttonholes

—F. WILLIAM VOETBERG, GRAND RAPIDS, MI

To get perfectly matched "lips" on bound buttonholes, start by cutting a piece of lip fabric long enough to make all of the lips for the number of buttonholes you plan to make (two lips per buttonhole), cutting the piece four times the width of one finished lip (usually ¼ in.). Before cutting the fabric into individual lip pieces, fold it lengthwise with wrong sides together. Then make a chalk mark lengthwise down the center of the folded piece. When stitching each lip in place, stitch along the chalkline. When the lips are turned to the inside of the buttonhole, they will match perfectly every time.

HOW TO MAKE LIGHT BUTTONHOLES IN HEAVY FABRIC

I designed a heavy denim jacket, which I embellished with 15 decorative buttons and corresponding buttonholes. In addition, I used the reverse side of the denim to add contrasting piping in the seams. In some places, I chose to add a decorative buttonhole where the fabric was thick even after trimming and grading because of the heavy fabric. No matter what I did, I couldn't get smooth, even ends on my buttonholes due to the fabric's bulk.

After much experimenting, I solved the problem. I stitched my buttonholes on two layers of tulle netting (the same color as my thread), then trimmed close to the stitching. Since the buttonholes weren't functional, they didn't need to support the stress of being buttoned and unbuttoned. I placed the tulle buttonholes on Steam-a-Seam®, then fused them to the jacket in each marked location and sewed my decorative buttons on top to give the appearance that the button was through the buttonhole! You couldn't tell that the buttonholes weren't stitched in the denim without scrutinizing each one.

—ESTHER D'ABATE, PAINESVILLE, OH

Create a Button Shank from Thread

—JENNIFER LOBB, NANAIMO, BRITISH COLUMBIA, CANADA

Sewing buttons on thick fabric usually requires a shanked button to allow the thick garment-front fabric to fit between the button and the front after it's buttoned. But sometimes a no-shank button is the best bet. To use a flat button on thick fabric, make a button shank from thread.

To start, attach the button with a knotted double thread, and take one small stitch on the right side of the fabric. (The knot will be hidden under the button, and the inside of the garment will be neat.) Then push the needle in and out of the buttonholes and back into the fabric, but don't pull the thread tight.

Next, choose a spacer. For thin fabrics, use a straight pin or toothpick. For thicker fabrics, use a heavy darning needle, bobby pin, chopstick, or thin pen. Insert the spacer between the fabric and button, and then tug slightly on the sewing needle to tighten the thread and secure the spacer. Keeping the spacer between the fabric and the button, continue to sew the button in the usual fashion. The spacer will ensure that there is ample space between the fabric and the button during stitching.

When the button has been sewn securely (with the needle on the wrong side of the fabric), remove the spacer and hold the button away from the fabric, keeping the threads taut. Then bring the needle up to the front of the fabric but behind the button, and wind the thread around the taut threads. Keep winding until the new shank is strong.

For a more finished look, particularly when a large spacer has been used, make closely spaced blanket stitches around the threads instead of simply winding the thread around the shank. When finished, secure the thread close to the shank.

Use Multiple Fabric Layers to Cover Buttons for Sheers or Knits

—KAREN ROTH WOLFF, ALISO VIEJO, CA

Stretching a knit or using a sheer fabric when covering a metal button can result in the button frame showing through. To prevent this, use multiple layers of fabric if the fabric is thin, or use a permanent marker to color the button frame first. This not only results in a perfectly matched button, but it also prevents potential metallic shine from peeking through.

Finish a Bound Buttonhole

—SUSAN HUTCHINS, SAGAMORE BEACH, MA

The quickest and least bulky method to finish the backs of bound buttonholes is to work a machine buttonhole on the facing that corresponds to the bound buttonhole. Then stitch in the ditch of the buttonhole lip seam to hold the layers together.

Sew on Buttons Using Transparent Tape

—DAVID MANGELS,
WOODINVILLE, WA

Sewing buttons on a shirt or blouse is easy with the use of transparent tape. First, sew the buttonholes; then rest a button on each hole precisely where desired. Carefully lay a piece of tape the length of the shirt front across the buttons so that the tape sticks to each button and the placket as you press it down. Adjust the buttons if necessary. Mark the tape at the bottom and top of the shirt front. Lift the tape with the buttons affixed, and move it to the opposite side of the shirt. Align the tape so the top and bottom marks are placed properly and the buttons are the correct distance from the center edge. Press the tape to the fabric. The buttons are now securely held by the tape and can be sewn to the garment right through the tape by machine or hand. The tape can easily be removed once the stitching is complete, and each button will be perfectly placed, ready to slip into the appropriate buttonhole.

Make a No-Seam Zipper

—JOHANNA ST. CLAIR,
PORT JEFFERSON, NY

Here's a neat way to install zippers in fabrics that don't fray, like Polarfleece®. The method allows the zipper to be placed anywhere on the garment, not just positioned under a seam, and the finish is secure, flat, and attractive.

First, lay the zipper faceup under the fabric where desired and pin it perpendicular to its length to hold it in place. Then staystitch a uniform distance around the zipper teeth, removing pins as you approach them, producing a stitched rectangle or an open-ended rectangle in the case of a neckline. Carefully slit along the center of the zipper teeth, stopping ½ in. from the rectangle's end(s). Clip the fabric diagonally at the ends of the long slit to meet the corners, which will look like the center drawing below. Fold back the cut edges away from the zipper teeth, and hold them with a pin or awl while staystitching them in place. Finally, satin-stitch around the zipper teeth to cover the staystitching, using a wide, short stitch and an interesting thread, such as a topstitching or a machine-embroidery thread.

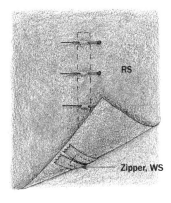

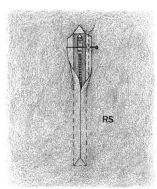

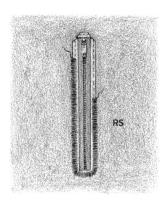

HOW TO USE MEDICAL PAPER TAPE TO ANCHOR BUTTONHOLE CORDING

I've never been able to get the cording (I use three single strands of embroidery floss) to stay put while using my machine's one-step buttonhole attachment. The foot's hook/anchor is not able to hold the floss securely as I manipulate the fabric.

Now I use translucent medical paper tape (Nexcare™ is my favorite) to tape the cording in place. I chalk-mark the ends and center of my buttonholes as usual. I make the marks extra bold so they will be visible through the tape. Then I fold the cording in half and place it on top of my buttonhole with one half on each side. I anchor it in place with a piece of tape at each end of the buttonhole. Although I've never left the tape on for more than a few hours, I've always been able to remove it easily, even from delicate fabrics, and it doesn't leave a residue. I sew each buttonhole slowly, in case I need to adjust the cording slightly to prevent it from getting caught in the stitches, although this rarely happens. For the occasional adjustment, I stop sewing with the needle in the fabric and use the sharp end of a straight pin to scoot the cording back into place and resume sewing.

—JULIE ORMSBY, MEMPHIS, TN

Get Precision Placement for Hooks and Eyes
—ANDREA L. MOORE, SPOKANE, WA

Here's how to precisely position the eyes of a hook-and-eye set: First sew on the hook, then lap the garment as it's intended to look when the closure is complete, pinning it in that position. Slip the eye onto the hook, then pin through the holes at each side of the eye, attaching the eye to the underlap so that it doesn't distort either layer, or offset them at their upper or lower edges. Take a few stitches to secure the eye before unpinning.

Install Invisible Zippers
—SHEILAH BARRETT-SANDLER, NORTHAMPTON, MA

Invisible zippers can be a real pain to install, but here's a technique that makes the process much easier. The key centers on a pintuck foot, which is available for any sewing machine model and is standard issue with some machines. After pressing the teeth of the zipper according to the zipper packet instructions, install the pintuck foot on your machine. The groove for the pintuck slides over the zipper teeth, providing perfect stitching every time. With this method, it might take less time to sew in an invisible zipper than a regular one.

Create Less Obvious Buttonholes First

—PAULA HUDSON,
GREEN VALLEY, AZ

Sewing the least-noticed buttonhole first and the most-noticed buttonhole last gives practice time to get the most noticeable one perfect. For blouses, sew the bottom buttonhole first and work your way up. And since the bottom buttonhole of a dress is noticed more than the second from the bottom, first sew the one second from the bottom.

Get a Perfect Lapped Zipper

—CHARLOTTE ANDREWS,
HAVERFORD, PA

Machine-stitching a lapped zipper can often cause the fabric to shift, thus distorting the grain and horizontal stripes. Here's a quick, neat method to correct that.

First, close the seam, backstitching at the end of the opening. Then press the seam open, including the zipper seam allowances. Inset the zipper on the right-hand seam allowance, leaving room for the tab to slide easily to the right of the seam. Baste it in place along the right seam allowance. Now open the zipper, and machine-stitch with the zipper foot in the crease on the left-hand seam allowance. Start sewing from the top. When you near the zipper tab, lower the needle, raise the presser foot, and slide the tab up out of the way; then finish sewing. No stitching will show on the garment's right side.

Close the zipper, and remove the basting thread. Turn the garment right side out, and pin the left side of the garment to the left side of the zipper, slightly overlapping the fold. With tiny backstitches, sew by hand, about ⅜ in. from the fold, manipulating the grain or stripes to match the other side. On the very top, consider moving the line of stitching a little to the left to give the slide more room.

If working with fine fabric, like crepe de chine or charmeuse, insert a narrow piece of organza or a similar suitable fabric before sewing to ensure a crisp look.

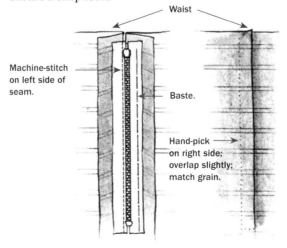

Waist

Machine-stitch
on left side of
seam.

Baste.

Hand-pick
on right side;
overlap slightly;
match grain.

Set an Invisible Zipper

—SANDRA VASSALLO,
ROZELLE, NEW SOUTH WALES, AUSTRALIA

Here's a simple yet effective method to accurately set an invisible zipper without basting. Serge the seam edges using a ⅛-in.-wide, three-thread overlock stitch. Then, align the zipper tape edge with the inside serged edge. The tape rests against the slightly raised serging without slipping and results in a perfect ⅝-in. seam allowance when inserted using an invisible zipper foot.

HOW TO CONCEAL A ZIPPER

I constructed a gown that called for a separating zipper in the bodice. I couldn't find a zipper in the appropriate color or weight, so I used a light, jacket-weight zipper instead. The technique I used was to double-cover the zipper by using the following procedure: After fitting the bodice, extend the seam allowance on the right side of the zipper by 1 in. Fold the seam allowance so that the teeth are totally covered, pin in place, and sew close to the right-hand side of the teeth. On the left side, using the ⅝-in. seam allowance, position the fold so that it just covers the first line of stitching. Finish the zipper application by stitching close to the left side of the teeth, making sure the lap on the right-hand side is not caught. The bodice I made had the zipper on the left side of the body. With this method, the teeth were completely concealed.

—MARY LONGREN, HOLTON, KS

TOOLS

Use Two Safety Pins to Pull Elastic or Cording

—BETTY BOLDEN,
BOLTON, CT

When pulling elastic or cording through a casing, if a safety pin is used to help guide it, the elastic or cording at the starting point can sneak into the casing. It can be difficult to "weave" back. If you try holding it in place with a straight pin, the pin can slip out in the process. Try using a second safety pin to secure the tail end of the elastic or cording to the casing. It holds securely, and you don't ever have to worry about it accidentally sliding into the casing.

Use a Ruler to Determine Grainline

—HEATHER TORGENRUD, ST. IGNATIUS, MT

Small pattern pieces are difficult to position on the straight grain because of their short grainline arrow. To help, place a ruler precisely along the arrow and attach it to the pattern tissue with removable tape. Then measure to the selvage from each end of the ruler. The longer line created by the ruler allows for more accurately positioning the piece on the straight of the grain.

Cut Inside Corners with Small Scissors

—EDITH FRANKEL, HANNAWA FALLS, NY

Cutting precise points and right angles with a rotary cutter is a snap if you can cut past the point on both sides, but for inside corners it's more difficult. Try stopping short of the corner and finish the cut with small, sharp scissors. Don't try to cut around the corner with the scissors. Cut up to the corner from one direction, then from the other. This will give accurate results every time.

Clip Curves with a Craft Knife

—PAMELA BEACH, DEARBORN, MI

When using scissors to clip curved seam allowances, it is easy to go too far and cut into the seam. To avoid this problem, try using a sharp craft knife instead of scissors. Place the curved fabric edge on a cutting mat. Starting one or two threads away from the seamline, slice toward the raw edge with the knife.

This procedure also works to prepare curved appliqué pieces for application. Start one or two threads away from the marked (not yet sewn) seamline, and slice as before. This technique prevents accidental overclipping because you cut away from the stitches instead of toward them. It's more precise and takes less time than using scissors.

Cut through Foam with a Rotary Cutter Instead of Scissors

—PEG PENNELL, OMAHA, NE

A 45-mm rotary cutter can cut through foam with ease, creating a nice, smooth cut along the cutting lines drawn with a permanent marker. It takes a fraction of the time to cut that scissors might, and the edges are not jagged as they often are when cut with scissors.

Color-Match Stabilizer

—JOANNE M. SPENCER, BROOKFIELD, CT

Machine embroidery requires the support of a good stabilizer, and stabilizers tend to come in only a few colors—black, white, and off-white. Even when the excess stabilizer is torn off, some may still show on the inside of the garment when it is worn. Try using a permanent-ink scrapbook pen that matches the fabric to color the stabilizer before sewing the embroidery, and there won't be black or white where you don't want it.

Turn a Point with Tweezers

—KAREN A. HURST,
ALTADENA, CA

A very easy way to turn a sharp point is to push the fabric into place with tweezers. Here's how: After carefully sewing a corner, pivoting rather than stitching across it, trim and then grade the seams, making three angled cuts at the corner to minimize bulk. Don't try to press the seams wrong side out. Instead, use a finger to push the seams roughly where desired. Then use a standard pair of tweezers (not surgical or other sharply pointed tweezers—those with an angled tip are particularly good) to grasp the corner point stitch and push in, teasing the corner into place. Now for the magical secret: Gently let the tweezers open, stretching open the seamlines at the corner, which allows you to push the corner out farther (push gently if your fabric is loosely woven). Repeat this push/stretch sequence until the corner is perfect, then press the seamlines and sharp new corner flat.

Try Spray Adhesive for Underlining

—LENORE ANDERSON,
ROCHESTER, NY

To tame slippery lining fabric when using underlining, use temporary spray adhesive found in the quilting section of craft stores (such as Sulky KK 2000). Spray the wrong side of the fashion fabric or lining material and place one piece on top of the other, wrong sides together. The spray holds pieces together smoothly while stitching. The adhesive allows for the fabric to be repositioned as desired. Then, like magic, the adhesive is gone, leaving a perfectly underlined, finished garment.

HOW TO USE A GLUE STICK FOR SEWING

I teach sewing to teenagers, and I find that a glue stick can be very handy when my students are learning a new skill. In fact, I often use glue sticks myself, because they make some sewing situations easier—even for me! Some of the ways we use the glue stick in class are the following:

- Holding down seam allowances on patch pockets to prepare the pocket for stitching.
- Holding a patch pocket in place on the garment as it is stitched.
- Holding straight seams together for sewing.
- Holding hems in place while they are stitched.
- Holding an appliqué in place as it is stitched.

The best part is that the glue washes out completely when the task is finished.

—JUDY LEATHLEY, TOOWOOMBA, QUEENSLAND, AUSTRALIA

Use a Lined Cutting Mat for Alterations

—PAMELA JOHNSTON, MCMINNVILLE, OR

To make length or width adjustments that require folding a tuck or cutting a spread in the tissue, begin by matching the pattern's grainlines to the lines on a cutting mat, and hold them together with pattern weights. Then, with a rotary cutter and a 2-in. transparent ruler, make straight alteration cuts to spread pattern pieces or fold them as needed. Matching the lines on the mat to the pattern grainline before cutting helps keep cuts or folds (which also follow the lines on the mat) squared with the grain, either perpendicular or parallel to it as needed.

Use Sticky Stabilizer as a Stitching Template

—TEENA WEDEMEYER, DAWSON CREEK, BRITISH COLUMBIA, CANADA

Water-soluble, sticky stabilizer makes an excellent stitching template. If a pocket or a placket needs a straight, sharp edge or a perfect curve, cut a piece of stabilizer to the finished shape of the pattern piece and stick it to the wrong side of the fabric (be sure the fabric is washable). Then fold the seam allowances around the stabilizer to the wrong side of the fabric; the stabilizer creates a firm, crisp line for stitching. After washing, the stabilizer will be gone, and all that will be left is a perfect line of stitching. This works particularly well for silky fabrics that have a tendency to pucker and slip. Small scraps of stabilizer are also great for firming up fabric when you're stitching buttonholes. With the water-soluble stabilizer, there is no residue and no puckers.

HOW TO MAKE A STATIC-FREE IRONING BOARD

I recently worked with some beautiful, hand-painted silk that needed its static tamed, and I wanted to press the fabric before I laid out the pattern pieces. I was afraid to spray Static Guard® directly on the silk because I didn't want to risk ruining the dye, and rubbing a cotton cloth treated with Static Guard didn't seem to help (although it works wonders on satins and other fabrics). Finally, I sprayed my ironing board with Static Guard before pressing (with a cool, dry iron), and that eliminated the static completely without harming the dye!

—JOCELYN SHORT, ARVADA, CO

TRY STABILIZER TO AVOID DISTORTING STITCHES

For drag-free sewing, I tried to use tissue paper between the machine and
an extraordinarily sticky vinyl, but found that tearing away the tissue paper
distorted my stitches. I then replaced the tissue with clear, water-soluble Solvy
stabilizer and discovered that I could see where I was sewing, the stabilizer tore
away without distorting the stitches, and any remaining whiskers of stabilizer
dabbed away with a bit of water. Subsequently, I found that older, slightly
dried-out Solvy works even better for this kind of sticky sewing.

—LINDA SOEDER, KITCHENER, ONTARIO, CANADA

ARMS, SLEEVES, AND CUFFS

Set In Sleeves
without Basting

—STEPHANIE TRELICK,
PITTSBURGH, PA

Here's a way to set in sleeves with a moderate amount of ease in the
cap, smoothly setting to the armscye without any ease basting. Match
and pin the underarm seams, the notches, the small dots, and the top
of the cap to the shoulder seam. Place the bodice piece uppermost and
the sleeve against the feed dogs and begin stitching at the underarm.

At the first notch, allow for ease in the sleeve by placing your left
hand between the two garment pieces and working the ease evenly
into the area between the notch and the first small dot pin with your
fingertips. Anchor the ease by pulling gently with your right hand on
the upper-bodice fabric from the next pin; this will flatten and control
the ease.

Maintain a gentle pressure on the bodice piece through each
section of the seam. Not only will you be surprised at how much ease
you can incorporate, but you also won't get those unsightly puckers
in the bodice that occur when a sleeve is inadvertently gathered too
much for the size of the armscye.

Set In Sleeves with a Continuous Armhole Seam

—ELEANOR L. SHIELDS, SANTA ROSA, CA

Here's a method of setting a sleeve that creates a continuous armhole seam with no underarm distortion. Sew the shoulder seam and press it open. Sew two rows of long stitches for easing between the notches on the sleeve cap. Then stitch the sleeve to the bodice, leaving approximately 1½ in. from the side seams unstitched, as shown in the top center drawing. Fold the right sides of the sleeve together and the right sides of the bodice together. Sew the sleeve and bodice underarm seams separately and press them open. Finally, match the underarm seam and stitch. This method can also be used for pants and three-piece sleeves—especially those that do not have seams to match in the jacket body. It works equally well with French seams.

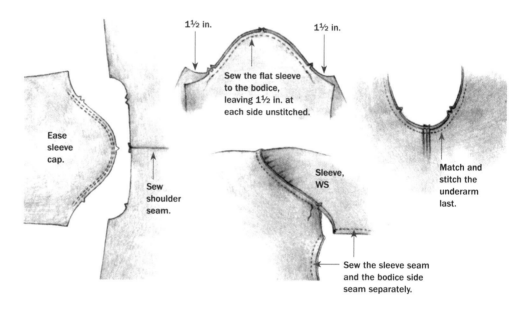

1½ in.   1½ in.

Sew the flat sleeve to the bodice, leaving 1½ in. at each side unstitched.

Ease sleeve cap.

Sew shoulder seam.

Sleeve, WS

Match and stitch the underarm last.

Sew the sleeve seam and the bodice side seam separately.

Machine-Baste Seamlines in Sleeves

—MARILYN BARKSDALE, REHOBOTH BEACH, DE

Here's a foolproof method to set in sleeves: Machine-baste the sleeve seamline (usually ⅝ in.) between the double and single notches of the sleeve. While stitching, gently ease the fabric by resting a finger on the fabric—not too tightly—behind the foot while stitching. Release your finger from the fabric every 2 in. or so. When the seam is complete, lightly finger-press the seam along the seamline to ease out any puckers that may have developed. Finally, attach the sleeve to the bodice using a normal stitch length, matching dots as appropriate. Remove the basting stitches, using tweezers to remove any stubborn threads.

Make No-Twist Sleeves

—MARSHA STEIN,
WATERBURY, CT

In jackets and coats, slipping and twisted sleeve linings can be avoided if they are joined to the sleeves before being stitched to the rest of the garment lining.

Stitch the underarm seam of the sleeve lining and press it open. Ease-stitch the sleeve cap, turn the seam allowance under, and baste. Then, wrong sides together, match the underarm seams of the sleeve lining and the sleeve. Pin one seam allowance of the lining to the corresponding seam allowance of the sleeve. Baste them together with thread that matches the lining, ending the stitching about 3 in. from the lower edge of the sleeve.

Now slip your hand into the sleeve lining from the armhole end of the sleeve, and grab the lower edge of both the garment sleeve and lining. Then pull the garment sleeve through the lining. Like magic, the sleeve lining will be right side out over the garment sleeve. The basting stitches on the seam allowances will prevent the lining from slipping.

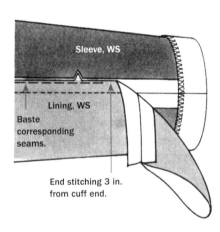

Sleeve, WS

Lining, WS

Baste corresponding seams.

End stitching 3 in. from cuff end.

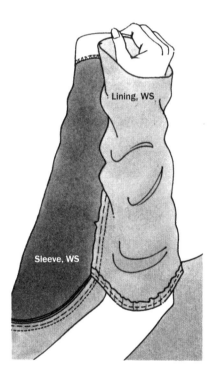

Lining, WS

Sleeve, WS

Produce Smooth Sleeve Insertion without Basting

—BERNICE YUTAN FIRESTONE, WINNETKA, IL

Here's a great way to produce a smooth, unpuckered sleeve insertion without adding basting stitches to the sleeve first. Place the sleeve inside the bodice with right sides together as usual. Stitch the lower portion of the sleeve between the notches to secure the underarm section of the sleeve. Instead of then easing the seam with the sleeve on the inside, turn the sleeve wrong side out, and put the bodice inside the sleeve (right sides together). Use your hand or fingers to bend the sleeve-cap seam as you ease the sleeve to the bodice. This effectively shapes the sleeve-cap edge as you work it, albeit wrong side out, and it can be more easily basted or pinned smoothly.

Lengthen Coat Sleeves

—MELISSA ENNIS, ARLINGTON, VA

Here's a tip for lengthening the three-quarter-length sleeves of vintage swing coats from the 1950s and 1960s: Knit faux-fur mohair cuffs in a contrasting color. Make a gauge swatch, measure the coat sleeve opening, and knit in reverse stockinette on a circular needle for twice the depth of the cuff. Cast off loosely, fold the knit cuff in half, and sew both edges to the sleeve edge.

HOW TO SEW A SLEEVE THE EASY WAY

Despite what the pattern directions indicate, sometimes I find it easier to set in a sleeve flat—that is, before the bodice side seam and the sleeve underarm seam are sewn. However, unless my fabric is soft and flowing, I don't like the way the underarm seams intersect or how the finished sleeve hangs. So I occasionally use a combination of flat and in-the-round sewing. I sew a line or two of easestitching along the upper cap of the sleeve, between the front and back notches as usual. I then ease and sew the sleeve into the armscye just in this area. With the top part of the sleeve cap stitched in place, I can sew the bodice side seam and the underarm seam, and finish setting in the sleeve by sewing the underarm section in the round. Both the inside and outside of the sleeve look better when I use this method.

—CAROL FRESIA, DANBURY, CT

Attach Bias Trim to Sleeve Edges

—MARTHA MCKEON,
SANDY HOOK, CT

Here's a quick, easy, secure method for attaching bias trim to gathered sleeve edges or bishop necklines:

Run a gathering thread along the sleeve edge ¼ in. from the bottom. Cut a strip of bias 2½ in. wide and the desired length (arm or wrist circumference plus ease and seam allowances). Press the bias strip in half so it's 1¼ in. wide. Pin the cut edges of the bias to the bottom gathered edge, distributing fullness and leaving 1½ in. on each side ungathered. Sew the strip to the sleeve just above the gathering thread with about a ⅜-in. seam (drawing below left—bias not to scale). Press the seam, and trim to ¼ in. Then turn the folded edge of the bias trim to the wrong side and pin, bringing it just beyond the seamline. Stitch in the ditch on the right side to secure it, leaving 1 in. on each side unstitched.

Next, attach the sleeve to the garment armscye. Sew the side and underarm seams as a continuous French seam, starting at the bottom of the garment side—wrong sides together—with a ⅜-in. seam allowance. Stop where the bias seam begins. Press, trim the seam to ⅛ in., and clip at the bias seam. Then turn, press, and seam the entire underarm and side—this time, including the bias edge of the sleeve with a ¼-in. seam. In the final step, trim the bias to the wrong side, pin it, and complete the stitching in the ditch.

This technique eliminates attaching bias to a cylindrical surface and hand-whipstitching the bias to the wrong side of the fabric—a tedious process and less sturdy finish.

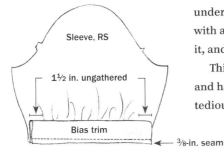

Sleeve, RS

1½ in. ungathered

Bias trim

⅜-in. seam

Sew bias onto flat garment piece.

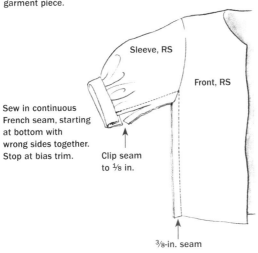

Sleeve, RS

Front, RS

Sew in continuous French seam, starting at bottom with wrong sides together. Stop at bias trim.

Clip seam to ⅛ in.

⅜-in. seam

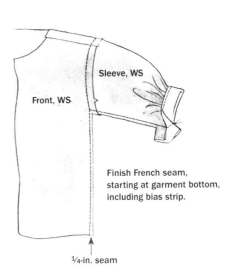

Sleeve, WS

Front, WS

Finish French seam, starting at garment bottom, including bias strip.

¼-in. seam

Make a One-Piece Sleeve and Cuff

—MARY HARDENBROOK, HUNTINGTON BEACH, CA

This trick is meant for short sleeves but can also work with long sleeves—just be aware that the cuff doesn't unbutton, so it needs to be wider than the hand. Also note that the finished cuff will have the same directional pattern as the sleeve. Add twice the desired width of the cuff plus ¾ in. to the length of the finished sleeve. Before sewing the sleeve seam, measure the cuff's width from the bottom of the fabric's wrong side, and press a fold. Press another fold where the raw edge meets the inside fold of the fabric, as shown below. Unfold the material and sew the sleeve seam, matching the foldlines. With the sleeve wrong side out, refold following the pressed foldlines, then topstitch ¼ in. to ⅜ in. from the lower folded edge through all layers. Finally, with the right side out, unfold the cuff downward as shown in the drawing, and press.

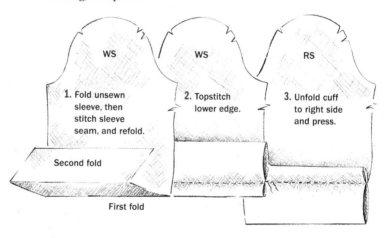

WS

1. Fold unsewn sleeve, then stitch sleeve seam, and refold.

Second fold

First fold

WS

2. Topstitch lower edge.

RS

3. Unfold cuff to right side and press.

Make Vest Armholes

—MARY LOUISE KOBE, MIDDLETOWN, DE

To avoid using bias tape on vest armholes, baste the fabric and lining right sides together all around the armholes, press the seam open, and remove the basting. When you turn the vest to the right side, just topstitch around the armhole, which is pressed to fit together perfectly.

Make a Quick Cuff Placket for a Lined Jacket

—EVELYN BLAKE, ROANOKE, VA

Try this technique to finish a sleeve-placket opening without making a real placket. Before doing any sewing on the sleeve or the lining, pin the lining to the sleeve with right sides together. Stitch parallel rows the length of the placket with two or three small stitches across the tip. Cut a slit between the two rows and diagonally into the corners at the top. Turn the lining to the inside of the sleeve, press, and proceed, treating the sleeve and lining as one layer.

Refine a Dropped Shoulder

—MARGARET KOMIVES,
MILWAUKEE, WI

Patterns for dropped- or extended-shoulder garments have straight shoulder seams, but similar ready-to-wear garments have rounded ones. Refine your pattern by taking off ½ in. from the armscye on both the bodice back and front at the shoulderline. Take 1 in. out of the sleeve pattern with a ½-in.-deep tuck along the shoulderline. The sleeve cap for this type of sleeve should have little, if any, ease. If the pattern being used includes ease, remove it at the underarm after stitching the sleeve to the bodice and checking the right side of the garment for appearance.

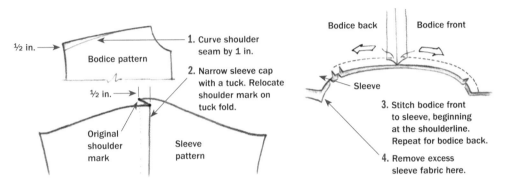

½ in.

Bodice pattern

½ in.

Original shoulder mark

Sleeve pattern

1. Curve shoulder seam by 1 in.

2. Narrow sleeve cap with a tuck. Relocate shoulder mark on tuck fold.

Bodice back

Bodice front

Sleeve

3. Stitch bodice front to sleeve, beginning at the shoulderline. Repeat for bodice back.

4. Remove excess sleeve fabric here.

HOW TO MAKE SMOOTHER SHOULDERLINES

By moving the shoulder seams of modern patterns so they're positioned like the shoulder seams I've seen in late-19th-century patterns and illustrations, I've achieved a smoother shoulderline on dresses and blouses. The older seam placement is typically about 1 in. behind the usual top-of-the-shoulder position most often used today. Moving the seam eliminates the bulky, wavy seam ridge that can mar the front of the garment. To do this, simply add 1 in. to the front seam allowance, and subtract the same amount from the back, stitching the pieces together as usual.

—GAIL MANNING, DON MILLS, ONTARIO, CANADA

NECKLINES AND COLLARS

Sew Crisp Knit Neckbands

—CINDY PETERSON,
MYRTLE POINT, OR

Here's a neat way to make professional-looking knit neckbands. Cut the collar or neckband pattern as usual out of commercial knit ribbing. Cut a piece of Wonder-Under® or other double-faced fusible half the width of the neckband, without seam allowances. Press the fusible to one-half of the neckband on the wrong side. Using the paper backing as a stitching guide, sew the neckband ends with right sides together. Trim the seams and corners, then turn and press. Remove the paper backing and press again, fusing the front to the back. Stitch the completed neckband into the garment as directed on the pattern instructions.

Streamline a Shirt Collar

—JUDY RAND,
COCONUT CREEK, FL

When cutting a shirt collar that has a straight edge, remove the seam allowance from the outer edge of the pattern piece and cut the collar on the fold. That way, there won't be any intersecting seams at the collar points, and the collar points come out nice and crisp.

How to Correct Shifting Necklines

—PHYLLIS ROSEN,
AIKEN, SC

Sometimes a heavy collar or an elaborate back treatment shifts the neckline of a garment as it's worn. To prevent that, slip small, round dress or drapery weights into the front points of covered shoulder pads to equalize the weight. Put the weights inside the pad on the body side to ensure a smooth bodice front.

WAISTBANDS

Make Waistbands More Comfortable

—BETTY J. MOORE,
NORTH BAY, ONTARIO, CANADA

Here's a tip for obtaining a better fit in sewn-on elastic waistbands: Mark the elastic waistband in even quarters, then move the side marks toward the back by $\frac{1}{2}$ in. When applying the elastic, match these adjusted marks to the garment's side markings. Most people have a larger front- than back-waist measurement, and this adjustment to the distribution of elastic on the waist puts a bit more elastic where it's needed for comfort.

Plan for Waistband Adjustments

—ARLENE SWAIN,
KISSIMMEE, FL

When making a pair of pants or a skirt, add a seam with an oversized seam allowance in the waistband's center back. It's helpful when making initial fitting adjustments and those required because of future weight loss or gain.

Make a Self-Interfaced Waistband

—JEANETTE BERNSTEIN,
CRANSTON, RI

For a neat, easy waistband, cut a strip from the selvage edge of the fabric three times the width of the finished band, plus the selvage itself, and 5 in. longer than the waist measurement (for overlap and seam allowances). Then, with the right side facing you and the selvage on the bottom, fold the band in thirds, as shown, leaving the selvage free. Stitch across the ends, turn the waistband right side out, and press. If the fabric is very soft, consider adding fusible interfacing to the wrong side next to the selvage.

To sew the band to the waistline in one step, pin it in place with the selvage on the inside and the folded edge extending over the seamline on the outside. Stitch it by machine from the outside, sewing very close to the fold and catching the selvage on the inside.

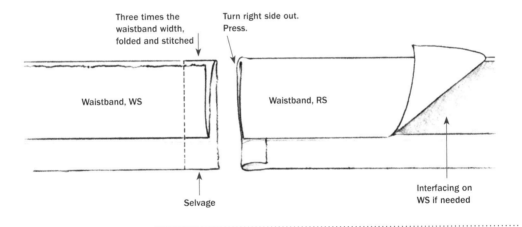

Three times the waistband width, folded and stitched

Turn right side out. Press.

Waistband, WS

Waistband, RS

Selvage

Interfacing on WS if needed

Thread Elastic through Waistbands

—CATHERINE NEFF,
MUSCODA, WI

In making pants or skirts with the waistband cut in one with the garment, threading elastic through the waistband can be difficult because it gets caught under the loose edges of the seam allowances. Try using fusible web like Stitch Witchery® to tack the seam allowances down before turning the waistband. Cut pieces a little narrower than the seam allowance and twice the waistband width. After pressing the seams open, put a piece of fusible web between the seam allowance and the garment on each side of the seam, and press again to fuse. With the waistband sewn and the elastic in, the web doesn't show, and inserting the elastic is much easier.

Reduce Waistband Bulk

—FRANCES COWEN,
ATLANTA, GA

To reduce bulk in a waistband, create a mitered "facing" on the inside instead of sewing square ends. First, add 4½ in. to the waist measurement (½ in. for ease, 1 in. for left side extension, and 3 in. to accommodate miters). Cut a band 3 in. wide by the length established above and interface it with a lightweight fusible.

1 Press each short end diagonally to the same long side to form a right triangle.

2 Cut off the triangles ¼ in. away from each fold. Serge-finish the shorter of the two long sides.

3 With right sides together and ¼-in. allowance extended, fold each diagonal end in half, perpendicular to the cut edge, so that cut edges align. Sew. Press the seam open.

4 Turn the band right side out and press. Sew the band to the garment as desired.

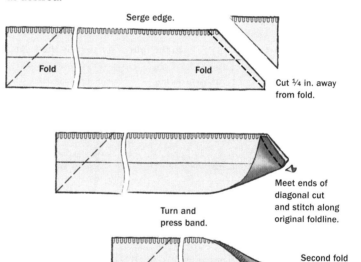

Serge edge.

Fold   Fold

Cut ¼ in. away from fold.

Meet ends of diagonal cut and stitch along original foldline.

Turn and press band.

Second fold

Use Strips of Fabric to Make Maternity Waistbands

—SANDRA THWAITES,
OAKVILLE, ONTARIO, CANADA

The patterns for maternity skirts and pants feature elastic waistbands and recommend using packaged bias tape to form the casing. This is because the top of the front curves so much to go up over your ever-growing stomach that it's impossible to simply turn under a casing. While bias tape is flexible enough to make the curved casing, it can be extremely irritating on increasingly sensitive skin by the last trimester. Try using strips of cotton knit fabric instead of bias tape. The casing has enough stretch to flex around the curved waistband—and it's much softer than the tape.

HOW TO MAKE PARTIAL ELASTIC DRAWSTRINGS

As an alterations professional and teacher, I always enjoy the opportunity to take apart my customers' fine garments and discover how the expensive ready-to-wear designers do things. Here's one idea I've come across and adopted: Drawstrings on pants may look as though they're made completely of fabric, but hidden inside that waistline casing the elastic takes over, making a garment more comfortable to wear and also accommodating minor weight changes. To make a partial-elastic drawstring, cut and sew it 12 in. to 18 in. shorter than the pattern calls for. Cut the finished drawstring in half, and securely sew each cut end to a 12-in. to 18-in. strip of narrow elastic. For more stretch, lengthen the elastic, but don't make it too long, or it will show when you tie the drawstrings.

—PATRICIA "T. C." FERRITO, ANGOLA, NY

Use Nonroll Elastic to Create a Smooth, Low-Bulk Elastic Waistband

—LISA WILLIS, HUNTSVILLE, AL

Here's how to create a tailored-looking waistband that has just the right amount of stretch, but in which the waistband interfacing is replaced by nonroll elastic. Cut the waistline and waistband of skirts and pants an inch or two bigger than your waist and replace the interfacing with nonroll elastic, marked in even quarters. To secure the elastic, bar-tack the elastic to the waist seam allowances (which have been pressed up and toward the waistband) at the ends, the center front, side seams, and center back, matching the quarter marks to the seams. Then sew the ends of the waistband, right sides together, creating an underlap on one end, and turn them right side out. Last, fold the waistband tightly down over the elastic, baste it in place to prevent shifting, and then stitch in the ditch from the right side to fasten the inner edge of the waistband in place, while enclosing the elastic.

Press Hems and Waistband Casing before Sewing

—SANDRA THWAITES, KILLARA, NEW SOUTH WALES, AUSTRALIA

Flat work is easier, so when sewing clothing, press up the hems and the elastic waistband casing prior to sewing the side seams. It's much easier to press up a 1-in. hem on pants or sleeves when the piece is flat rather than trying to press the hem after the leg has already been sewn.

Add a Waistband in a Sheer Skirt without Adding Bulk

—JOANN BROWN, HARRISBURG, PA

Flowing skirts with sheer overlays are fashionable and pretty. Here's a way to add a narrow elastic waistband without adding bulk. Sew the skirt lining and overlay side seams as the pattern instructs. Pin the waists together with the right side of the sheer fabric facing the wrong side of the lining. Sew a scant ⅛-in. seam around the waist. Turn the sheer layer to the other side of the lining and press. Stitch ¾ in. from the edge to form a casing, leaving a 1-in. opening. Thread ½-in. elastic through the casing, join the ends of the elastic, and stitch the casing opening closed. Anchor the elastic by sewing a few stitches at each side seam.

Attach Lining and Waistband at Once

—SAMINA MIRZA, KATY, TX

Here's a slick method for attaching the lining and waistband all at once to a skirt. Prepare each piece separately: skirt (seams sewn, zipper installed), lining (seams sewn, pleats formed or ease-stitched at waist, and the opening for the zipper pressed back), and waistband (interfaced and very carefully marked with notches). Sew one long edge of the waistband to the skirt, right sides together, easing in the skirt as usual, then press the seam toward the waistband. Sew the other long edge of the waistband to the lining, right sides together, and press this seam toward the lining. Fold the waistband along the foldline, wrong sides together, at the same time inserting the lining inside the skirt. Press the foldline, making sure that the lining/waistband seam is ⅛ in. higher rather than aligned with the skirt/waistband seam. Now fold the waistband on the foldline so that right sides are together (this can probably be done without having to pull out the lining), and sew just the short ends of the waistband. Turn the band right side out and press.

To finish the lower edge of the underlap, clip the waistband seam allowance where the lining ends and the underlap begins. Stitch in the ditch from the right side to finish the rest of the waistband, then slipstitch the underlap and finish the rest of the skirt as you would any other lined skirt.

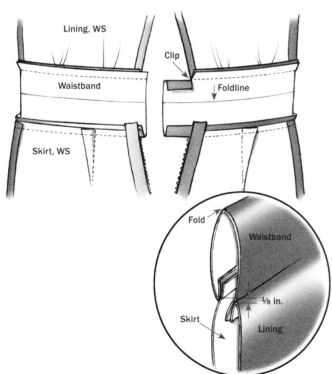

Lining, WS

Waistband

Skirt, WS

Clip

Foldline

Fold

Waistband

Skirt

⅛ in.

Lining

PANTS AND SKIRTS

Install a Removable Skirt Lining

—PHILIPPA YOUNG, BUSBRIDGE, GODALMING, SURREY, ENGLAND

Instead of attaching a skirt to the lining at the hem with a hand-stitched chain, try instead attaching a small length of narrow, lightweight stay tape to the seam allowance of the skirt (near the hem) with a small snap stitched on the end. Stitch the other end of the snap onto the lining at the appropriate place. This means the skirt and lining can easily be separately pressed after laundering—not an easy job if they are linked!

Make Pull-On Pants Sleek

—JILL SMITH, LINCOLN, NE

Here's a ready-to-wear trick for pull-on pants that's quick to sew and results in a smooth, secure finish that looks like a faced waist. Adjust the pattern to have a cut-on casing by measuring the width of the elastic and adding that amount above the waist seamline. If the pattern doesn't already have front and back darts, add faux darts by sewing pintucks on the inside of the pants where the darts would go. When it's time to finish the waistline, place the elastic on the wrong side of the fabric and serge it to the unfinished top edge of the pants. Then fold the elastic to the inside of the pants on the waistline, and hand-tack it to just the seams and each dart. The result is a smoothly finished waistband with no apparent stitches, with elastic that won't twist or bunch.

Elastic

Pull-on pants can be as svelte as those with faced waistlines.

The waistline is the foldline.

Hand-tack the elastic to the seams and darts on the inside.

Serge the elastic inside the pants.

Foldline

Create No-Show Pockets

—DOLORES BROBERG,
SHELTON, WA

Before you cut out side-seam pockets for pants or a skirt, sew a 2-in. width of fashion fabric to a length of lining fabric. Then cut the pocket backs with the fashion fabric on the side-seam edge of the pocket pattern. When the garment is worn, this pocket looks better because any gapes are less evident when the wearer sits, and the bulkiness from heavy layers doesn't show through the front.

HOME ACCENTS

Create Lump-Free Accent Pillows

—MARTHA MCKEON,
SANDY HOOK, CT

Stuff free-form accent pillows with polyester fiberfill, and underline the front and back pieces for a lump-free look. The underlining also helps distribute the filling. Machine-baste a scrap of sturdy woven fabric to the wrong sides of the cover pieces close to the edges. Consider also fusing interfacing to the cover pieces or use double-sided fusible interfacing to fuse a woven fabric lining to the pillow front and back pieces.

Use a Flannel Sheet to Protect Your Cutting Table

—MARGARET C. STORY, GOODRICH, MI

A twin-size fitted flannel sheet is a perfect covering for a cutting table, as the flannel prevents pattern pieces and fabric from sliding around as you work with them.

Prevent Piping Puckers on Slipcovers

—PATRICIA "T. C." FERRITO, ANGOLA, NY

The key to preventing piping in a seam from puckering or bunching up and changing the shape or size of a slipcover is to not sew the piping into the slipcover as its own step. All those extra rows of stitching can cause problems. To install the piping, cut seam allowances to an exact $\frac{1}{2}$ in., draw a line on the slipcover where your piping belongs, and pin it loosely to one layer. Cover it with the second layer, align the edges, and sew the three layers together in one step. It takes some practice to hold the three layers and sew at the same time; use your fingers between the layers to hold the cording in place as you stitch. Even though it seems awkward at first, it's really worth the effort.

Collect Inspiration

—HÉLÈNE MURIEL DOYLE,
VALCARTIER VILLAGE, QUEBEC, CANADA

Keeping a scrapbook of garment pictures is one way to stir one's imagination; another is to sketch interesting garment details while watching movies at home. Keep a sketchpad and pencil next to your remote control—it might just make all the difference on your next sewing project.

HOW TO MAKE EASY-CARE BALLOON VALANCES

I don't use expensive, unruly shirring or ring tape to construct balloon valances for decorative window treatments that remain stationary. After preparing the fabric—including heading and hems—and marking the places for the shirring, I sew the widest, longest zigzag stitch on either side of each marking over a string or cord. I zigzag only the length that will be shirred. To complete the valance, I pull up each pair of cord ends and tie them off. Besides looking good, this valance is much easier to launder and press.

—MARTHA MCKEON, SANDY HOOK, CT

Get Perfect Narrow Mitered Corners

—CHERYL LICHT, PALMER, AK

Do you become frustrated when trying to make garments or home décor items with perfect narrow ¼-in. mitered corners? Here's a foolproof method that results in perfect corners every time. First, fold the fabric's corner to the wrong side, making each edge of the folded "triangle" ¾ in. long, and then press the fold. Trim the pressed triangle so ¼ in. remains along the fold. Then turn each side fabric edge in ¼ in., and press. Finally, fold the sides in another ¼ in., and press again. The end result is a perfect mitered corner and the ability to stitch the pressed edge in any manner for a perfectly finished mitered corner.

SHORTCUTS

SEAMS

Batch Seams to Save Time

—CATHERINE NEFF, MUSCODA, WI

Here's a manufacturing technique that can save time in garment construction: Sew all the seams possible at the same time with a continuous line of stitching. Pin or baste any seam that doesn't intersect another and arrange the seams in your lap one on top of the other so you can reach for them quickly. Sew the first seam; backstitch at the beginning and end. There won't be any thread tails to tie off, because you are going to butt the next seam up against the first. Continue sewing all seams prepared. When all the seams are sewn, cut them apart and press the seam allowances open. Repeat the process till the entire garment is sewn.

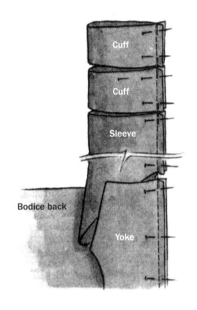

Use Your Fingertip as a Seam Gauge

—TERRY GRANT, ASHLAND, OR

Eyeballing a seam while hand stitching isn't always accurate enough, especially when doing precision piecing, but marking every seamline is very time-consuming. Try sticking a ¼-in.-wide piece of masking tape to the thumbnail of the hand that holds the pieces being sewn. It's easy to line up the edge of the fabric with the outside edge of the tape and to use the inside edge as a moving marker for stitches. Some quilting sources sell ¼-in.-wide tape for marking entire seamlines. Use this tape for its width, and you only need a tiny length for a day's worth of stitching. This method is much faster than sticking all that tape to the fabric.

Use Pattern Samples as Linings

—LIZ VIOLANTE, MARCO ISLAND, FL

Make pattern samples out of preshrunk cotton batiste in the same color as the garment-to-be and then use it as an underlining. This works well with dresses made of lightweight silky polyester material. The lining makes garments easier to handle and more comfortable to wear.

Use Tape to Keep Layers Straight While Making Seams

—MARCY TILTON, CAVE JUNCTION, OR

Here's a fast, clean, and easy technique to keep the layers from shifting when making lapped seams with fleece, melton, or wool jersey. Place the piece that has the underlapping edge right side up on a paper-covered worksurface. Mask the piece using paper and tape so only the seam allowance is exposed, and spray it evenly with a temporary fabric adhesive. It doesn't take much, although textured fabrics may require a thicker coat. Cut the seam allowance off the overlapping edge and place the overlap on top of the sprayed underlap allowance; finger-press the pieces together. The adhesive keeps the fabric from slipping sideways and lengthwise. Try using a few pins to keep the layers from separating before stitching. To sew, lengthen the stitch length, use an edgestitch foot, and set the needle in the position farthest from the center to yield a stitch along the edge of the fabric.

Make a Multilayer Masking Tape Seam-Allowance Guide

—LESLIE PELECOVICH, STAMFORD, CT

Looking for an easy way to create an effective seam guide? This trick is especially helpful when seam allowances don't correspond to the marks on your throat plate. Slightly flatten a roll of masking tape, and use a rotary cutter or craft knife to carefully score across the tape in two places an inch apart to a depth of three or four layers of tape. Peel off all of the layers as one unit, and affix the tape stack to your machine at the appropriate seam allowance. The depth of the tape unit is a helpful guide that prevents seam allowances from wavering during sewing.

HOW TO KEEP NOTCH INFORMATION VISIBLE

I always serge the edges of my seams—even when I plan to press them open. To keep the notch information visible, I cut the notches pointing away from the fabric and slightly longer when I'm cutting out my pattern. Then, as I'm overcasting the edge on the serger, I fold the notch away from the edge right before it passes through the serger blade. I can still see the notch through the stitching and use it to align my seams.

—PEGGY BARNES, EL PASO, TX

Get Easy Turning
through the Seam

—SHIRLEY SCHOEN,
SAN FRANCISCO, CA

When you leave an opening in a seam to stuff or turn the lining through, shorten your stitch length where you want one end of the opening positioned, pivot, and sew perpendicular to the seamline and off the raw edge. Then repeat the same process from the other end of the opening. This stitching in the seam allowance makes the opening fold neatly inside, and is particularly useful when stuffing because the edges hold without popping stitches, even if stuffed firmly.

POCKETS

Attach a Patch Pocket
without Topstitching

—M. ELAINE MACKAY,
THAMESFORD,
ONTARIO, CANADA

Here's a neat way to attach a patch pocket without having to topstitch. Place the prepared pocket on the garment and pin it securely. Then take a basting thread and baste around the edge of the pocket, making sure to secure the thread ends. The trick is to pick up only a thread or two of the pocket with each stitch. Now machine-sew exactly along the inside edge of the pocket. The basting line is the sewing line, and it holds everything firmly and flatly in place. Although it can be tricky, it is possible to sew the base of the pocket this way, too, and this method can even be used to attach sleeves to a garment.

Sew Rounded Pockets

—HELEN DE ROO,
SILVER SPRING, MD

It's a challenge to sew perfectly symmetrical pocket curves so both the left and right sides of the pocket are identical. Here's a hint that makes the job easy. First, fold the cut pocket in half lengthwise. Then machine-baste it along the stitching line from the fold around the curve and about halfway up the side of the pocket, making a half pocket. Next, trim the seam allowance to $\frac{1}{4}$ in. and clip the curve to $\frac{1}{16}$ in. from the basting stitches. Roll up a sock and stuff it firmly into the half pocket, or use a June Tailor® pressing board and press the seam open and flat, avoiding the fold. Remove the basting and open the pocket flat, being certain that the clipped edges are neatly tucked underneath. Re-press the perfect pocket curves. Finish the upper edge of the pocket and attach it to the garment as directed by your pattern guide sheet. Preparing a pocket in this way takes a little extra effort, but the time is well worth it.

BUTTONS AND BUTTONHOLES

Sew Quick-and-Easy Button Loops

—ELIZABETH BLODGETT,
MORRISTOWN, NJ

Hate to sew thread loops for a back-neck opening? Here's a tip. Cut ½-yd. lengths of elastic thread and fold them in fourths. Next, stitch over the bundle with a narrow, dense zigzag stitch in a color to match the garment. After cutting a loop to the correct length, sew it by machine to the wrong side of the finished back-neck opening. For a smooth finish, press a small piece of fusible interfacing over the ends. The loop stretches easily over the button and matches the fabric nicely.

Check the Undersides of Your Flat Buttons

—DONNA DAVIS,
STEUBENVILLE, OH

Sometimes even the most seasoned sewers may take for granted this little surprise: Flat buttons have two sides. Can't find a perfect match in your button box? Take a look at the backs of the buttons. This nearly doubles the size of your button stash.

Make Quick Bound Buttonholes

—KATHLEEN MORRIS,
AUGUSTA, GA

To shorten the task of making bound buttonholes, consider using this quick method, which looks as good as the real thing. Simply mark the buttonhole as usual, place the facing material on top and stabilizer underneath, and sew a standard buttonhole on top of the facing. Carefully slit open the buttonhole, clipping into the corners of the bar tack, then turn the facing to the inside. Press, using the machine buttonhole stitches as support for the lips, and complete the bound buttonhole as usual.

Use Folding to Space Buttons

—JULIA PICKETT,
HOUSTON, TX

To evenly space blouse buttons, measure by folding. Mark the "avoid-gaposis" button position (at the bust point level) and the neck button placement. Then fold the blouse to bring these points together and mark this fold. Use these three evenly spaced marks as the guide for spacing the other buttons. Make sure there's at least as much space from the bottom button to the finished hem edge as there is between the other buttons.

HOW TO ELIMINATE A BUTTONHOLE IN A COLLAR BAND

I fought with buttonhole placement on a collar band every time I tried it, but now, when I make shirts and blouses with collars, I eliminate the troublesome buttonhole in the collar band. I replace the buttonhole with a snap closure. Then I sew a button on the right side, over the snap—it looks just like all the other buttons and I no longer have to fuss to get a perfectly placed buttonhole. Most of the shirts I make are casual, and many have mandarin collars, so I usually keep them snapped. Yes, if the collar is open, the snap shows, so I use a black snap on a dark shirt, and silver or clear nylon snaps on light colors.

—LOIS HANNULA, HILLSBORO, OR

Make Fast One-Stitch Buttons

—BARBARA NOWICH, KANSAS CITY, MO

To sew the long row of buttons sometimes worn down the back of wedding dresses, many dressmakers thread a needle with three or four threads at once and then sew the buttons with one stitch and a knot in each before moving on down the row. This is a quick way to sew on any button, snap, or hook and eye, and the stitching stays even. Sew with the four threads doubled for extra strength.

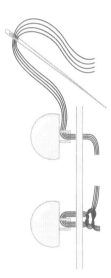

Stitch Speedy Buttons

—NANCY WHITING, LANCASTER, PA

Threading multiple strands of thread in a needle will speed up hand sewing of buttons, hooks and eyes, or snaps. Having three or four doubled threads knotted together makes it possible to firmly attach the button with only three or four stitches. In places where a button will have a lot of stress, reinforce the back with fusible interfacing, add a backing button, and use several strands of carpet thread. If you can't find matching carpet thread, mix a similar-colored carpet thread with strands of matching thread.

PLEATS

Eliminate Knots with Pleater Threading
—JUDITH BRANDAU, BUTLER, PA

Try threading the pleater for a single smocking project with the gathering threads twice as long as needed, threaded through the eyes of two adjacent pleater needles. Threading the pleater in this way eliminates the need to tie knots along one side of the pleated fabric.

Make Easy Gathered Pleats
—PAMELA TALLMAN, HUNTINGTON BEACH, CA

Cartridge pleating is difficult to do evenly and frustrating if the thread breaks before the gathers are finished. To avoid this difficulty and speed the process, stitch over a thread. Press the seam allowance or facing at the top edge under. Set the sewing machine to its widest blind-hem stitch. Place a length of button-and-carpet thread at the desired start point in the first row of pleating, and blind-stitch over the thread. Do a second row exactly like the first, keeping the rows evenly spaced and the blind stitches matched one below the other. Pull both threads evenly.

Notch to Make Mirror-Image Pleats
—LORRAINE SINTETOS, FELTON, CA

Ever have trouble getting pleats on skirts (or pants) equally deep and evenly spaced from the center of the garment? Solve this problem by notching the pleat positions on both the skirt and the waistband. After notching the skirt fabric, fold the skirt pattern piece along the pleat lines and, aligning the center fronts, lay it next to the cutout fabric waistband. Notch the waistband at the outer edge of each pleat, then pin or baste the skirt to the waistband, matching the notches to space and balance the pleats.

SERGING, THREADING, AND DARTS

Thread Multiple Bobbins for Efficient Sewing
—ROBIN MAZZOLA, FORMER *THREADS* ART DIRECTOR

When winding a bobbin with a basic thread color such as white or black or with a color that's used often, always wind a few extra bobbins, too. This way you won't have to stop sewing and rethread the machine to wind another bobbin later.

HOW TO USE A SERGER TO COMPLETE NOTCHED COLLARS

As a sewing mother, I've found it necessary to take advantage of shortcuts whenever I can. I've been using a serger for many years and find it invaluable for completing a notched collar. Patterns for a notched collar without a back yoke frequently require that the top layer of the collar be clipped to the seamline at the shoulder seam. The clip must be exact for acceptable results, and if the material is loosely woven, the collar will be at risk. Fray Check can solve this problem but may leave a scratchy residue.

My method eliminates the clip. I first apply the collar to the garment, right sides out. Next, I fold the front extensions to the outside to form the self-facings. Then I overlock or serge. I also serge the shoulder edge and the long edge of the self-facing for a quick, easy finish. All that remains is to turn the facings to the inside. No clipping is necessary. The serged seam will show on the back neck, but not when the garment is worn. Using one of the new serger threads, such as woolly nylon or Metrolene, guarantees a smooth seam that won't irritate even the most delicate skin.

—ROBBIN KOLLER, PATTERSON, NY

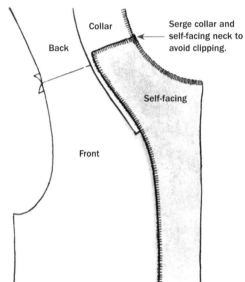

Collar

Back

Serge collar and self-facing neck to avoid clipping.

Self-facing

Front

Thread Your Machine Quickly

—JEAN GUNNELLS, DOVER, DE

Here's a quick machine-needle threading tip for a sewing machine that orients its needle with the groove facing the front or side: Snip the tip of the thread at an angle, and hold it about ⅜ in. behind the cut end. Now use that convenient groove that every machine needle has as a guide for the thread. Slide the cut end of the thread down the center of the groove; when it reaches the needle's eye, it will just slip through like magic. Works every time, unless your thread is too heavy for the needle (it's a good way to find out).

Easy Threading for Sergers

—ERIN NESMITH,
ENID, OK

It's easier to slip threads through all the tricky loops and holes of your serger when Fray Check is used first to stiffen the thread ends. Put a drop between your thumb and forefinger and draw the last 3 in. or so of thread through the drop. Drying only takes a moment.

Sew Darts with a Clean Look

—M. ELAINE MACKAY,
THAMESFORD, ONTARIO, CANADA

Here's a fabulous method of sewing darts that's perfect for sheer fabric or just a clean look. Pull up the bobbin thread (a foot or so for an average dart), then thread the needle with it from the side opposite the groove. Tie the bobbin thread to the top thread and, retracing the path of the top thread, pull the bobbin thread up through the tension guides, removing the slack. This way the machine sews with only one thread, so there are no loose ends when sewing the darts at the tips.

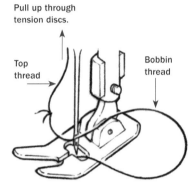

Pull up through tension discs.

Top thread

Bobbin thread

STRAPS

Use a Bobby Pin to Turn Spaghetti Straps

—ILYA SANDRA PERLINGIERI,
SAN DIEGO, CA

An easy and handy way to turn spaghetti straps is to use a bobby pin. Cut fabric either on the straight grain or on the bias, fold it in half, and stitch it at the desired strap width, making sure that each end of the seam is backstitched for strength. Depending on the desired effect, trim the seam allowances. Next, cut a small wedge out of one side of the fold and insert the bobby pin so that one leg of the pin goes outside the fold, but into the wedge. The pin will be able to move easily through the fabric to the other end, where there will be no trouble pulling it through completely.

Create Easy Elasticized Swimsuit Straps

—NANCY JACKSON, SHALIMAR, FL

Cut elastic for the strap as long as the desired finished strap plus two seam allowances and 3 in. Cut the fabric (with its greater stretch going lengthwise) the length of the desired strap plus two seam allowances and twice the width of the elastic plus ½ in. To sew the strap, fold the fabric in half lengthwise with right sides together. Place the elastic on top of the fabric with one edge of the elastic aligned with the raw edges of the fabric and the extra 3 in. extending off one end. Sew along the long edge of the fabric and elastic with a zigzag stitch. To turn the strap right side out, attach a bodkin to the end of the 3-in.-long extension and feed it back through the tube. This technique works with fabrics other than stretch swimsuit fabrics, including extremely narrow elastic with woven fabric and wider elastic with bias-cut woven. It also works with ribbon instead of elastic.

PIPING AND RIBBING

Create Easy Piping Strips

—CORINNE SHOULDERS, MADISON, MS

Here's an easy way to make piping. Cut the bias strips as usual, then attach double-sided fusible tape on the wrong side of one long edge. Fold the strip in half over the cord with the wrong sides together, and fuse the raw edges together by pressing. This simple process makes stitching the piping into a garment quick, easy, and more accurate than pinning.

Cut Extra Bias Strips for Piping

—DRUANN GREER-CISNEROS, COSTA MESA, CA

Cutting the bias strips needed to make piping is time-consuming, so why not cut extra strips at the same time? Often the scraps that remain after cutting out a pattern are enough for a few strips. Sew the pieces together and roll them on old thread or ribbon spools. You'll be able to easily see what you have, and more important, when you're on a roll sewing, you won't have to stop to cut fabric if you want to add piping to a project.

Make Fabric Ribbing

—CHARLENE PIERCE, MARSHALL, SASKATCHEWAN, CANADA

To make children's clothing with ribbing for cuffs, waistbands, and neckbands, use a rotary cutter, yardstick, and grid mat to cut several strips at once in standard widths. Keep the strips in a basket, and just cut off the length required when you need it.

Use Fusible Webbing for Seamless Piping

—FRANKIE LEVERETT, ATLANTA, GA

For fast, easy, stabilized piping, cut a bias strip of fabric the desired length and place it right side down on your ironing board. Cut strips of fusible webbing, such as Stitch Witchery, ¼ in. to ⅛ in. wide and place them along the center of the bias strip. Then cut the piping filler 1 in. longer than the bias strip and tie a simple knot in each end. Put pins in the knots, position the filler over the webbing, and use the pins to anchor it to the ironing board at the ends. Lightly steam by holding your iron above the filler to begin the fusing process. Now fold the bias strip in half over the filler and press, keeping the edge of the iron in the crease formed by the filler thread. This seamless piping is very easy to apply precisely.

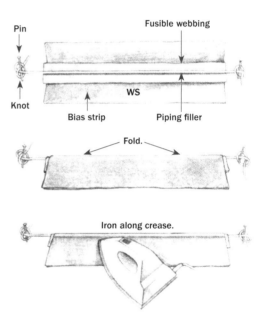

Use fusible webbing to seal piping filter inside a bias strip.

Pin

Fusible webbing

Knot

WS

Bias strip

Piping filler

Fold.

Iron along crease.

GATHERING

Use a Double Needle to Speed Gathering

—CECELIA SCHMEIDER, PELHAM, MA

Did you know that using a double needle speeds gathering and saves both time and thread? This method requires a little fussing and sampling at the beginning, but it's worth it. With the double needle in the machine and the tension set slightly tight, sew along the line to be gathered. Adjust the stitches by pulling the thread ends, just as if they were two separate lines of stitches. If the fabric puckers into a tuck, try a narrower double needle, like a 1.6 mm, or loosen the bobbin tension.

Attach Gathered Material to a Nongathered Piece

—KAREN WOLFF, LAGUNA HILLS, CA

It can be difficult to gather fabric in order to attach it to a nongathered piece, such as gathering a skirt to a waistband or bodice. Here's how to simplify the process. First, determine how long the finished gathered piece should be, including seam allowances (i.e., the length of the adjoining waistband or bodice), and cut a piece of ⅛-in.- or ¹⁄₁₆-in.-diameter cording the same length. Secure the cord to the wrong side of the fabric to be gathered at the start of the seam. Next, using a wide zigzag stitch, continue stitching the cord to the fabric along the gathering line. Use one hand to hold the cord taut in front of the needle as you zigzag over it. With the other hand, feed the fabric into the machine, allowing the feed dogs to gather it. Be sure the stitches do not go through the cording. Continue until your fabric and the cord ends meet at the other end of the garment seam, and secure the cord. The resulting gathered fabric will be the desired finished length, ready to attach to the rest of your garment.

CASINGS

Sew Elastic and Casing in One Step

—LINDA VIELHABER, STERLING HEIGHTS, MI

Make an easy job of sewing a casing for elastic by inserting the elastic and sewing the casing at the same time. To do this, press the casing in place, mark any matching points on the elastic and the casing, and then fold the casing around the elastic before sewing. Anchor the elastic at the starting point of the casing by stitching through the elastic and fabric. If desired, pin the elastic to the casing at the marked points. Stretch the elastic as you sew, and keep it within the casing space, but clear of the stitching line. Use this technique for sewing casings in the round or those that are constructed flat and later sewn into a seam (i.e., doll waists or cuffs). This method also works well for casings with drawstrings.

Make a Quick Casing for an Elastic Waistband

—NELLIE DERY, VAN WERT, OH

This is a fast method for sewing an elasticized waistband with a cut-on casing. Turn down the waist casing allowance, press, and edgestitch the top edge. Attach a large safety pin to each end of the elastic, lay the elastic between the casing layers, stitch the bottom edge to the garment, leave an opening for the elastic to come out, and feed the elastic from both ends to the opening.

TRICKS

THREAD

Make Tighter Knots

—JOAN T. BENSON,
MIDLAND, MI

There's a very simple way to get a knot that really holds. Draw the needle through the first loop twice, pull it tight, then repeat this step. The knot will be much tighter than a single-loop knot and won't require a second finger to hold things in place. Also, if knots usually end up 1 in. or more away from where you need them, move the knot down to the fabric's surface by inserting a needle (or pin) through the knot's loop, place the needle's point on the edge of the loop, and draw the knot down to the fabric.

Neaten Your Knots

—ILYA SANDRA PERLINGIERI,
SAND DIEGO, CA

Here's a way to eliminate unsightly knots in double threads for handwork or embroidering. Put both ends of the thread or floss through the needle's eye. Then pull the thread so that its looped end is longer. Make a stitch in the fabric in the direction in which you'll be stitching, and pull the needle through until the loop is almost at the point where the needle was first inserted into the fabric. Now put the point of the needle through the loop and pull the thread until you have secured it.

String Beads with Dental Floss Threaders

—CLAUDE ENGLISH,
SEBASTOPOL, CA

Plastic dental floss threaders, sold at drug stores, make wonderful needles for stringing small beads. Put the thread being used through the loop. Then put the first bead on the tip and push it to the "eye" to hold the thread more securely. After a number of beads have been placed on the needle, push them onto the thread at once.

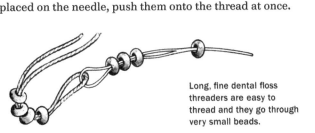

Long, fine dental floss threaders are easy to thread and they go through very small beads.

In-a-Pinch Substitute for Topstitching Thread

—DOROTHY MADIAS,
HAMPTON, SC

Sometimes if all that's needed is to replace just a few inches of topstitching, regular-weight thread can do the job.

First, using thread that matches the color of the original topstitching, wind and load a bobbin. Then place the spool of thread on the machine's spindle, and unwind a length that's sufficient to replace the topstitching times two (plus a few extra inches just in case). Tie the free end of the unwound thread to the thread close to the spool, and rewind this doubled section of thread back around the spool. Thread the doubled thread as if it were a single strand, and resew the topstitching.

NEEDLES

Use Nail Polish to Identify Needles

—AUDREY LEAR,
COMOX, BRITISH COLUMBIA, CANADA

Using inexpensive nail polish, paint the shaft of each machine needle a different color or combination of colors to quickly and easily identify its size and style. Record the size and style of each needle next to a brush stroke of each color on an index card that serves as a master list. The nail polish is easy to see, is amazingly durable, and is available in a wide range of bright colors.

Identify Used Needles at a Glance

—GAIL LEONE,
CEDAR, MI

Some projects require changing needles after they've been used briefly, for example, switching from a lightweight needle to a heavyweight one. To know if a needle is slightly used or brand new, return used needles to the needle packet flat-side up. This way, you can distinguish a new needle (for that special project) from one that's slightly used.

BUTTONHOLES, BUTTONS, AND SNAPS

Use a Dry Pen Refill for Easier Button Shanks

—JULIE BRADY,
CHANDLER, AZ

When sewing on buttons, slip an old, dry ballpoint-pen refill between button and fabric to raise the button and create a shank, instead of using the traditional wooden matchstick. The plastic is an ideal size for a button spacer, and it will slip out easily before it's time to wind around the loose thread shank.

Cut a Buttonhole with a Seam Ripper

—DOROTHY MADIAS, WILKES BARRE, PA

It's easy to accidentally cut a buttonhole opening too far when using scissors. To ensure careful cutting, try using a seam ripper at each end of the buttonhole slit. Push the point of the seam ripper in one end of the buttonhole and cut as many fabric threads as possible toward the center of the buttonhole, then go to the other end and repeat. Then safely cut the remaining center of the buttonhole with scissors.

Pop a Button with a Comb

—SUZAN L. WIENER, SPRING HILL, FL

Slip a thin comb under a button, then use a razor or other sharp knife between the button and the comb to cut the threads and remove the button without risk of nicking the fabric.

SEAMS

Flatten Thick Seams with a Vise Grip

—D. SELF, AURORA, CO

Sometimes thick details of a sewing project (such as the corner where two narrow hems meet) are impossible to fit under the presser foot. Before stitching, compress these areas with a pair of vise grips. Clamp the vise grips on the problem spot and turn the adjustment knob to flatten the area as much as possible. Be sure to protect your fashion fabric by wrapping the jaws of the vise grips with sturdy scrap fabric.

Give Seams an Easy Start

—MARGE PFEIL, ARROYO GRANDE, CA

Working with fabric that needs help starting through the machine, just pull gently on the needle and bobbin threads to guide the fabric until it can be grasped.

Maintain Shape When Ripping Seams

—MARILYN A. JENSEN, FREMONT, CA

In ripping apart an old garment to make a pattern, first treat the seam allowances with spray starch and iron them. This will prevent the fabric from losing its shape when pulling the seams apart.

Remove Holes Left from Seam Ripping

—SUZAN L. WIENER, SPRING HILL, FL

When removing a hem or ripping apart a seam, lots of little holes remain. To remove them, dampen a cloth with white vinegar, spread it flat under the material, and press.

Use a Visual Aid for French Seams

—JANET MCGLYNN, NEENAH, WI

It's a lot easier to see the first seam of a French seam to trim before turning it if it has a contrasting thread sewn in. This will allow for trimming closer without worrying about catching a thread.

Make a Better French Seam with Extra Pressing

—DEBORAH C. LITTLE, ALVA, FL

Take the time to press a French seam open flat after trimming. Fold the seam over, right sides together, and press again. The first pressing is an extra step, but it helps roll that first line of stitching to the exact outer edge.

TAPE

Pin with Double-Sided Tape

—MARLI POPPLE, ARMADALE, VICTORIA, AUSTRALIA

Use double-sided sticky tape when sewing leather, velvet, or silk. It holds two layers together without allowing shifting, and it can be removed easily after a seam has been stitched.

Make a Ruler Out of Tiger Tape

—SUZANNA SANDOVAL, BELLEVUE, WA

For a tiny ruler you can't lose, put a ½-in. piece of Tiger Tape™ on your left thumbnail (if you're right-handed; on your right if you're left-handed). Then, when you're hand stitching or hand embroidering, the way you hold your thumb allows you to gauge stitches quickly and effortlessly. Now your stitches will have even depth and width.

Use Masking Tape as a Topstitching Guide

—SUSAN MORGAN, SALT LAKE CITY, UT

Sew perfectly straight topstitching on fabric without marking it with chalk by putting some masking tape on the fabric and stitching along the straight edge of the tape.

HOW TO USE TAPE TO KEEP THE BUTTONHOLE FOOT FROM SNAGGING

When I tried to sew buttonholes on a piped vest, the buttonhole foot kept snagging on the piping as the machine stitched. To eliminate the problem, I covered the buttonhole area with transparent tape that extended to the edge and over the piping. Then I stitched right over the tape. It gave me a smooth surface with no hang-ups—and an unexpected bonus. I could mark the buttonhole placement on the tape and easily reposition it to ensure perfect buttonhole alignment. The needle stitched through the tape easily, and the tape came off with no difficulty after the buttonholes were sewn.

—DEBBIE NACEWICZ, WILBRAHAM, MA

Use Blue Painter's Tape as a Sewing Aid

—PATRICIA ARMSTRONG, PRESCOTT, AZ

Blue painter's tape (not masking tape) can be a valuable tool for working on garments and quilt pieces that vary in seam-allowance size (¼ in. and up) because it adheres well to fabric without leaving a residue. Use it to write a note, for example, to indicate the right side/wrong side of the fabric or to remind yourself of something you want to do to the piece. Tape a strip to your sewing machine to indicate the sewing needle size being used, so you know which needle is in your machine.

TOOLS AND AIDS

Get Help from Your Sewing Machine Screwdriver

—DIANE SCHULTZ, ST. PAUL, MN

A tiny sewing machine screwdriver makes for an excellent extra finger to hold down and control the edge of an appliqué as it's sewn in place with a satin stitch or other decorative machine stitch. It's possible to allow the point of the screwdriver to ride the fabric right up to the foot and under the upturned edge until the last second, when the fabric is firmly between the presser foot and throat plate. You won't sew a finger, and your line of vision is clear.

Use a Hammer to Flatten Denim

—LINDA SOMMER, WHITBY, ONTARIO, CANADA

Before attempting to sew over multiple layers of denim, hammer the hem flat at the points where the side seam creates a really thick spot. This breaks up the fibers and flattens out the multiple layers. Place the pinned seam on a sturdy surface, and give it a good number of blows with the hammer. When you attempt to sew the hem, the machine needle will be able to go right through those hard spots.

Keep Scarf Mesh Fibers Snag-Free with Paper

—ANN MARIE FROEHLE, ST. PAUL, MN

Scarf mesh is an ultrasoft mesh fabric that can be cut to size. When sewing scarf mesh, the fibers and yarns sometimes get stuck in the throat plate or snagged in the needle during stitching. To prevent this, sandwich the scarf between two pieces of paper and then stitch back and forth over the entire scarf. Simply add paper as you continue to sew down the scarf. When finished, rip off the paper, and a perfectly stitched scarf remains. This is a great way to use up small pieces of yarn, trim, and fabric from your stash and to make a scarf to go with a specific garment.

HOW TO USE SIMPLE PAPER TO GET A HANDLE ON SEWING

I always had trouble edgestitching shirt collars on my zigzag machine. When I got to the point of the collar and turned the work to sew the long edge, the needle would push the point down into the slot in the throat plate or pull it up into the slot in the presser foot. It was also hard to guide the collar for neat stitching because there wasn't much fabric for my fingers or the feed dogs to grasp. I solved this problem by slipping a piece of paper (from a small note pad) under the collar about 1 in. before reaching the point. I sew through the fabric and paper, using the paper as a handle to help guide the stitching. The paper tears away easily after stitching. This works for all pointed construction details, such as cuffs, sashes, belts, and lapels.

—D. SELF, AURORA, CO

Hold Fabric in Place with Magnets on Metal Ironing Boards
—SUSAN NUNN, RALEIGH, NC

When pressing large items, the weight of the fabric hanging off the ironing board tends to pull the rest of the fabric off as well. Because most ironing boards are metal, consider using a strong magnet (available inexpensively at electronic-hobby shops) to hold the fabric to the board. The magnets hold the fabric firmly—right through the fabric and the ironing board cover—but are easy to move and don't damage the fabric.

Extra Tape Helps Prevent Mishaps
—MARY LONGREN, HOLTON, KS

When using hook-and-loop tape as a closure, the tape often catches on itself or on the fabric while the project is under construction. To avoid this frustration, place an extra piece of hook-and-loop tape on top of each of those already sewn. Simply remove the added pieces when the project is complete.

Make Vinyl Glide with ChapStick
—SANDRA LEE WOODS, EL PASO, TX

To prevent a presser foot from sticking or dragging, apply a bead of ChapStick® in front of the stitching. This eliminates inconsistent stitch lengths, and it's easy to wipe off when finished.

Keep Press Cloths Damp
—CAROL STONER,
DENVER, CO

Here's a good way to keep a good supply of press cloths that are just the right dampness handy when doing a lot of pressing. Cut three identical rectangles of press-cloth material, then wet one well and wring it out loosely. Sandwich the wet cloth between the two dry ones and wring them all together thoroughly and firmly. After a little practice, it will get easier to get all three equally damp, and none too wet or too dry.

....

Use Correction Fluid to Reduce Glare
—PATRICIA JINKENS,
OXFORD, OH

If glare from sewing-room lights makes it difficult to clearly see all of the engraved markings on your sewing machine throat plate and attachments, try dabbing enough white correction fluid to fill the indented markings, then wipe off the excess. You'll be able to see the markings without difficulty or glare.

....

Try Graph Paper for Pockets
—JOAN MEYER,
BRUNSWICK, GA

When making bound buttonholes or welt pockets, place a sheet of graph paper (ruled 8 squares to an inch) on the wrong side of the garment. Using the lines as a sewing guide, stitch perfectly straight seams and square corners; the paper is easy to remove when finished.

HOW TO USE GLAD WRAP TO SECURE THREAD

Over the years, I've tried everything the market has to offer to prevent my serger thread from coming off the cone in storage and creating a mess. Nothing really worked particularly well until I tried using the new Glad® Press'n Seal® wrap (available in most grocery stores). It works like a charm because the wrap sticks to itself as well as to the cone thread without leaving a sticky residue.

—JEAN C. SMOLENS, WILMINGTON, DE

Use Quilter's Gloves to Protect Hands

—JEAN WACHS,
ANDERSON, SC

A pair of quilter's gloves can be a sewing aid for all sewers. When pressing small seams, slip a quilter's glove onto your left hand (if you're right-handed) and steam and press with your right. Use the kind of gloves that cover the entire hand and have lots of little rubber nubs on the palm side. These nubs will help you to spread seams and hold on to small trim. Although the gloves are not heat resistant, they do protect fingertips from the steam and heat and save time in the process.

Use Pins to Protect from Burns

—COLLEEN MURPHY,
LOUISVILLE, KY

To ensure inexperienced sewers do not burn themselves while pressing fabric, have them stick glass-head or all-metal pins through the fabric into the ironing board. This holds the fabric in place as they iron, prevents the fabric from sliding off the ironing board, and keeps their fingers away from the bottom of the hot iron.

Use Wax to Lubricate Zipper Teeth

—ANDREA L. MOORE,
SPOKANE WA

Metal zippers open and close more easily when the metal teeth are lubricated with a paraffin wax such as Parowax™, found in most houseware stores. Simply glide a bar of the household wax back and forth over the teeth on both sides of the opened zipper. The wax is transparent and will not wash off in the laundry.

HOW TO HOLD RICKRACK ON YOUR WRIST

When I used to stitch long lengths of binding, rickrack, or other trims to a garment or quilt, the trim often got caught under the wheel of my chair or became tangled before it reached the sewing machine needle. Now, I loosely roll the trim, and place it over my wrist so it gently unwinds as I stitch it in place. I'm right-handed, so I place the roll on my left wrist. As long as the roll is loose enough, it revolves around my wrist, feeds smoothly, and doesn't twist as it unrolls itself.

—CAROLYN AURAND, DIXON, IL

HOW TO SEE "NORTH" MORE CLEARLY

Machine-embroidery hoops must be reassembled correctly, matching the "north, south, east, and west" markings on the inner and outer hoop. On my hoops, north is noted by a small triangle that is difficult to see. To make it easier and quicker to match the north triangles, I have colored them with a permanent marker. Now I always know which way is up!

—PATRICIA JINKENS, OXFORD, OH

Pin Layers Safely

—MARY HARDENBROOK,
HUNTINGTON BEACH, CA

When pinning layers (fabric, pattern pieces, and so forth) together, burying the point of the pin between the layers after the initial pinning makes it less likely you will prick yourself.

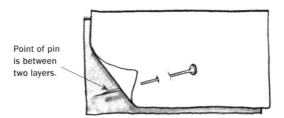

Point of pin is between two layers.

THREAD

Mark Thread Spools to Remember Settings

—CYNTHIA DUNN, NEDERLAND, CO

If the thread on your sewing machine gets changed several times a day, note the tension settings and needle sizes used on the end of each spool of thread with an indelible marker to make easy readjustments.

Dental Floss Holders Help Thread Serger Loopers

—KATHIE HOLLAND, MORRIS PLAINS, NJ

An additional use for a dental floss holder is to thread the looper threads on sergers.

Mark Your Spool Notches for Better Visibility

—T. J. PIKE, HURST, TX

Mark thread spool notches with a permanent marker as soon as you buy a new spool to make the notches easier to see.

ALTERATIONS

Mark Where the Folded Edge Will Meet

—MARTHA FEE, CENTERPORT, NY

Whenever you need to press a fold on any cloth, don't mark the foldline. Instead, mark where the folded edge will meet. You won't have to worry about burned fingers or hard-to-see marks; just fold the edge to the marked line, and press.

....

Work with Asymmetric Miters

—SHIRLEY MCKEOWN, ADELPHI, MD

Using this method, any two hemmed edges coming together at a corner can be neatly mitered. The hems may vary in size, and the seam need not be at a 45-degree angle to the edges, but the miter will be perfect. Press the fabric along the hemlines, and clean-finish the cut edges by turning them under or zigzagging. Mark the intersection of the hems with pins or clips. Open the hems and fold the fabric right sides together, matching the two pins. Stitch from the pins to where the hem creases intersect at the fabric fold. Press the seam open on a point presser. Turn the miter right side out, refold the hems, and flatten the excess fabric inside the hem corner. Press. You may trim the excess fabric after pressing the corner, but be sure you don't need it for weight in the corner. Also be certain you'll never want to adjust the garment's length, because once the corner is trimmed, it is no longer possible to lengthen it.

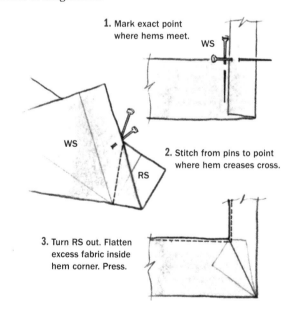

1. Mark exact point where hems meet.

WS

WS

RS

2. Stitch from pins to point where hem creases cross.

3. Turn RS out. Flatten excess fabric inside hem corner. Press.

TWO WAYS TO SET IN SLEEVES WITH A PENCIL ERASER

Method One

Staystitch the entire sleeve cap, then clip the bobbin thread at the front and back notches and pull up the ease. Sew with the sleeve on top, right sides together. To manipulate the ease so the cap will be perfectly rounded with no tucks or puckers, use the tip of a pencil eraser to ease in the fullness on the seam-allowance side of the needle close to the staystitching as you machine-stitch.

—DOROTHY RICHARDS, ESCONDIDO, CA

Method Two

Pin the sleeve to the bodice, matching the dots and notches. Using a regular stitch with the sleeve piece on top, sew the seam as usual until you come to an area where the sleeve needs to be eased. Then, hold the eraser against the back of your machine's foot, resting the eraser gently on the top fabric. The eraser slows the fabric as it moves through the feed dogs, causing it to ease as it's stitched. Release the eraser where easing isn't required and complete the seam. The sleeve is finished in no time with no tucks, no pleats, and no broken threads—just a perfectly eased sleeve cap that isn't puckered and doesn't have a gathered appearance.

—JOANN ARMOR, GOODRICH, MI

Press Altered Seamlines before Stitching

—LINDA DORAN, GREENDALE, WI

When ready to restitch altered seamlines, press the layers of fabric together with a warm iron before stitching. This will temporarily stick them together and smooth the old seamlines.

Sew with the Needle Down

—KATHY ZACHRY, SPRINGDALE, AR

Many newer sewing machines have an option to specify whether the needle will stay down in the fabric or stop fully up whenever you lift your foot off the control. You'll be amazed at how much more control you'll have when you turn "needle-down" on for all your sewing, disengaging it only at the end of a seam. When topstitching, easing sleeves, or any time you're stopping midseam to adjust fabric layers or check their position, having the needle down when you stop totally prevents slippage, even on the silkiest fabrics that presser feet alone can't keep secure.

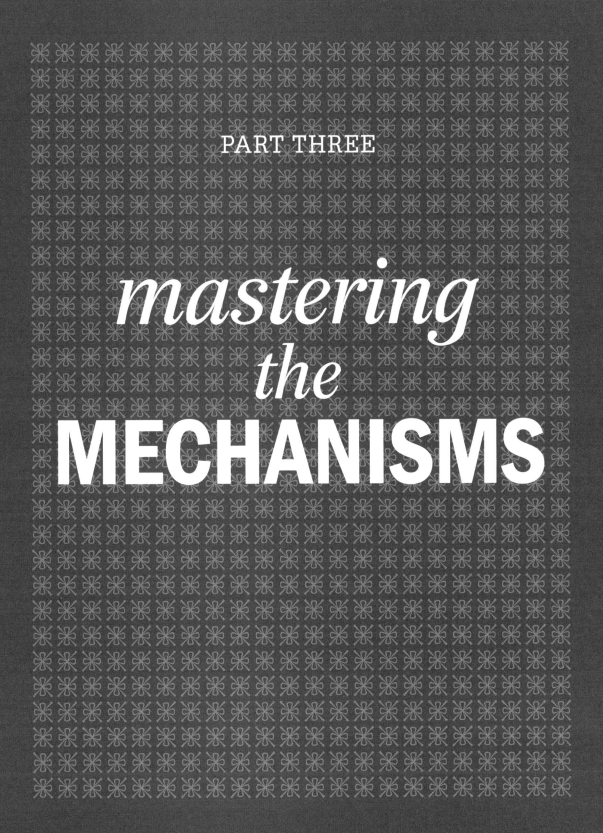

PART THREE

mastering
the
MECHANISMS

SEWING MACHINES

WORKING PEDALS AND FEET

Get to Know Your Feet

—PATRICIA ANN VAN MAANEN,
FRIDAY HARBOR, WA

Whether you're a home sewer or making a living sewing, it's important to keep a record of what your machine can do. One way is to make samples using most of the machine's bells and whistles, showing, for instance, how the various hemming feet or the bias-tape foot works. Use both woven and knit fabrics for the samples, because each produces very different results. Also, practice with various types of needles, from wings to doubles. On each sample, note the stitch number, the tension combinations that produce the best stitch, and possible applications. Store the samples inside your sewing machine's owner's manual for easy reference.

Make Samples from Your Presser Feet

—MICHELLE NEWCOME,
ATLANTA, GA

Here's a fun way to get acquainted with a new machine, practice new stitches, use up extra fabric, and get presser feet organized. Make a little fabric bag for each foot. Use the built-in alphabets to write the name of the foot on each bag, and decorative stitches for embellishment. Put the foot and a small blurb about what it does and how to use it inside the bag and store them all in a small box near your machine.

Use Your Sewing Machine as a Handy Third Hand

—MARIANNE KANTOR, BONDVILLE, VT

Your sewing machine can double as a third hand, or "sewing bird," for easier ripping and hand sewing. Put work under the presser foot—feed dogs and needle up—and drop the foot. If the fabric is fragile or slips, put a wide rubber band between the fabric and the presser foot.

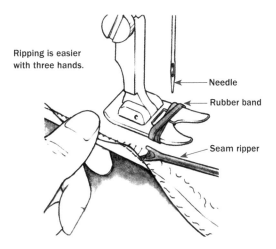

Ripping is easier with three hands.

Needle

Rubber band

Seam ripper

HOW TO PIN-TUCK WITH A BUTTONHOLE FOOT

If you can't get a pin-tuck foot for your sewing machine or wouldn't use it enough to justify the cost, you can use the buttonhole foot of your zigzag machine. Its limitations are that there is only one channel size, and no more than two tucks can be made side by side. You'll also need a 2-mm left-position twin needle and a machine with a front- or top-loaded bobbin and the ability to shift the needle position left and right (see drawings below). The narrow channels of the foot provide enough stability, so a fabric stabilizer isn't needed for most fabrics.

Turn the flywheel by hand to lower the needle until it just pierces the fabric. If you are using a cord, make sure it's between the two needles and moves freely. Grasp the three sewing threads firmly while taking the first two to three stitches. Once you've started, you can concentrate on guiding the work. As I complete each tuck, I pull the cord through until the excess at the top is eliminated before I cut the work from the machine.

To use the foot as a guide for spacing single tucks, set the needle position at whichever channel gives the desired distance (left drawing below). The center needle position makes use of the right channel, which spaces the tucks rather close. The left needle position uses the left channel and spaces them a little farther apart.

For pairs of tucks, set the needle to the left, sew the first tuck, move the tuck into the right channel, and sew the second tuck (center drawing below). You can continue this way, spacing the pairs of tucks the distance from the right edge of the foot to the left channel. Or you can space them a little closer by shifting the needle between center and left positions and working first in the right channel and then in the left (right drawing below). Or you can space the tucks without regard to the presser-foot width. As with a special pin-tuck foot, you can also do cord quilting.

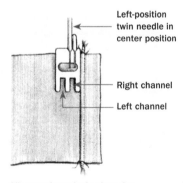

Left-position twin needle in center position

Right channel

Left channel

Align previous single pin tucks along the right edge of the buttonhole foot. Putting the needle in center position uses the right channel of the foot and spaces tucks closely; the left position uses the left channel, spacing them farther apart.

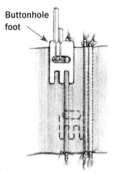

Buttonhole foot

Working pairs of tucks with the needle in the left position only spaces them the farthest. The first tuck moves into the right channel while the second tuck is made. (The dashed foot shows the position for making the first tuck.)

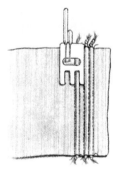

Space pairs of pin tucks the distance from the right side of the foot to the right channel by shifting the needle position from center to left and working first in the right channel, then in the left.

—ELIZABETH LEE RICHTER, HUNTINGTON, CT

Use a Knee-Operated Foot Pedal

—CAROL STONER,
DENVER, CO

A knee-operated control can be much less tiring than the typical foot pedal. Here's how to set it up so the control rests at knee height. Fasten two screw eyes to the right side of your sewing desk's knee opening, positioning them slightly farther apart than the width of the pedal. With the machine unplugged, thread wire into a vent hole on either side of the pedal case, pulling the wires taut against the case to avoid contact with any of the interior apparatus. Snug the control to the desk through the screw eyes, where it will stay without wiggling when pressed.

Customize a Teflon Foot for Sewing Leather

—ANNA MAZUR,
AVON, CT

If a Teflon® foot is too bulky to cover the area needed to see for close stitching when edgestitching, try customizing the foot. Teflon is fairly soft; it can be easily shaved with a knife. Consider wearing an oven mitt in case the knife slips, and shave the foot to the shape you need. Mark guides on the foot with a permanent marker. The seam will show better, and with the aid of the markings, you'll be able to sew very straight edgestitching.

Use a Hemmer Foot for Piping

—JULIETTE KIMES,
DRIPPING SPRINGS, TX

If the nonadjustable zipper foot that came with your sewing machine is too wide for sewing piping, try using the adjustable blind-hem foot. It works great! The foot has more clearance, the guide runs right along the cording, and it's possible to adjust how closely to the edge you stitch.

Stitch a Narrow Hem Using a Narrow Hem Foot

—NANCY MILLER,
ATWOOD, KS

It can be a challenge to stitch a narrow hem using a narrow hem foot because it's so hard to ease the fabric into the curl of the foot. Here's a method that works well every time.

Start with a cleanly cut fabric edge. Make sure long thread tails are coming from the machine's needle. Sew an inch or two close to the hem's raw edge using a straight stitch and a regular foot, and cut the ending thread close to the stitches. Insert the narrow hem foot into the machine, and use the long thread tails to feed the fabric into the narrow hem foot, pulling the thread slightly to help ease the fabric into the presser foot's curl.

This method also works in the same manner to ease bias strips into a bias binder.

Pleat with Pin-Tucking Foot
—ELLEN J. RIGGAN, GLOUCESTER, VA

If you don't own a pleater and don't want to pay someone to pleat for you, try threading your sewing machine with a triple needle. Using the pin-tucking foot, stitch as many rows as you need. With these lines as your guide, you can make very pretty hand or machine smocking.

Make Perfect Gathers with a Cording Foot
—TERESA SIMPSON, KNOXVILLE, TN

Sometimes when zigzagging over cord, then pulling the cord to create gathers, the needle goes slightly off track and stitches through the cord, which interferes with the gathering process. To eliminate this problem, try using a cording foot. Thread the cord through one of the center holes on the foot, and tie the starting cord end to a large safety pin so it can't accidentally slip out of place. Then snap the cording foot onto the machine, and set the machine to a wide zigzag stitch. Hand-walk the first couple of stitches to make sure the needle doesn't strike the foot or the cord. Then sew a few reverse stitches to lock the zigzag stitches. The cording foot protects against accidentally hitting the gathering string. At the end of the zigzag stitches, lock the stitches again, then cut the end of the gathering cord, tie it to another safety pin, and adjust the gathers as usual. This process makes gathering quick and easy without any unanticipated fumbles.

Restrain Pedals with a Rubber Drawer Liner
—JENNY WESNER, INDIANAPOLIS, IN

To hold serger and pedals firmly in place, try using the nonslip rubber drawer liner made for use in the kitchen. The liner is easy to find in any discount store, is very inexpensive, and will keep your equipment from moving around when you sew.

HOW TO MAKE AN ERGONOMIC PEDAL

I do a lot of sewing, and after a while, the top of my foot develops an ache from always being arched. I found that if I turn the pedal around so that my toes are lower than my heel, the new position relieves any building pain. When I rotate the pedal in this way, I use my heel instead of my toes to do the pushing. Frequently, I leave my pedal turned around the entire time I am sewing because I find it more comfortable.

—LORELEE SIENKOWSKI, PACKWAUKEE, WI

HOW TO USE OLD SEWING MACHINE FEET

My husband and I own several antique sewing machines, some acquired with a full complement of original attachments. After trying out a few antique feet that fit on my contemporary sewing machine, I found that some actually worked better than the new versions. For example, I use the zipper feet (one for the left and another for the right) from a Singer Featherweight to make piping. The old feet were made all in one piece without a joint or sliding mechanism. I find them more stable, and they make it easier to stitch close to piping cord. If someone you know has an unused, older sewing machine, ask to treasure-hunt among the accessories.

—DAWN A. JARDINE, RED HOOK, NY

Secure an Odd Foot with Sticky Putty

—BONNIE BLEDSOE FUCHS, CHAPEL HILL, NC

Sticky putty is truly a modern wonder, and really comes in handy in a sewing space. The putty comes in white or blue, kneads into any shape, and never loosens unless the user wants it to. Use plastic adhesive putty (Plasti-Tak®) to hold a generic presser foot (that might not quite fit your sewing machine) to the presser bar. The putty becomes tacky when worked by hand, and a pinhead-size ball of it on the presser foot creates a tight fit. When it's time to change the foot, just pull it away—the tacky putty easily comes loose. Also try using plastic putty to adhere a small film canister to your sewing machine to hold a dust brush.

USING A SERGER

Insert a New Serger Needle

—F. NOVARRA, TUALATIN, OR

To put in a new needle more easily, thread the needle before inserting. Then, holding the thread taut in one hand and guiding the needle with the other, insert the needle into the needle bar. The tension on the thread will hold the needle in place while you tighten the screw, and if the needle drops, it won't get lost.

HOW TO EASILY THREAD A SERGER

I've tried all of the tricks suggested by friends and sewing teachers to thread my serger. Tying the new thread to the old thread worked best, but the knot got stuck in many places along the threading path, which became annoying. Instead, I rethread the serger simply by following the path of thread that's already in the machine.

One at a time, I lift the thread spool that's no longer needed from its spindle and place it on the side of the serger without removing the thread from the machine. Then I place the new thread spool on the spindle and thread the machine following the path of the old thread until I get to the needle/throat plate area. At this point, there are two threads along each step of the threading path. There are no knots, and there's plenty of room for both threads.

When I've reached the needle/throat plate area with the new thread, I hold on to it tightly while I ease the old thread out. If the new thread is one of the serger's needle threads, I thread the needle before following the same process with the next thread to be replaced. This method works especially well if one of the threads is about to run out during a serging project. As long as I replace the thread before the last of it leaves the spool on the spindle, adding new thread is a breeze.

—KAREN WOLFF, LAGUNA HILLS, CA

Quick Serger Threading
—SHIRLEY A. NOOYEN, ELK GROVE, CA

To thread a serger needle, remove the needle, thread it from the grooved side, and replace it in the serger.

....

Hassle-Free Serger Thread Changing
—SUSAN RILEY, SUDBURY, MA

Cut old color threads close to the cones, place the new color on the thread stand, and tie the new color on with an overhand knot. Serge slowly until the new color comes through.

....

Replace Your Serger Blade
—BELVA BARRICK, GLENDALE, AZ

It's time to change your serger blades when, while serging through a knee-high stocking or pantyhose leg, a scrap of tricot, or a piece of slinky knit fabric, the serger chews rather than cuts clean. This means the blades are dull and should be replaced. Keep an old knee-high stocking in your serger case for this purpose.

Use a Loop-Turner Tool for Serger Tails

—RITA JACOBSON, FOUNTAIN VALLEY, CA

Consider using a loop-turner tool, a long piece of stiff wire with a latch on one end, to avoid cutting the tail off a serged seam and leaving a frayed edge. Run the latch of the loop-turner under the loops on the underside for about 2 in., up to the edge. Catch the tail with the latch, and, making sure it closes, pull the tail through the loops.

Use Nail Polish to Premark Tension on Knobs

—SUSAN STRANGE, GLENCOE, IL

To avoid having to return serger tension knobs to zero each time you rethread your machine, mark the recommended tension settings required for standard-size thread on each knob with red nail polish. After threading the serger, it will be quick and easy to return the knobs to their original tension settings by aligning the machine guides with the red marks. In addition, this will provide quick reference points for adjusting the tensions up or down to accommodate a special technique, such as a rolled hem, or nonstandard thread weights.

HOW TO PRACTICE SERGER STITCHES

I bought a serger, but for months I was comfortable doing only one type of stitch. To overcome my phobia of changing threads, tensions, and using new stitches, I threaded the machine with four different colors to match those shown on the machine's color-coded diagram, and made myself sew all the stitches on white cloth, following the adjustments listed in the manual. Then I labeled the samples and taped each to its corresponding page in the manual. I jotted down helpful notes about what I learned.

Now I'm more comfortable with the threading, tension settings, and adjustment requirements of changing stitches, and I always find the stitch I need in my sample manual.

—ANNA ZAPFFEL, KEY WEST, FL

TOOLS & AIDS

SEWING SAFELY

Wear Safety Goggles

Consider wearing safety goggles when doing certain types of machine sewing, such as machine embroidery, topstitching, and sewing seams on densely woven fabrics, as needles can sometimes break and pop up, causing eye damage.

—JANE CONLON, EUGENE, OR

Use Reading Glasses to Magnify and Protect

Try wearing over-the-counter reading glasses when machine sewing. They provide just enough magnification to prevent eyestrain and improve sewing accuracy while protecting eyes. In the event of accidentally sewing over a pin or breaking a needle, the glasses shield eyes from flying fragments of metal.

—EDNA KISH, EPWORTH, GA

Cover Your Magnifying Glass

A magnifying lens is a great help for doing close work, but if the lens isn't properly covered or stored, it can direct an intense ray of sunshine, which could cause a fire. Solve this potential hazard by making a hood for your lens, which will allow you to leave the lens positioned wherever you want it, with no danger.

—MRS. O. W. OLSON, MILL BAY, BRITISH COLUMBIA, CANADA

RIPPING AND CUTTING

Rip Threads with a Rotary Cutter

—BARBARA LENZ, SEATTLE, WA

Here's an efficient, speedy alternative to the traditional ripper: Position a rotary cutter with its blade upright in a small vise, or clamp it to the side of a drawer, which will make both hands available to spread the seam and bring the threads over the blade. Just a quick touch is all it takes to snip them, and with a little practice, you can rip the seam as fast as you can reposition your hands.

Use a Rolling Ruler to Make Rotary-Cut Strips

—ELIZABETH RYMER, HURRICANE MILLS, TN

Consider acquiring a draftsman's 12-in. rolling ruler, available in various models at most art stores. Designed to roll without pivoting or slipping, rolling rulers are ideal for guiding multiple parallel cuts. The rolling mechanism makes them easier to grip and hold steady than most rulers.

Bias Cut on a Drywall Square

—TONYA CAMPBELL, ST. JOSEPH, MO

To cut large pieces of fabric on the bias, try using a jumbo drywall square (an oversize T-square). It's big enough to mark or cut long bias strips, and holds the fabric securely in place.

Use Cork as a Cutting Surface

—GWEN JONES, NIAGARA FALLS, ONTARIO, CANADA

Cork sheeting or tiles (available in hardware stores) affixed to plywood make a good nonslip cutting surface. Cork surfaces are especially good for cutting silk and other slippery fabrics with scissors. The fabric doesn't move around the way it does on a table or a rotary mat, and pins can be jabbed right into the surface to hold fabric in place.

Sheathe a Tracing-Wheel Blade

—ZANY ASLAM, NEWARK, DE

Here's a tip for sewers who want to prevent the spikes of their tracing wheel from inadvertently poking something while in storage. Put the wheel into a toothbrush holder (usually available where travel-size products are sold in drugstores) so that it doesn't get caught on fabrics or other items in the sewing box. This also eliminates the possibility of it poking your hand when you're searching for another sewing notion.

PRESSING

Try Velvet Board Substitutes

—SHIRLEY J. CROOKS, WALNUT CREEK, CA

When sewing with velvet, experts recommend pressing on a velvet board. An inexpensive substitute is a lint brush with a fuzzy surface, the kind that gets brushed in the direction of the arrows on top. Lay the brush, fuzzy side up, on the ironing board and place the seam of the velvet garment over the brush. Steam it without touching the fabric. Finger-press the seam and move the brush to the next section. This works well enough but takes time. For long seams, stick a strip of self-adhesive hook-and-loop tape (either side will work) on a wooden pressing stick. Work up the seam as described above. Reminder: Always test a scrap of the actual fashion fabric before trying anything on the garment.

Make Tailor's Pressing Tools

—STANLEY HOSTEK, SEATTLE, WA

Two traditional tailoring notions that most tailors make for themselves are a dauber for dampening limited areas, like seams, and a sleeve pad, which slips into awkward places to simplify pressing.

A dauber is a strip of soft or medium woolen cloth about $3\frac{1}{2}$ in. wide and long enough to roll tightly into a cylinder about 1 in. thick. The long edges should be unfinished. After rolling it up, whip the dauber closed with a strong thread. One dauber should last a lifetime, and it will get better (and more ragged looking) with use. Simply dip it into water and wipe it along the area needing to be pressed.

Pressing pads of various shapes can be made to augment the press buck, the tailor's primary pressing aid. The ends should be rounded. Cut enough layers of an old woolen blanket in this shape to make about a $\frac{3}{4}$-in. stack. Fasten the layers loosely together with a few stab stitches, and cover the whole thing in a smooth cotton or heavy lining rayon. This is a big help for pressing sleeve heads, sleeve hems, and elbow seams.

Use a Dowel as a Pressing Surface

—MARY HARDENBROOK, HUNTINGTON BEACH, CA

If regular sleeve rolls seem unstable and never long enough, make one out of a $1\frac{1}{2}$-in. wooden dowel, which can be found in building-supply stores. Make the pressing surface any length, and cut off $\frac{1}{4}$ in. of its diameter. Sand and smooth the pole to remove any burrs.

Create a Portable, Lightweight Ironing Surface

—PAT STORLA, MOSCOW, IN

Make an easy-to-grab, easy-to-store ironing board that's great for quick jobs and pressing from the cardboard forms that fabric bolts come wrapped around. Your fabric store will probably be glad to give you an empty form. Cotton flannel, toweling, drill, and sheeting would all make serviceable covers.

Measure a long strip of your covering material that's exactly as wide as the form, not including the ends, and that's long enough to wrap around it the way yardage would at least twice (more wouldn't hurt, if you've got the fabric). Before you cut, measure one more length that's about 3 in. wider on each end. Use the extra width to wrap around the ends, then hand-stitch the whole cover to itself, folding under the raw edges.

Protect Your Ironing Board When Using Fusibles

—KAREN WONG, ROUND ROCK, TX

Try using quick-release aluminum foil to protect your ironing board when fusing interfacing or fusible web. The little bits of adhesive, which can ruin an ironing-board cover, won't fuse to the nonstick side of the foil. The foil also reflects the iron's heat, which helps with the fusing process.

USE A CLOVER MINI IRON TO PRESS PLEATS

I was working on a pleated bodice and discovered the perfect tool for pressing the varied-width pleats in place—my Clover Mini Iron™. I layered the bodice pattern piece and the to-be-pleated overlay on a pinnable pressing surface, then pinned the horizontal pleats exactly where I wanted them. The tiny iron, with its triangular head, fit perfectly between the pins, and working from the top to the bottom, I was able to press the folds crisply. Then I machine-basted both sides of the front and back bodices (in the seam allowances), anchoring the pleats permanently in place. The iron made a challenging task simple.

—LINDA MCCOY, OOSTBURG, WI

THREADING

Use a Paper Clip to Keep Bobbin and Thread Spools Together

—ANNEMARIE MACFADYEN, CHESTER, UNITED KINGDOM

It's possible to buy gadgets to keep bobbin and thread spools together, but here's something that's simple and practically free. Partially straighten an ordinary paper clip. Push one end inside the thread spool and feed the other through the bobbin. It's a cinch to join the two and just as simple to separate them. When you reach for thread, you'll know the bobbin thread will be an exact match in color and thread type.

Maximize Use of Machine Needles

—EDITH CLARK, NEPEAN, ONTARIO, CANADA

If a sewing-machine needle has been used, but it's not ready to be thrown out, return it to its package for reuse, leaving a short length of thread in the eye of needles that have been sewn with to easily distinguish between new and used needles.

Thread Needles Easily

—MILDRED BOWLES,
FRAMINGHAM, MA

Clip the end of the thread for a clean cut, and raise the sewing-machine needle to its highest position. Place the nail of your right thumb directly behind the eye of the needle. Thread the needle with your left hand (even right-handers) by essentially pressing the tip of the thread against the eye, which is covered by your thumbnail. As you pull your thumb away, the thread pushes through the eye more easily than with the typical threading process, because it has no place else to go. It works great.

Tame Flyaway Threads

—JOYCE A. HALL,
HORIZON CITY, TX

I recently encountered a situation in which my thread continually looped over the thread spindle as my embroidery machine stitched. I had used this thread successfully many times before with no trouble. In addition, I noticed that every time I touched the machine, I got a static shock. Putting two and two together, I realized that static electricity was the cause of my thread "fly away." My solution was to spritz my sewing area with a mixture of fabric softener and water. For the rest of the day, I was able to stitch smoothly with no static shocks or misbehaving thread.

HOW HOOK-AND-LOOP TAPE AND THREAD LUBRICATOR HELP SEW FANCY FABRICS

I've been sewing a lot of glitzy fabrics with glued-on sequins, metallic fibers, and other like materials. I found that sequins popped off as I sewed, and I was getting lots of skipped stitches. Sewer's Aid thread lubricant helps, and I've discovered a great way to apply it continuously as I'm sewing: I stick a strip of the loop side of self-adhesive hook-and-loop tape to my sewing machine, just above the needle area, and apply Sewer's Aid to it. As the thread slides down from the take-up lever and through the needle, it passes over this tape patch and collects a dose of thread lubricant. My sequins stay stuck, my needle isn't sticky, and my machine no longer skips stitches.

—ELIZABETH SHELTON, CEDAR RAPIDS, IA

USE A BOBBIN WINDER TO FILL THREAD SPOOLS

I like having matching thread on my serger but hate buying four cones of the same color—that's a lot of thread. I can use one cone to fill a handy bob (for keeping matching bobbin and thread together) to fill empty, regular-size thread spools.

First, I snip off the little thread holders around the outer edge of the handy bob so they won't catch on the machine. Then I put a bobbin on the sewing machine, as if to fill it. Next, I put the handy bob on top of the bobbin (a little double-faced tape makes it adhere well) and place the empty spool on top of the handy bob with the thread groove on top. The bobbin turns the handy bob, which turns the spool, and I guide the thread by hand to fill the spool evenly. This way, I can use one cone to fill as many spools as I need.

—SHIRLEY HASTINGS,
KAMLOOPS, BRITISH COLUMBIA, CANADA

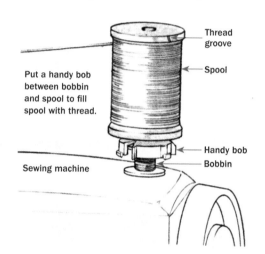

Thread groove

Spool

Put a handy bob between bobbin and spool to fill spool with thread.

Handy bob

Bobbin

Sewing machine

Stop Thread from Getting Strangled in the Machine

—LOUISE ALLEN, DURHAM, NC

When thread gets caught in the slit on the spool cut by the manufacturer to catch the thread tail when the spool was new, the result is a machine screeching to a halt. This is easy to fix, but because it can ruin an important seam or row of topstitching, it's best to prevent it before it happens. Here's how: Take five seconds to mark the slit on each new spool, and on those currently being used, with a bright-colored permanent marker (like a Sharpie®). Be careful not to get ink on the thread. When threading the machine, place the spool's marked end at the right-hand end of a horizontal spool holder and at the top on a vertical holder.

MEASURING

Customize Your
Tape Measure

—LUCY THOMPSON,
LIVINGSTON, TX

If you've got a few measurements that you use all the time, such as the hem length you like for skirts or the inseam length on finished pants, you can keep a permanent record of them with marks on your tape measure at these lengths. Try using a colored marker to make a thin line across the tape and label each one a short code, like "H" for hem, and "I" for inseam.

HOW TO MAKE ONE TAPE MEASURE INTO TWO

While checking the straight of grain as I cut out a pattern using a rotary cutter, I accidentally sliced through my high-quality, 60-in. tape measure. With frustration and annoyance, I stuck the two cut pieces in my drawer and finished the project. About two weeks later, I reached into my drawer for the tape measure and realized I would have to work with a shorter piece. As it turned out, the shorter piece was much easier to work with, stayed out of the way better, and didn't need to be frequently rolled up. I still use that same piece when I cut out pattern pieces. I also discovered that the second half works really well in my knitting bag. It, too, is more convenient to tote around than the original longer tape measure. In fact, there are many times when a standard 60-in. tape measure is simply not necessary. If I were going to do this on purpose, I would cut one piece 36 in. long to have a full yard and use the other 24-in. piece for smaller measuring tasks.

—ROBIN PEABODY, NAPERVILLE, IL

THIMBLES

Make a Thimble Liner from a Rubber Finger
—VICKI TATUM STAMMER, ARLINGTON, TX

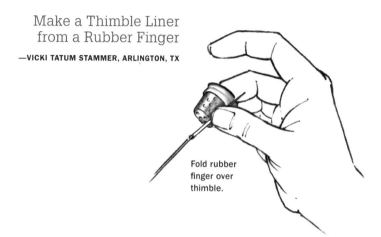

Fold rubber finger over thimble.

Line an oversize metal thimble with a "rubber finger" from stationary stores to create a double-duty device that makes grabbing needles as easy as pushing them, with no need to reach for or find an extra tool. Turn the excess length of the rubber fingertip over the bottom edge of the metal thimble. Secure the excess in place and position a layer of rubber where it can be used to pinch and pull a needle.

Use a Rubber Finger Instead of a Thimble
—DAWN LESLEY STEWART, HOLLISTON, MA

Not everyone is comfortable using the classic metal thimble. One alternative is to use an inexpensive rubber finger cover (sold in an office-supply shop), used to help in sorting and counting paper. The rubber is typically thicker at the tip than on the sides, offering almost the same protection from needle ends, plus the sides provide increased grip, useful for pulling stuck needles through.

Use Liquid Bandage as a Thimble
—SUZANNA SANDOVAL, BELLEVUE, WA

Consider using New-Skin® Liquid Bandage on the hand held under a project when hand sewing or hand quilting. No more pricks and no blood on the fabric. It takes several coats, but the results are well worth the effort.

Alter Your Thimble to Fit
—DOROTHY ZALESKI, SOUTHINGTON, CT

Thimbles are round, but if your fingers are oval, try bending the thimble with a few gentle taps of a hammer to make it fit better.

NEEDLES AND PINCUSHIONS

Use a Whetstone to Remove Burrs
—TERRI RAGOT, GROTON, MA

Try using a whetstone (usually designated for sharpening kitchen knives) to remove needle burrs that catch in fabric—it works beautifully and can even extend the life of your needles.

....

Use an Emery Board to Remove Burrs
—ALETA GIDDINGS, SURREY, BRITISH COLUMBIA, CANADA

Keep needles sharp using an emery board. A few gentle strokes along a needle's surface result in a perfectly honed needle and save the expense of purchasing new needles. These work equally well on straight pins.

HOW TO ORGANIZE NEEDLES

With the variety of machine needles on the market today, it's a challenge to keep them organized. So I created a "needle cushion," a simple-to-make item that not only stores and classifies a growing collection of new and barely used needles, but also identifies the needle currently installed on the machine. I keep two of these holders handy, one for universal needles and the other for specialty needles.

To make a needle cushion, sandwich a layer of thin batting between two pieces of light-colored fabric (I like unbleached muslin), both cut to 6-in. squares. Stitch a series of straight vertical, horizontal, and diagonal lines that intersect neatly in the center. I use the multimotion stitch, but any stitch will do. If your sewing machine has lettering capabilities, machine-stitch each section with the names and sizes of the needles you frequently use. (A fabric marker does the job for sewers whose machines don't read and write.) To complete, serge, zigzag, or bind the outside edges.

To store needles, simply stick them through the appropriate sections of the needle cushion. To remind yourself which needle is currently on the machine, affix a straight pin to the section that identifies that needle.

When you finish sewing, put the needle cushion under the presser foot and lower the foot for the night, just like sewing-machine dealers do to prevent the feed dogs from nicking the bottom of the foot. When you next sew, the type of needle on the machine won't be a mystery.

—CAROL S. DEBAETS, CHARLOTTE, NC

Make a Ham Out of a Pincushion

—ELIZABETH FERGUSON, CANAL WINCHESTER, OH

If you don't own a ham, try using a pincushion to press curved seams. Remove the pins and turn it on its side, then lay the seam on top and press. For long seams, simply roll the pincushion along the underside of the seam as you go.

....

Hold Your Ham Up Straight

—TESS EDWARDS, ST. CLAIR PARK, DUNEDIN, NEW ZEALAND

Using a tailor's ham to press the top of a sleeve is much easier if the ham remains upright. No ham holder? Wedge one end of the ham in the drawer of your sewing table with an extra towel on each side to prevent it from shifting. Pressing the sleeve cap will be a breeze, and there won't be additional equipment to store!

....

Sew over Pins Correctly

—ROSEMARY BOWDITCH, ANN ARBOR, MI

When sewing over pins, by choice or necessity, the smoothest way is to have the pins enter and exit the fabric on the underside, as viewed by the sewer. This way, the pins will be in plain view, so you can slow the machine to stitch over or remove them.

....

Hold Hand-Sewing Thread with a Bill Spike

—VIOLA CLARA VAUGHAN, INDIANAPOLIS, IN

When hand sewing, try using a bill spike to hold spools of thread. They are available in stationery catalogs and can help you keep spools readily accessible without rolling away, while offering the freedom to pull off as much thread as needed. You can even place more than one spool on the spike at a time.

HOW TO RELEASE YOUR PINS

My magnetic pin holder secures my silk pins so tightly that it's difficult to remove them, so I push a knitting needle or stiletto under the pins to sculpt them into a tepee shape. Then I can remove individual pins effortlessly while the rest remain securely attached to the magnetic base.

—ELIZABETH SHELTON, CEDAR RAPIDS, IA

HOW TO WEAR YOUR SEWING AIDS

When I sew, I like to have the notions I use most often close at hand. I wear a wrist pincushion to keep my pins readily available, and I "wear" my sewing gauge and 4-in. Gingher® scissors around my neck so that I don't have to hunt for them when they're needed. The scissors are attached to a lanyard with a short piece of ¼-in. elastic. I keep a sheath on the scissors so that they're not a hazard. When I want to snip, I simply remove the sheath and cut. The sheath is also attached to the lanyard so I don't misplace it when I remove it. The sewing gauge has a hole at one end, and I have threaded it with a piece of 50-in.-long, ¼-in.-wide elastic that I've tied in a circle. The loop is large enough to slip over my head, but the elastic's stretch allows me to access whatever I'm measuring, even if I have to reach across my cutting board. Whether I am sitting at my machine, standing at the ironing board, or working at my cutting table, the pins, scissors, and gauge are always at hand.

—NANCY BORGER, WASHINGTON, DC

TAPE

Keep Snips Ready with Hook-and-Loop Tape

—BRENDA BLACKWOOD, BURLINGTON, ONTARIO, CANADA

To eliminate the problem of losing snips when sewing, attach snips to a long, curly cord designed for keys. Stitch the nonadhesive side of a strip of hook-and-loop tape (the loop side) to the key ring, and attach a 1-in. square of adhesive hook-and-loop tape (the hook side) to your sewing machine and one to your serger. Your snips will be close at hand whenever you need them, and you'll be able to move them easily from machine to machine. The snips and hook-and-loop tape are available at sewing centers and hobby stores. The curly cord, which comes with the clasp and the key ring attached, is available at most dollar and hardware stores.

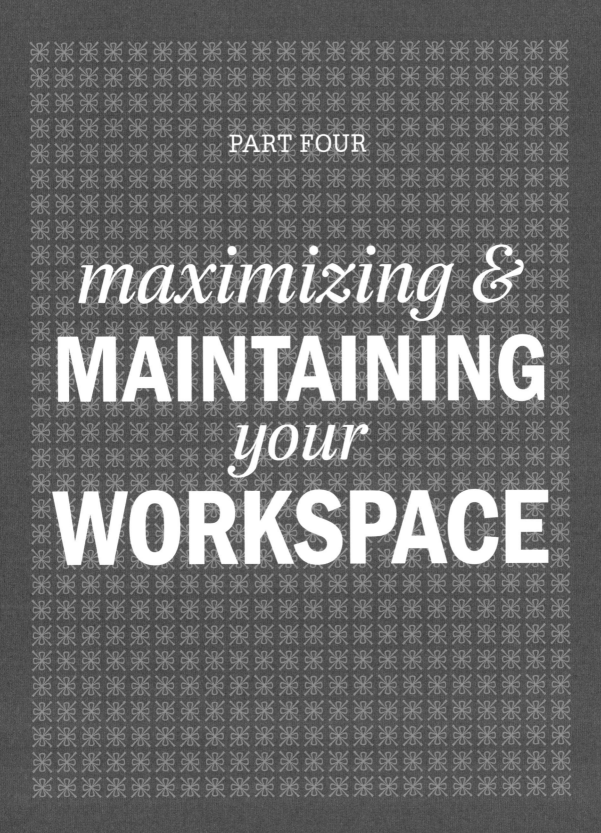

PART FOUR

maximizing &
MAINTAINING
your
WORKSPACE

SETUP

CREATING SMART SURFACES AND SEWING STATIONS

Hang Inspiration on an Upholstered Wall

—SUSAN MACKENZIE,
GRANTS PASS, OR

A wonderful sewing aid, which also lightens and brightens a small, dark sewing room, is an upholstered wall. To create one in your sewing space, staple a layer of medium-weight polyester batting directly to the wall or paneling, using a staple gun and medium staples. The staples usually leave minimal holes. Cut a king-size sheet to cover the batting, leaving enough allowance to turn under the edges. Staple the sheet to the batting. Long quilting pins are ideal for hanging sketches, photos, swatches of fabric, notes, and reminders. Pin up an entire garment's pieces, along with notions and pattern tissues, to the surface, preventing wrinkles. Best of all, all the pieces are kept out of the way till sewing time.

Make a Building Board Cutting Table

—EVA BRASWELL,
BLOOMINGTON, IL

Make your own cutting board from a sheet of building board from the lumberyard. Building board is a lightweight, porous cardboard about $\frac{1}{2}$ in. thick that pins can easily penetrate. It can be cut to size with a drywall knife. Consider covering it with a close-fitting cotton cover to keep the edges from being damaged. The board is easy to store against the wall when not in use.

Create a Temporary Light Table

—DORIS KOURT,
BARTLESVILLE, OK

Need a light table, but don't have the room to store one? Try making a temporary light table with items found around the house, including a table that pulls apart (to accommodate expansion leaves) and glass from an end table or dresser top (Plexiglas® from a storm window or door will do). Open the table, lay the glass over the opening, and set a tall table lamp on the floor underneath. Instant light table—at least until suppertime.

Extend a Table with Cardboard

—MARGARET MARINUCCI,
LANGHORNE, PA

To get more support when working on wide, bulky, or stretchy fabrics and to keep them from drooping off the worktable, insert a heavy cardboard cutting board (the folding kind that you can get in most fabric stores) between the mat and the tabletop so that it sticks out the required distance along the long side. The cardboard extended up to about half its width will give adequate support. With very heavy fabrics, clamp the mat and board together down against the tabletop with a couple of C-clamps for even more stability.

Use Foam Board as a Portable Cutting Surface

—KATIA TSVETKOVA,
SAN FRANCISCO, CA

For easy tracing and cutting when there isn't a lot of space to work in, consider using a large white foam fold-out display board (available at office-supply stores). Lightweight, easy to store, inexpensive, and readily available, it can also be great for slippery fabric, because fabric and pattern can literally be pinned to the foam board. Lay it out on a bed or table for an instant sewing prep area.

Use a Jelly Roll Pan to Corral Tools and Notions

—PATRICIA CHAPMAN,
DOYLESTOWN, PA

To reduce havoc around your sewing machine, try putting it on a large cookie sheet with sides—sometimes called a jelly roll pan. Set the machine 3 in. to 4 in. from the edge of the sheet, leaving a space to set scissors, seam rippers, pins, and so on. The sides of the cookie sheet keep notions from rolling away. Pad the sheet with a couple of layers of felt to help keep things from rolling and to muffle the machine noise a bit.

Make a Taller Table

—HELEN M. SCHMIDT,
BROOKS, ALBERTA, CANADA

Turn any table into a cutting or layout surface of the perfect height by placing an empty or full 1-gal. paint can under each leg of the table. For class or large projects, a Ping-Pong® table is ideal. When the table is needed for another use, one person can easily remove the cans by quickly lifting the table and scooting the cans with a foot.

Use an Air Mattress as a Worksurface

—MARY-ANN BIELEC,
NIAGARA FALLS, NY

If you're short on room, consider using an air mattress as a worksurface. It can add 8 in. of height to your bed and makes a great cutting surface. Cover the mattress with a pad, then a cutting board (for a flat and sturdy base), and top it with a self-healing cutting mat. All of the pieces easily slide under the bed for storage. If additional height is needed for comfort, there are also bed risers (a set of four cups) available that raise a bed another 6 in. to allow for even more under-bed storage.

Fashion a Mobile Workstation on Wheels

—MRS. NAT DEAN,
SANTA FE, NM

Adjustable rolling tables that pull over a bed, used in hospitals, make great mobile workstations. They are handy to extend over cutting tables and keep sewing tools close without getting buried. A table carrying your sewing projects can even be rolled to other areas of the home, parked by the TV or a window, or set up anywhere in a fresh environment (even on your bed). The tables are easy to find at office/business furniture liquidators, secondhand stores, or commercial display hardware resellers. Cover the laminate tops with recycled cutting mat scraps for a bonus cutting surface.

Create a Folding Design Board

—JUDITH NEUKAM,
THREADS CONTRIBUTOR

A 4-ft.-high folding screen makes a great design/display board for sewing projects. Here's how to make one—so easy! Slide four 24-in. by 48-in. panels of ½-in. foam core into a large fabric envelope divided into four pockets. (The pocket stitching forms the hinges and allows the panels to swing in both directions.) Just hand-stitch the bottom closed and it's ready. To use it as a design/bulletin board, nail it right to the wall or stand it on a cutting table. Fold it up and slide it under the bed or store it in a closet when not in use. The screen zigzags open for double-sided displays or a privacy screen. It can be arranged as a column or used to keep the dog or toddlers out of your sewing room.

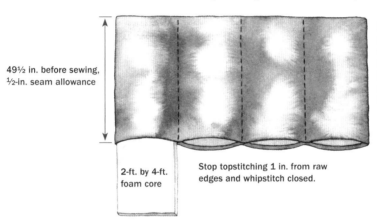

49½ in. before sewing, ½-in. seam allowance

Sew the two seams with the fabric right sides together, and then turn right side out before topstitching.

2-ft. by 4-ft. foam core

Stop topstitching 1 in. from raw edges and whipstitch closed.

Make a Rotating Platform

—ALIS M. WINTLE SEFICK,
BALDWINSVILLE, NY

Here's how to make a rotating particle-board platform to hold your serger and sewing machine. Purchase a 6-in. metal turntable unit that can support 300 lb. from a home center. Figure the size of board needed by placing both machines on a table back to back and measuring depth and length. Mount the turntable on the center of the particle board with the corners rounded off. To lock the turntable in place so it doesn't spin, drill a hole through the board into the tabletop and insert a 3-in. bolt. Then remove the bolt and rotate the board until the other machine is in place. Now insert a marking pen up through the tabletop hole and mark a second hole on the board. Drill the second hole. You may have to unplug the front machine to rotate the platform.

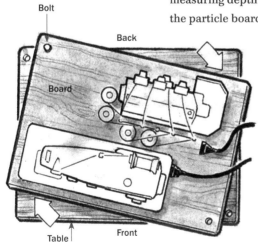

Bolt

Back

Board

Table

Front

Use an Ironing Board as a Workspace

—TOMASA JIMENEZ, LYNDHURST, NY

To create extra workspace when needed, use an ironing board. Adjust it to table height so it's comfortable to work on. Because it's portable, just fold it up for easy storage when finished.

......

Use Kitchen Furniture in the Sewing Room

—JUDY GORDON, ELK GROVE, CA

In the sewing room, consider using cabinets designed for use in the kitchen. A kitchen island with drawers is a perfect height for a cutting table. A kitchen counter gives added workspace. Counters lining the walls enable you to place rolling drawers or plastic bins underneath. The combination will function beautifully and look lovely, too.

......

Reuse a Mattress Pad

—MYRA C. PROPST, SHELBY, NC

A quilted mattress pad, ideally the size made for a crib, can perform many jobs in the sewing room. Placed under a portable sewing machine or serger, it controls noise and vibration. Use it as a large pincushion, as well as a handy pressing pad for small projects. Put it to use to help anchor slippery fabric and also to protect the table from dropped scissors.

......

Make an Ironing-Board Sewing Kit

—BETTY BOLDEN, BOLTON, CT

Take a canvas bag and fill it with a pair of scissors, a clear ruler, a small box filled with pins, a square piece of organza for use as a pressing cloth, and anything else you might need for sewing, and attach it to the end of your ironing board with safety pins for a quick "sewing kit."

HOW TO MAKE A HINGED CUTTING TABLETOP

Like many sewers, I don't have a large sewing area, and I like to be well installed when cutting out a pattern. Last Christmas, my better half had a great idea. He purchased a shelf that was 16 in. wide and had it cut into two pieces measuring 51 in. long. He then joined the two along their long edges with a piano hinge. The finished product opens into a cutting tabletop that fits perfectly on my ironing board. It measures 32 in. wide by 51 in. long. When folded, the tabletop can easily be stored in a closet or under a bed or couch.

—CATHERINE LAPLANTE, MONTREAL, QUEBEC, CANADA

MAXIMIZING YOUR MACHINE

Make No-Slip Foot Controls
—MARIE VAN BOCKERN, SPOKANE, WA

To make some "handy" machine foot controls, take a piece of carpet remnant and position sewing-machine foot controls on it. Mark closely around the controls with masking tape, then cut inside the masked pattern with a sharp utility knife. After cutting the holes and removing the tape, put the carpet back under the sewing table with the foot controls now snug and contained in the cutouts.

....

Create Hook-and-Loop-Tape Foot Controls
—RENE SIMPSON, BRIGHTON, SOUTH AUSTRALIA

Put hook-and-loop-tape dots under your sewing-machine and serger foot pedals. They'll stick to the carpet beautifully.

....

Prevent Foot-Pedal Meandering
—LOIS JOHNSTON, CALGARY, ALBERTA, CANADA

Tired of machine foot pedals "wandering away" on the carpet? Purchase a heavy fiberboard chair mat, then glue a section of hook-and-loop tape on the mat where you want the foot pedal to stay put. The other half of the tape sticks to the bottom of the pedal. The pedal won't move, but you'll also be able to detach it when you need to.

....

Use an iPod Grip Pad to Stop Foot-Pedal Movement
—CANDY SCHWARTZ, GREENFIELD, WI

Try using a 4-in.-wide by 6-in.-long iPod® grip pad to prevent sewing-machine and serger foot pedals from moving while you're sewing. The pads are available at most office-supply stores and are meant to hold an iPod on a car dashboard or other hard surface. They have a tacky surface on both sides, and they attach easily to the bottoms of foot pedals. The pads work well on both carpeted and noncarpeted floors to eliminate pedal movement. You may also consider keeping a larger version next to your sewing machine to prevent scissors and other items from falling due to the vibrations from sewing.

....

Try Hook-and-Loop Tape to Help a Foot Pedal Stay Put
—GAIL YANO, POTOMAC, MD

To keep a sewing-machine foot pedal stationary when it rests on a carpet, apply the hook side of hook-and-loop tape to the bottom of the pedal.

Keep Your Sewing Machine Still

—DIANNE HILLEMEYER, ANCHORAGE, AK

Keep your serger and machine in place, even when rapidly stitching rolled hems on yards and yards of fabric. Try using the heavy-duty bumpers usually placed between glass-topped tables and wooden bases. Find them in the furniture accessories section of hardware stores. They look like clear, $\frac{1}{2}$-in. half-balls, but they come in several other shapes as well. They are self-sticking, which makes them easy to apply. Place one of these bumpers under each corner of your serger, and your serger will stay where you want it. The bumpers also work wonders on sewing machines.

Quiet Serger Vibrations

—DIANE MCNEVICH, NEWARK, DE

Do the vibrations from your serger seem to rock the entire house? Here's a solution: Purchase an inexpensive mouse pad at a computer store and place it under your serger. The pad—just the right size for a serger—will ensure quiet, vibration-free serging.

MAKE A "MEMORIES" COVER

Every time I start a new sewing project, I cut a 3-in. by 3-in. swatch of the fabric and thread it onto a large safety pin along with all of the swatches from previous projects. It gives me a lot of satisfaction at the end of each year to see how many things I've sewn. It's almost like a colorful journal of my sewing projects. After five years of collecting these swatches, I noticed my storage drawer was too cluttered. I needed a new cover for my sewing machine, so I decided to sew these squares together in a patchwork cover. When my grandchildren come to visit, they love finding the squares of fabric that were used in the garments I made for them and/or their dolls and teddy bears. I, too, enjoy a trip down memory lane each time I remove or replace the cover when I sew.

—CHANA ZWEIG, PHILADELPHIA, PA

STORAGE
&
ORGANIZATION

WORKS-IN-PROGRESS

Hang Projects on a Drying Rack
—BETTY BOLDEN, BOLTON, CT

Try using a collapsible clothes drying rack to store projects and fabrics that are currently being worked on or planned for use. By draping fabrics or garments-in-process over the rods of the rack, creases don't form as they would if the project were folded. Each project is clearly visible, which means no rummaging through piles.

Store Sewing Stuff in a Suitcase
—MARTY KORWIN-POWLOWSKI, WEST CHESTER, PA

Keep a few projects organized with patterns, fabric, thread, interfacing, notions, and any special sewing tools required in a small suitcase, which can eliminate those last-minute dashes to the store for a critical missing item.

FABRIC

Mark to Keep Track of Yardage
—DARLEEN A. CLEMENTS, SEATTLE, WA

Ever look at a stack of fabric in your stash and wonder how much yardage is on that piece buried near the bottom? Instead of pulling it out to measure it, store fabrics so you'll know at a glance how much you've got. After every fabric purchase, prewash, then mark the number of yards and fabric width at one end of the selvage with a permanent marker (in case the fabric is washed again later). Fold and shelve the fabric with the notations clearly visible. To use a selected fabric, cut from the marked end, and mark the selvage with the new length.

Keep Stabilizer Accessible
—BARBARA KELSEY, VALLEY VILLAGE, CA

Use pants hangers to store stabilizer. Put a different stabilizer on each rung and keep the instructions and brand information wrapped inside the stabilizer. The filled hanger is easy to place on a hook or closet rod for quick and easy access.

Store Fabric in Dishpans
—CHERYL HILBRANDS, GEORGE, IA

To make it easy to sort and organize fabrics, put them in dishpans in a shelved cabinet. Take out each dishpan to easily browse through the fabric choices without having to refold each piece. Organize the dishpans by type or color—whatever works best. This method allows easy access to fabric without making a mess.

HOW TO KEEP TRACK OF A FABRIC STASH

When I buy fabric, I immediately cut a 2-in.-square swatch and fuse it to a same-size piece of white iron-on interfacing. I record fiber information, width, length, and care directions on the interfacing side with a permanent pen. Then I slide a safety pin through one corner and attach the swatch to a round, split key ring. You can, of course, place more than one swatch on a safety pin and will likely fill more than one key ring as you compile your fabric collection reference.

This "stash-and-carry" system has many benefits: You can carry a huge collection of swatches; each grouping can be sorted by color or fiber on separate pins or multiple rings; and you're sure to find an accurate match when purchasing coordinating fabrics, threads, zippers, and buttons. This system allows you to hold your entire fabric collection in one hand, by a finger, so your other hand is free to shop for more fabric. Store the rings on a hook in your sewing room or keep them in your shopping carryall for unexpected trips to the fabric store. And after sewing, when a garment requires cleaning, the relevant information will still be on the back of a swatch.

—JUDY LESLIE, COQUITLAM, BRITISH COLUMBIA, CANADA

Store Interfacing in "Envelopes"
—LYNN TEICHMAN, LEWISBURG, PA

Anyone who sews has to solve the problem of sorting and storing interfacings. Here's a handy solution. Make an envelope for each type from the plastic instruction sheet. Fold the sheet and machine-sew the sides. Not only are these pockets, or envelopes, quick and easy to make, but it keeps interfacing easily accessible with the instructions. It's also a great method for storing scraps.

Use Foam Pipe Insulation Tubes to Roll Up Interfacing
—JEAN YAEGER, NOVATO, CA

Consider rolling and storing interfacing on foam tubes that are meant to be used to insulate pipes. They are inexpensive and reusable, and the texture of the foam holds the fabric well. The tubes come in 6-ft. lengths; simply cut the length needed with a serrated knife. These tubes have a shallow, lengthwise slit; stuff ¼ in. of the cut end of the interfacing into the slit. The fabric is held securely and is easy to roll evenly onto the tube. Store the tubes standing upright in boxes.

Label Fabric for a Swatch Book

—PATRICIA MEEKS, WHITE SALMON, WA

Carry computer labels when shopping for fabrics. Just after the fabric is cut, while the bolt is still in the cart, write down the fabric content, price, size, and so forth on a label and affix it to a corner of the fabric. At home, cut a swatch of the fabric, add the label, and add them to a swatch book. Whenever you need information about a fabric, the complete details will be readily accessible.

Use Closet Organizers for Storing Fabric

—JUDY ZIFKA, BEND, OR

A vinyl shoe organizer, hung from a closet rod, is an ideal storage container for scraps of fabrics and other miscellaneous sewing items, while a sweater organizer is a great way to store flat folded yardage.

THREAD

Use a Shelf Edge for Extra Thread

—WENDY WITTER, PEACE RIVER, ALBERTA, CANADA

Have an overabundance of thread? Here's a great storage idea: a shelf edge. A shelf edge is one of those things that do-it-yourselfers use to edge shelves. They're made of plastic, with a built-in "grip" that holds a lot of thread spools. A piece of ¾-in. shelf edge, with a hole punched at one end, hangs from a piece of pegboard, keeping countless spools in place and visible. Try grouping threads by color in several strips.

Find "shelf edge" at home centers and home-improvement stores. Cut it into strips, and load it with thread spools.

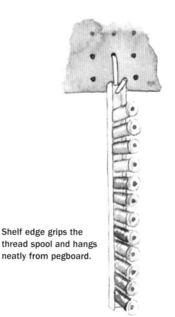

Shelf edge grips the thread spool and hangs neatly from pegboard.

Remove shelf, and lay on fabric to find color match

Tame Tangled Embroidery Threads
—K. C. SAXE, SIOUX CITY, IA

Anyone who does a lot of embroidery or cross stitch knows how quickly leftover thread scraps can pile up and tangle. Here's a simple way to keep them organized and easily at hand: Lay out strands straight and together in an unsorted bundle, trimming any unusually long strands. Fold the bundle in half and tie a thread loosely around the center. Anchor the center loop and braid all the threads into a big, loose braid. From now on, whenever a thread of a certain color is needed, pick it up at the middle tie and slip it out. If the braid isn't too tight, the thread will come right out without disturbing the braided threads around it.

Use Drinking Straws to Extend Spool Pins
—NELLIE DERY, VAN WERT, OH

Get maximum spool storage by adding drinking straws to the pins on your spool rack. Just be sure to compare the size of the straw to your pins because they are not all the same.

Use a Plastic Rolling Drawer Unit to Organize Thread
—E'ANNE FRYE, TOPEKA, KS

Store thread and related items in an inexpensive plastic rolling drawer unit, preferably one that is short enough to fit under the sewing table. Use the large bottom drawer for serger cones, and sort threads into separate drawers by type: regular sewing, embroidery, silk, cotton, and quilting, and then by color within each drawer. Line the drawers with a rubber shelf liner so the spools don't shift when you pull out and push in the drawers. In each drawer, consider also placing a little box for bobbins. The spools of thread will stay dust-free, won't fade or deteriorate in the light, and will also be handy.

Stash Thread in a Pie Keeper
—CHERYL HILBRANDS, GEORGE, IA

A sturdy plastic pie keeper can store forty 300-yd. thread spools. Perfect dust-free thread storage.

Keep Bobbins and Spools Together with Rubber Bands
—KAREN D'ALESSANDRI, POMONA, NY

Here's an easy way to keep a wound bobbin together with its matching spool of thread. Slide one end of a rubber band through the bobbin hole and loop it through its other end; this holds the bobbin securely. Wrap the loop end of the rubber band (with the bobbin on it) around the spool. The bonus: The rubber band prevents both the spool and the bobbin from unraveling.

Adapt a Thread Rack to Create More Storage

—LESLIE PELECOVICH, STAMFORD, CT

I store my thread on a standard wooden thread rack covered with multiple wooden spindles. I found it frustrating that each spindle only held one thread spool with no room to add a bobbin, so I decided to adapt it. Using a pair of pliers, I replaced the rack's short, stubby spindles with longer ones. First, I twisted each spindle out and discarded it. Then, I cut a $^3/_{16}$-in.-diameter dowel (the same diameter as the discarded spindles) into lengths appropriate to hold my thread spools along with each matching bobbin. I sanded the ends, then tapped a dowel into each existing hole. Now I can stack the bobbins on top of each respective spool, and the rack looks just as nice as it did before, without taking up additional space.

Make a Thread Organizer

—ADELINE D. FARMER, SUPERIOR, WI

My homemade thread organizer is a handy gadget for doing stitchery. It has a revolving platform mounted on a post about 34 in. high that stands on a 14-in.-sq. plywood base. I mount a short dowel into the top of the post to hold a platform for a Rubbermaid turntable. I drill holes for $^1/_4$-in. dowels all around a circular board that rests on the turntable, and I glue the dowels in place. I hang each skein on a dowel and stick a label below the dowel on the edge of the circular board to identify the color's symbol. I usually sit on the couch with my embroidery frame supported. The work goes faster because I can use both hands.

Store Thread on a Pegboard

—CAROL WALLIS, BEVERLY, MA

Make a thread board to hold spools and bobbins out of a 24-in. by 48-in. piece of pegboard. Insert $^1/_8$-in. wooden dowels into the holes, which can be widened with the twist of a sharpened pencil. Cut as many dowels as you will need into lengths that will hold your larger spools of thread easily. A dab of glue on the back of each dowel will lock it securely to the board. On the bottom row insert pegboard hooks to hang notions and sewing tools.

Use Multipurpose Bobbin Thread

—ANNA MARIA BALZARINI, BREWSTER, MA

Keep a full bobbin of transparent thread handy for little sewing projects or alterations that require only a small amount of colored thread. Thread your machine needle with the proper color and pop in the transparent bobbin thread. No more winding bobbins partway.

Make Little Labels for Bobbins	To label filled bobbins, use self-adhesive, loose-leaf reinforcement
—LINDA VELSOR, CATAWBA, NC	rings. Write the thread name, color number, and weight on the label. They fit perfectly around the bobbin holes.

HOW TO STORE CONES ON AN OVER-THE-DOOR SHOE RACK

When I first got a serger, I started collecting cone threads. Whenever cones went on sale, I'd buy four of each color, since my serger uses four threads. Well, as you can imagine, what I ended up with was a big, cumbersome boxful of jumbled thread cones.

While in a department store one day, I noticed shoe-storage units with 12 to 18 clear plastic sleeves, intended to be hung on a closet rod. This was the perfect solution for organizing my threads! Each pocket holds several cones, depending on their size.

—JAN EDE, PENDER ISLAND, BRITISH COLUMBIA, CANADA

PINS AND NEEDLES

Stash Lightly Used Needles in Fabric	To store a slightly used sewing-machine needle for future use, stick it
—JENNY LEWIS, PORTSMOUTH, NH	in a scrap of the fabric for which it's appropriate. For example, stick a 100/16 jeans needle into a scrap of denim, or a 60/8 sharp into a scrap of silk. This way it will be known at a glance whether used needles are still usable and what they're to be used for.

Create Easy-Access Storage for Machine Needles	Here's a way to store sewing-machine needles to quickly find the
—LYNN M. SCHELITZCHE, BURNSVILLE, MN	right size, requiring only a black, felt-tip marker and a pincushion, preferably a divided cushion like the familiar tomato. Label the sections with frequently used machine-needle sizes and types: 8, 10, 12, double, straight, ball, and so on. Then just stick the needle into the appropriate section when removed from the machine.

USING SOAP AS A PINCUSHION

A bar of soap is a great way to hold pins and needles and keep them lubricated to glide right through fabrics (even canvas).

—ANNA VICTORIA REICH, ALBUQUERQUE, NM

When using a bar of soap to hold pins and needles, don't use a soap with moisturizers in it, as they cause rust.

—LOUISE WORMAN, DEPOSIT, NY

Use a Candle to Store Pins and Needles

—BEVERLY HILTON, PEMBROKE PINES, FL

Keep a favorite scented candle (the soft type that comes in its own container) near your sewing machine, and store needles with their points down in the candle wax when you're not using them. This keeps them rust-free and lubricated, and also keeps your sewing room smelling great.

Create a Safe Box for Needle Storage

—GRACE B. WEINSTEIN, LOS ANGELES, CA

A simple, effective needle "safe" can be made out of an empty paper clip box and a few strips of self-adhesive magnetic tape (sold in sewing-notion stores). Cover the paper clip box with decorative paper and apply strips of the magnetic tape to the inside bottom. If the box tips over, the needles will be held fast by the magnetic tape.

Use a Tackle Box for a Sewing Box

—MRS. MARY ANN JAMES, OWEGO, NY

A large fishing tackle box that has multilayered trays is ideal for organizing sewing accessories. The small compartments are useful for needles, pins, buttons, and beads. The bottom of the box can hold sewing books, instruction manuals, and patterns. Fishing tackle boxes are well balanced, can be left open for easy rummaging, and can be packed up quickly for taking to classes.

Try Double-Sided Tape for Holding Needles

—KATHRYN RAY, RICHMOND, VA

Don't waste time digging in a box for sewing machine needles of the right size. Use double-sided tape to secure each of your needle containers to a piece of cardboard, placing them in size order. It will be easy to see which needles you have on hand and which you need to restock, and you'll be able to find the needle needed in no time.

Use Zip-Top Bags for Needle Storage

—LOUISE BUSHELL, CHESHIRE, CT

To store needles conveniently, purchase a small pack of 2-in.-wide by 4-in.-long zip-top bags, available at craft stores. Punch a hole in the corner of each bag and use a split ring from an old key chain to join the bags. Place one pack of needles in each plastic bag. Notebook split rings or even a short ball chain or piece of ribbon can also be used to keep the bags together. It will make it so easy to find the exact needle size you want and also easy to see which needles you need to buy the next time you're at the fabric store.

Use a Business-Card Holder for Needles

—ELISA DALRYMPLE, AUSTIN, TX

I have never been happy with storing and organizing all of the different kinds of machine needle cases I own. I found the perfect solution at an office-supply store: A clear page-protector-style business-card holder allows me to easily see the needle cases, and they're also easy to get to.

Note Needle Size with an Adhesive Dot

—PATRICIA CUNNINGHAM, BALLWIN, MO

When I put a needle into the sewing machine, I write the size on an adhesive dot (the kind you buy at an office-supply store) and put it on the sewing machine. No more guessing which needle is in the machine.

Keep a Stash of Threaded Needles

—KAREN WOLFF, LAGUNA HILLS, CA

Here's a great way to make use of long strands of thread: Keep a pincushion of needles handy when sewing. When you're ready to remove a spool of thread from your machine, clip the thread at the spool and pull the thread out of the machine through the needle. Take that strand and thread it through one of the hand-sewing needles in the pincushion. Whenever you need to baste, make tailor's tacks, or sew on a button, snap, or hook and eye, there will be an assortment of threaded needles all ready to go.

HOW TO ATTACH A PINCUSHION TO YOUR SEWING MACHINE

When I sew, I often remove pins as I go. I used to end up with an annoying pile of pins that got in my way, fell on the floor, got lost in the machine's base, and generally drove me crazy—until I came up with this solution. I made a 3-in. by 5-in. cushion from a scrap of material and stuffed it firmly with polyester filling.

I sewed the fuzzy half of a piece of hook-and-loop tape onto the back of the cushion and sewed the other side midway along a 15-in. length of ½-in.-wide braid. I wrapped the braid snugly around the body of my sewing machine and secured it with a safety pin. (You could also just glue the tape right to the front of the machine.) Now I have a pincushion in just the right place to receive the pins I take out midseam, and it's removable for use at the cutting table or elsewhere.

—MARY APPLEGATE, BELCHERTOWN, MA

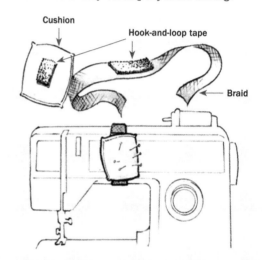

Sew hook-and-loop tape onto a small, tightly stuffed cushion and a long braid strip. Pin it comfortably to your sewing machine.

Make a Sewing-Machine Pincushion
—PHILLIDA B. MIRK, ISLESBORO, ME

Form a small cushion—about 1½ in. by 3 in.—from leftover fabric and stuff it with cornmeal or ground coffee. (Either substance gives the pins just enough oil to prevent rusting.) Then attach the cushion to a narrow strap, made of the same material, with a buttonhole or a slit in one end. The hole slips over the spool holder on top of the machine, and the cushion hangs either in front of, or behind, the body.

TOOLS

Create a Permanent Tape Measure
—SHIRLEY W. BELLERANTI, MESA, AZ

Wasting a lot of time rummaging through drawers looking for a tape measure, then more time unwinding and rewinding it? Here's an easy solution. Glue a tape measure made of heavy-grade paper to your worksurface. It works like a charm and saves both time and frustration when something needs to be measured quickly.

Magnetize Serger Screwdrivers
—BARBARA WORDEN, MECHANICSBURG, PA

Consider keeping serger screwdrivers on a magnetic pin holder, such as a Grabbit®. It makes it easier to maneuver those tiny screws when changing needles, feet, and so forth. It's also especially helpful for anyone with arthritis. Also consider using this technique for sewing machine screwdrivers. Be careful: If your machine is electronic, it may be sensitive to magnets.

Keep Scissors Handy
—RACHEL PFAFFENDORF, CLEAR LAKE, SD

How can you keep scissors from wandering away from your sewing machine? Cut a length of ¼-in. elastic, 24 in. to 48 in. long, and tie the ends together. Fold the elastic in half, and place about 3 in. of one end through the scissors handle. Then open this part of the elastic to make a small loop and pull the other end through the loop to form a knot. Tug on the long end of the elastic to secure the knot. Next, slide the free end of the elastic through the handle of your sewing machine and tie it in the same manner as the scissors. Now the scissors will stay with your machine even when it travels—and they never get left behind. You can also make a scissors holster for your ironing board using a kitchen pot holder folded into a cone. Stitch the cone together with the hanging loop up, and then pin the loop to the ironing board.

Store Stabilizers on Wooden Curtain Rods
—JANE TUTTON, VERO BEACH, FL

To free up workspace and keep stabilizers organized, try hanging wooden curtain rods on the wall. The dowels will sit just the right distance from the wall for rolls of stabilizer—pieces can even be cut off without having to remove the rolls. To make it easy to identify the type of stabilizer, slip the name of the stabilizer inside the tube. But don't do this with water-soluble stabilizers or those with water-activated glues. Keep those together in a large zip-top bag.

HOW TO SET A METAL TOOL CHEST ON WHEELS

After years of using stackable plastic organizer drawers, I purchased a red metal tool chest on wheels—the type typically used by woodworkers. I use it to organize threads, buttons, zippers, and other sewing miscellany. The drawers slide smoothly and easily on ball bearings and are supported with secure drawer glides. The chest is on wheels so I can move it around my sewing room easily to keep it close at hand. Each drawer has a rubber lining that helps to prevent my stored items from shifting as it travels from place to place. If I ever get weary of it or (gasp) quit sewing, it'll be a natural in the garage.

—KATHY WALKOWSKI, PEWAUKEE, WI

Hook-Hang Shears and Scissors
—ZEE PERRY, ESCONDIDO, CA

3M™ Command™ adhesive hooks are a great solution for organizing sewing scissors and shears to keep them at hand while maintaining a very specific, uncluttered storage place. Attach them without screws or nails, and remove them easily without leaving a residue. Place two hooks side by side spaced 1½ in. apart—the distance between the two holes on your shears. The shears slip easily over the hooks and are ready to grab when needed.

Use Pegboard Storage in Cramped Quarters
—DORIS HARRIS, SEARCY, AR

A handy notion and sewing tool board can be made from a 4-ft. by 8-ft. pegboard. To attach the board to your wall, make a frame smaller than the pegboard out of 1-in. by 2-in. wooden strips. Screw or nail the frame through wall plaster or drywall into the wall studs. This will prevent the weight of the loaded pegboard from pulling away from the wall. After the frame is secured to the wall, fasten the pegboard to the frame with screws. At a hardware store, you will find all sorts of brackets and hooks made especially for pegboards. There are even holders for carpentry tools that you can easily adapt for sewing; a screwdriver holder, for example, will hold scissors.

Organize Fine Tools Using a Toolbox and a Lazy Susan
—JAN SCHOLL, STATE COLLEGE, PA

To make a tool holder for my sewing equipment, I cleaned up an old toolbox caddy and put a lazy Susan under it so that it could spin to within my reach. The drawers hold fasteners, safety pins, thimbles, seam rippers, tweezers, bobbins, chalk, and so forth. I hang my scissors on the outside hooks. The bins are great for tapes and trims, rulers, and glues. With a twist of the wrist, I have all my sewing supplies within reach, and it takes up little space behind my machine.

PATTERNS

Take Patterns to the Store
—SUSAN STONE, AMELIA ISLAND, FL

Bring patterns with you to the fabric store with this simple system: Keep the contents of the pattern envelope in a 6-in. by 9-in. manila clasp envelope. Label these with the pattern company, number, size, and comments (for a visual reference, photocopy the pattern envelope, and tape it to the manila envelope). The real pattern jackets go into clear plastic sheet protectors in a binder that can easily be taken along to the fabric store, for reading yardage and notions requirements and knowing instantly how much fabric to buy.

Store Patterns in a Binder
—JANE SERIGHT, COLDSTREAM, BRITISH COLUMBIA, CANADA

Remove the pattern and instruction sheets from the original pattern envelope, put them in a brown 9-in. by 12-in. envelope, and mark the name of the pattern company and the number on the top corner of the envelope. Store them in numerical order in a letter-size filing cabinet (rarely are there two patterns with the same number from two different companies). Put patterns without numbers in alphabetical order at the end. Place the original pattern envelope in a three-hole plastic sheet protector (along with any vital information from the pattern sheets), and put the sheet protectors in a three-ring binder, divided by category, as they would be in a pattern catalog. This way you can look through your entire pattern collection easily, at your leisure, and even take it fabric shopping.

Store Patterns without Folding
—LINDA KURAS, PORTLAND, OR

Here's a great solution for storing patterns that eliminates the need to iron them each time they're used. Instead of folding them back into their small envelopes, roll them up and slip them into cardboard tubes from kitchen and gift wrap.

Use Plastic Folders to Stash Patterns

—**LYNN MALLY, IRVINE, CA**

Making patterns is fun, but it can soon present a storage problem. Here's a solution: colorful plastic file folders, called "tabbed project viewers," available at office-supply stores. Choose durable ones that are open at the top but sealed on the bottom and on one side, with a simple security flap on the other side. This clever construction protects the pattern pieces and allows for easy identification via the included adhesive index tabs.

Store Pattern Pieces on Hooks

—**MERYL S. WYNNE, VICTORIA, BRITISH COLUMBIA, CANADA**

Separate cut pattern pieces into sections (front with back and facings, sleeves with cuffs, and so forth), then attach each section to a C-clip (a plastic clothespin that's attached to a hanger-hook designed to fit on a closet clothing rod—available at dollar and home-goods stores). Hang all hooks on one hanger for easy closet storage. For large pattern pieces, use two hooks to prevent the pieces from stretching. This is a particularly good way to store cut fabric pieces for projects you are not able to finish immediately. As the garment begins to take shape, it can be hung on the same hanger for storage until the next sewing day.

Make a Binder Index for Sewing Patterns

—**KRISTINE KADLEC, LOS ANGELES, CA**

Organizing sewing patterns into categories makes browsing easier. This can be done by photocopying the pattern envelopes and arranging them in a three-ring binder. If you are unable to get double-sided copies of your pattern envelopes, glue or staple the fronts and backs together. Plastic photograph sleeves that fit a three-ring binder, found in stationery stores, are a convenient way to display your copies. Attach any fabrics, notes, or other reminders to the patterns.

Devise a Pattern Reference System

—**SUE BOGAN, SPRINGFIELD, VA**

Here's how to remember which pattern a fabric find will work great for. Cut open each pattern envelope and unfold it so both front and back are visible. Put two opened envelopes back-to-back in a clear sheet protector and store them in a three-ring binder, organized by garment type. Place the pattern directions, which contain the pattern number, on top of the pattern pieces in a resealable plastic bag, and file them by number in a carton. Take your binder with you to the fabric store so you're ready to identify the patterns that work with the fantastic fabrics you find.

Keep Track of Successful Patterns

—DAPHNE DOOLING, BURLINGTON, ONTARIO, CANADA

If you have trouble remembering which patterns from your collection you've sewn that have been successful, here's a foolproof system: Date and write a description of the pattern on an index card, record the details you want to remember about sizing or other anomalies, staple on a remnant of the fabric you used, and insert it in the pattern envelope for easy future reference.

....

Store Patterns in Manila Folders

—CAROL CLAIRE STEVENS, JACKSON, MI

Patterns never fit neatly back into the envelope that they came in—especially when there are multiple garments. Here's a solution to this problem, which will also help you organize your patterns as well.

Make an envelope from a manila office folder by machine stitching the side edges together using a size 16 needle and quilting thread. Cut the original pattern envelope apart along the left and bottom edges, so it opens flat, and glue it to the manila folder envelope. When you're ready to store patterns, stack the pieces from one garment and fold them together, so the printed identification is on the outside of the bundle, and then put them in the folder envelope. The next time you use the pattern, the various garments will be easy to sort out. As you sew, write notes on the folder envelope front for future reference. The folder envelopes will fit perfectly in an office file or box, and the patterns will be organized and easy to find.

....

Use Comic Book Sleeves to Organize Paper Patterns

—ANNE RUBY, BROOKLINE, MA

Comic book sleeves are a great option for boxing and arranging patterns. Head to your local comic book store to find 7-in. by 10-in. plastic comic book sleeves and an assortment of storage boxes. Since the boxes come in a variety of lengths, you may be able to find just the size box you need for each category. Inside each sleeve, put the pattern, the original photo of the garment, a master sheet containing all pertinent measurements, and a swatch of fabric.

TRIMS AND NOTIONS

Use a Magnetic Dish to Hold Notions

—HOLLY ROWE FABER, WILLIAMSBURG, VA

An inexpensive 6-in. magnetic parts dish, which can be purchased at an auto parts store, can be ideal for storing scissors, pins, a small metal ruler, and more, and it can also be adhered firmly to sewing surfaces.

HOW TO ORGANIZE TRIMS ON A FELT-WRAPPED PIPE

I needed a way to disentangle and organize my stash of by-the-yard novelty trims, elastics, and ribbons. So, I glued several thicknesses of felt around the outside of a 2-in.-diameter PVC pipe. I wrapped strands of ribbon, seam binding, and other such notions around the pipe, offset the end of each strand, and pinned it to the felt. I mounted the pipe onto a café-style curtain rod and hung it on the wall. When I want trim, I simply unroll a length, snip off what I need, and repin the end. It's easy to see my inventory, and my trims and ribbons don't get tangled, wrinkled, or damaged.

—MARY MOONEY, NEW YORK, NY

Magnetic Bars Help Keep Notions in Order
—JULIENNE LAMBRE, ROME, ITALY

Hang a magnetic bar on the wall behind your sewing machine to hold threaded needles, a single-edged razor blade (for rapid ripping out), small scissors, and so forth. Magnetic bars can be purchased inexpensively at home-supply stores, and they make notions simple to store and easy to find.

Store Notions in a Spice Rack
—MARY E. GREEN, TOLEDO, OH

A beautiful wooden spice rack with fitted glass jars that I found at a garage sale has been reborn in my sewing room as storage for all those tiny items that previously were jumbled in the bottom of a drawer. Buttons can be sorted by color, needles by size and type, and so on. Labels aren't necessary, and the whole thing can be hung in plain sight but out of the way on a wall.

Use a Jewelry Organizer for Small Notions
—CAROL FARRANT, SAN FRANCISCO, CA

Here's a great way to keep small sewing tools and supplies visible and easy to grab. Try using a hanging jewelry organizer. It makes it easy to locate each item at a glance, and it takes up little room hanging in the closet.

Store Notion Directions in a Binder
—JAN MAHUSKY, PAINESVILLE, OH

Whenever you buy a new notion or gadget, consider saving the manufacturer's directions in a plastic pocket sheet that snaps into a three-ring binder. That way the directions will always be handy. As your collection grows, organize the directions into categories to make them even easier to find.

Use Empty Paper Towel and Toilet Paper Rolls for Trim Storage

—STACEY CALLAHAN,
TOULOUSE, FRANCE

Here's how to prevent elastic, cording, and laces from tangling together, while keeping them visible but protected from dust and direct light: Slide empty paper towel and toilet paper rolls over a wooden or metal dowel from the hardware store. Suspend each end of the dowel beneath a shelf using wire, long-shaft cup hooks, or whatever is most appropriate for your shelving, so the dowel is removable. When the dowel is secure, wrap notions around the tubes and roll them up. The farther toward the back of the shelf, the more protected the tubes will be.

Store Trims in Plastic Takeout Containers

—ELIZABETH SHELTON,
CEDAR RAPIDS, IA

The clear plastic containers that restaurants use for takeout make wonderful see-through storage for gathered laces and other trims. After you roll the trims, they will look like floating roses in the container, and with a rubber band around the container, the attached lid can't flip open, even if a container is dropped. The stash will be visible through all sides, and the containers will be easy to stack.

Use Empty Thread Spools to Store Short Trim and Elastic

—EMILY MCNAMARA, GOODHUE, MN

Store shorter pieces of ribbon and trim on empty thread spools. The filled spools fit on a spool rack in plain sight or anywhere thread is stored. Mark the length directly on the spool top before wrapping the trim around it. That way you won't have to unroll the piece to consider it for a project.

Stash Long Trim on Shower-Curtain Hooks

—MARSHA M. KITT,
TWO HILLS, ALBERTA, CANADA

Recycle (or buy) shower-curtain hooks to store ribbons and other long trims. Hang the hooks on hangers or stationary hooks—whichever is convenient. Simply drape the trims over the hooks. If a trim is extra long, fold it in half or in quarters first. If it's slippery, tie it with a half-hitch knot at the hook to secure it. By putting similar trims together on one hook, they are automatically sorted. This helps keep all by-the-yard items untangled and easy to find.

BUTTONS AND BAUBLES

Match Buttons to Fabric

—JEANNIE K. MCCORMIC,
MANY, LA

Don't get frustrated trying to match a card of buttons to your fabric swatch because you can't really lay the button on the fabric. Snip a 1-in. slit in your swatch and button the card of buttons onto the fabric.

HOW TO ORGANIZE A BUTTON STASH WITH SAFETY PINS

My button box used to be a total disaster. The buttons were loose and disorganized, so I could never find two of the same button without dumping out the whole box. Then I tried stringing them together in logical groups on button thread, but the threads tangled if I kept them too loose, and if I just wanted a few buttons, I had to cut the strand and then restring it. Finally, I found the perfect solution by "stringing" my buttons on safety pins.

There are lots of different-size safety pins available that work well for all but the largest buttons. The safety pins are effective for either shank buttons or those with holes, they don't get tangled in the box, and I can clearly see how many buttons I have. It's a snap to take off as many or as few buttons as I need, then simply close the pin again. If I have more buttons than will fit on one pin or if I have two or more sizes of the same style, I just link the pins together through the coil end. This storage method makes button selection a pleasure.

—ELIZABETH MERRITT, ST. PAUL, MN

Store Buttons in Hanging Jars
—JANET HOMEC, HUDSON, WY

Here's a foolproof method for organizing buttons. Mount the lids of small jars (pint, quart, or baby-food-size) by screwing them to the underside of an overhead shelf (it looks best if several of the same size jars are used in a row). Fill the jar with buttons and screw it to its lid. Sort buttons by color and give each color its own jar. All will be easily identifiable and out of the way.

Wear Bead Samples
—LINDA BOSTON, *THREADS* CONTRIBUTOR

At a recent gem trade show, I saw a woman with the perfect way to carry samples of all her seed beads. Around her neck was a cord holding a wire shower-curtain ring. The ring held samples of her bead collection, strung on 3-in. lengths of monofilament thread with a loop at one end. I have too many seed beads to recall the colors in my stash, and this method helps prevent buying duplicates. I sort my beads by type: natural stones and pearls, delicas, metals—but they could be sorted by size, color, or whatever works for you. So far, not a single strand has ever broken, making this a very durable and compact system.

Reuse Old Buttons

—JEAN MARGOLIS,
SEBASTOPOL, CA

To reuse the buttons on a worn-out garment, cut off the strips of fabric with buttons still on them (cuffs, openings) and pin them together. It's a handy way to keep sets together while you store the buttons.

....

Organize Spare Buttons

—CLAUDETTE TAYLOR,
ELLSWORTH, IA

Whenever you make a garment with buttons, always make at least one sample buttonhole to confirm that the thread and fabric combination chosen produces the look you want. After you've finished a satisfactory test buttonhole, use a zigzag rotary cutter or pinking shears to trim a small rectangle (about 2 in. long by 1 in. wide) with the buttonhole in the center. If the extra buttons are on a card, simply slip one of them through the buttonhole in the swatch. If the buttons are loose, stitch them to the trial buttonhole fabric. Store the extra buttons and the swatch in a container marked "Finished Garments."

BOOKS AND MAGAZINES

HOW TO GET EASY ACCESS TO *THREADS* MAGAZINE

To keep track of all the wonderful information in *Threads*, here's a system that not only gives you fast access to a particular topic but also provides a review of information found in past issues. Create a Microsoft® Word document (Excel would work just as well) that contains reference information for every issue of *Threads* you have:

THREADS NO. ——— Month/Year ————

1. Tips: Page #

2. Notions: Page #

3. Articles of Interest: Page #

4. Advertisers' Addresses: Page #

5. Patterns: Page #

When you want to find an article, tip, advertisement, or anything else of interest, just go to your computer, search the list, and, when you find what you want, you can quickly locate the issue.

—GERRI JURISSON, SUN CITY, AZ

DOCUMENTING AND ARCHIVING YOUR WORK

Photograph Your Projects
—KAREN MCCORMIC,
MANY, LA

Always take photographs of your finished projects. In time, you will have an album full of accomplishments to look back on, and a handy reference when duplicating a past project.

....

Make Reference Labels
—CARLA H. JOHNSON,
BALTIMORE, MD

To keep track of what pattern(s) you used to make garments, make labels from satin ribbon, using the alphabet embroidery feature on your machine. With a strip of tear-away backing under the ribbon, sew the first three letters of the pattern company name and the pattern number in contrasting thread. After treating the cut edges with a fray preventive, attach your "custom reference" to the inside of the garment.

....

Use a Photo Album to Create a Portfolio and Swatch Book
—SUZIE ELLIOTT,
NEW YORK, NY

A small photo album, the kind that holds one photo per page, makes an ideal portable place to keep photos of completed projects and swatches of yarns or fabrics used, but it can also make a handy place to keep swatches of fabrics and yarns you haven't used, to check for compatibility with goods you may be thinking of buying in shops.

....

Record Bolt Information for Reference File
—FRED SHULTZ,
BURTONSVILLE, MD

Carry a camera with you when fabric shopping. After you've made your selections and before taking them to the cutting table, take a photo of the information on the label at the end of each bolt. Fold the fabric up over the top of the bolt, so the right side shows above the label, and capture the pattern and color of the fabric in the shot. The photos make a great fabric collection reference file.

....

Keep Fabric Requirements in a Planner
—DANA ZARUBA,
COBBLE HILL,
BRITISH COLUMBIA, CANADA

The beautiful fabrics I find while shopping inspire me, but I'm often uncertain of how many yards to buy for the patterns I have at home. I used to look through the pattern books at the store to find the yardages, but that took too much time. Now I keep a list of the fabric requirements for my favorite patterns in my daily planner, which I carry everywhere I go. When I discover a wonderful fabric, I can easily locate how much to buy. Another way I streamline my shopping is to shop pattern catalogs online before I go to the store. I find all of the information I need online so I can go directly to the pattern drawers when I get to the fabric store. This saves me a great deal of time, and makes shopping very efficient.

Track Patterns in a Sewing Album

—SUSAN SMITH,
DELPHI, IN

To keep track of patterns, make and trim reduced copies of pattern envelopes and insert them into a 4-in. by 6-in. purse-size photo album. In this album, also keep yardage and notions information, and the front and back sketches of the pattern. Use extra photo sleeves in the back of the album for fabric swatches and also a yardage converter. It will make shopping for fabric and buttons so easy.

Create a Fashion Show Screen Saver

—JULIA MESNIKOFF,
COLORADO SPRINGS, CO

Consider creating a digital "Sewing Inspiration" file on your computer, and set your screen saver to link to that file. Whenever you pass your idle computer screen, a medley of beautiful garments and details will scroll past, urging you back to the sewing machine.

Make a Personal Sewing History

—TOMASA JIMENEZ,
LYNDHURST, NJ

Whenever you complete a sewing project, record the date, pattern company and number, size, sketch of the garment sewn, fabric content and care, and comments about the garment, and attach a swatch of the fabric you used. File your records in a binder, which can help you easily look up fabric care or the pattern used. It will be both a handy reference tool and a chronicle of the growth of your sewing skills.

Keep a Pattern Catalog in Your Computer

—LINDA ROCK,
WINNIPEG, MANITOBA, CANADA

Technology can aid you in your sewing room in more ways than just having a computerized embroidery sewing machine. You can scan—or take digital photos of—the front and back of pattern envelopes, then sort them into electronic folders in your computer. View the pictures as thumbnails so that you can see, at a glance, what's in your pattern collection. You can even print out these files to display many patterns on a single sheet of paper. Paste the thumbnail sheet on the front of your storage box to indicate its contents. It cuts down on time spent searching through boxes of patterns.

CLEANUP

SPRUCING UP YOUR SPACE

Prevent a Mess with Plastic Bags

—SHIRLEY HASTINGS, KAMLOOPS, BRITISH COLUMBIA, CANADA

Tape a plastic bag to the table you work at to catch clipped threads and trimmings. Here's how to keep the bag open: Cut a ¼-in. circular strip from around a plastic bleach bottle. To make it fit the bag opening, cut the circle apart, and fit it inside the plastic bag with ends overlapping. Fold the bag over it twice, and staple around the bag right through the plastic. Tape or staple the open bag where it will be a convenient mess-catcher. You can sew a fabric bag for a coordinated sewing room.

You can also create a similar system for your serger if it doesn't have a catch bin, slipping a bag with a ring under the serger at the spot where the trimmings fall.

Use Laundry Baskets to Organize

—JOYCE DELOCA, MEDFIELD, MA

Consider using laundry baskets for organizing the diverse items in your sewing studio. Laundry baskets stack well and can be marked. Jumbo 3½-gal. zip-top bags store, neatly and visibly, all the pieces needed for an entire project (fabric, pattern, thread, and embellishments). These bags also keep notions, fabric scraps and remnants, shoulder pads, underlinings, zippers, stabilizers, and trims sorted and organized. File the bags in laundry baskets labeled "future projects," "work in progress," "notions," and so forth.

Catch Scraps in a Sheet

—SHERRI BROWN, BROOKSVILLE, FL

Put an old sheet on the floor beneath the machine to catch scraps and threads. When you finish, fold up the sheet and shake it into the trash can.

Use a Hair Dryer to Clean Your Machine

—RENE SIMPSON, BRIGHTON, SOUTH AUSTRALIA

For a quick, easy cleanup of your sewing machine or serger, don't blow on it—your breath contains moisture that may harm your machine. Instead, get rid of the dirt and dust that collect with a quick blast from your hair dryer.

Make Your Own "Canned" Air

—CYNTHIA DUNN, NEDERLAND, CO

An empty, clean dish detergent bottle makes an inexpensive and effective substitute for canned air. Just squeeze the bottle to get a squirt of air.

Dispose of Sharp Objects Safely

—JESSICA KRAKOW, SAN FRANCISCO, CA

Take a cue from hospitals and labs, which dispose of used needles in special puncture-proof containers, by setting up a "sharps" container for your sewing room. Take an empty metal canister, label it "SHARPS!" on all four sides, and place it near your sewing machine. You'll be able to easily—and safely—dispose of used rotary-cutter blades, razor blades, needles, and other sharp items. A tight-fitting lid will prevent dangerous spills if the container is dropped. When it's full, tape the lid securely to the container and dispose of it.

TOOLS AND MATERIALS

Remove Lint with Pipe Cleaners

—JUDITH E. SMITH, FANWOOD, NJ

An ordinary pipe cleaner is a great tool for cleaning out the feed-dog and bobbin-race areas of your sewing machine. Available in craft stores, dime stores, and tobacco shops, the wire is stiff enough to go where you point it, yet flexible enough to go around corners and reach into tiny recesses. Lint clings immediately to its fuzzy surface, instead of simply being pushed around as it is by a brush. When the end gets dirty, simply snip it off with a wire cutter or kitchen shears, exposing a clean tip.

Clean Plastic with Nail Polish Remover

—JEAN KAPLAN, PHOENIX, AZ

If red-dyed fabrics leave a red residue on the plastic parts of your sewing machine, try taking it off with a non-acetone nail polish remover that contains ethyl acetate and alcohol. Don't use one with acetone, which will damage the plastic parts on your machine.

Use Cosmetic Brushes to Clean Sewing Machines

—JULIE PLOTNIKO, PARKSVILLE, BRITISH COLUMBIA, CANADA

Cosmetic brushes for applying makeup are wonderful for cleaning a sewing machine. Use the largest brush for allover dusting, a medium-size one for removing lint from the inside of the machine, and a small one for cleaning those tiny, hard-to-reach places. Some sets come with ceramic holders, but a toothbrush holder will keep the brushes handy.

Clean Your Machine with a Watercolor Paintbrush

—NANCY BROCKLAND, ST. LOUIS, MO

Try using a size 2 fan-shaped watercolor paintbrush, available inexpensively at any art-supply store, to clean your sewing machine. The brush's long handle will enable you to reach out-of-the-way places easily. When used sideways, it can brush off larger areas much faster than a standard brush will. A fan brush may also be narrow enough to clean the tiny crevices in the bobbin case.

Vacuum Sergers and Sewing Machines

—ELIZABETH RYMER, HURRICANE MILLS, TN

To clean your serger and sewing machine, attach a flexible drinking straw to the crevice attachment of your regular vacuum cleaner. Close the space between the straw and the crevice tool with masking tape before you vacuum.

Keep Pinking Shears Free of Lint

—FAY M. DORR, WEST PALM BEACH, FL

Over the years, it's sometimes difficult to keep pinking shears working properly, even with periodic sharpening. This is because lint accumulates along the edge of the cutting surface as well as on the little shelf above the cutting edges. Use a soft brush to wipe away the lint, and the pinking shears will be good as new.

Preserve Your Vacuum Cleaner

—YVONNE PAUL, WINTER SPRINGS, FL

Before you vacuum after a sewing project, run a lint roller over the area where you sewed to pick up threads, lint, and even stray pins. This prevents the threads from wrapping around the brush on your vacuum cleaner.

Tend to Your Serger

—STEPHEN WISNER, MAPLEWOOD, NJ

Before you put your serger away, vacuum and air-blast the lint out. Lubricate the parts recommended by the manufacturer and run the machine for a short time with a small scrap of fabric to distribute the oil. While the machine is running, carefully lower the telescoping thread arm as the thread is taken up. This way, the dust cover fits easily over the machine without you having to put the telescoping arm through the slit in the cover. When you serge again, the cover comes off and the thread arm pops up, ready to stitch tangle-free.

HOW TO "FLOSS" YOUR MACHINE

My sewing machine technician recommended a care routine to keep my sewing machine's tension disks free of lint. When I'm finished sewing with a particular thread, I cut the thread near the spool, then I pull it down through the needle, essentially "flossing" the tension disk and pulling any lint away from the disk. My machine's tension disks are now routinely lint-free, and I use the precut thread lengths for basting, hemming, mending, etc.

—MERRILYN SCOTT, JACKSONVILLE, FL

REMOVING STAINS AND SPOTS

Use Ice to Get Out Bloodstains
—MARY ANN HICKEY, CHICAGO, IL

Here's a way to remove both fresh and dried bloodstains without laundering. Rub an ice cube into the fabric, using a circular motion. Blot up the resulting moisture with a Q-tip. Start rubbing around the stain and gradually work your way into its center until the bloodstain disappears. Blot frequently so you won't leave a watermark.

The ice-cube method works just as well on embroidery thread with one additional step. After the surface stain disappears, separate the strands of thread with the eye of a needle, and continue to rub onto the underlying threads with the ice cube until all traces of the stain are gone. Remember to blot regularly.

CLEAN YOUR IRON

Remove Fusible Adhesive with a Dryer Sheet

If you accidentally iron the adhesive side of fusible interfacing, the best way to remove the sticky goo from your iron's soleplate is with a fabric-softener dryer sheet. To protect your ironing board, make a thick pad of paper towels or newspapers and place a couple of dryer sheets on top. Heat up the iron, and iron the sheets. The interfacing glue will come off, and the soleplate won't be scratched.

—MEG ALLEN, ROCHESTER, VT

Use Cooking Oil to Clean Your Iron

If you've ever touched interfacing or synthetic fabrics with a hot iron, you are familiar with the sticky, messy residue that forms instantly on your iron's soleplate. Rubbing the surface with a cloth or paper towel moistened with cooking oil will clean it very inexpensively. Rub the cooled iron plate until the surface is free of sticky residue, then wipe it with a cloth moistened with dish detergent or liquid soap. Finish with a wet cloth using water only. Before using the iron on good fabric, heat it up, and run it over an old cloth a few times. This technique works, and you don't have to buy any special products.

—LESLEY TUCKER, SARNIA, ONTARIO, CANADA

Use Peroxide to Clean Up after Pinpricks

—WANDA RICE, LYONS, CO

To remove blood from garments caused by pinpricks, saturate a cotton swab with hydrogen peroxide. Then touch the swab to the bloodstain and blot the stain with a tissue or paper towel. If the stain is stubborn, use the swab to wet it completely, while holding a scrap of fabric behind the stain to absorb any excess moisture. Keep applying the peroxide and blotting the stain until it disappears. This works best when the stain is fresh, but it will also remove most stains even after they have dried, and it works on all types of fabric, including silk georgette and satin, without harming the fabric. Use it on light-colored fabrics as well, but only after testing the peroxide on a scrap.

Use Grease to Dissolve Label Glue

—BETTY SAGER, SPRING VALLEY, CA

Even sewing tools are now plastered with those pesky price labels. When you try to peel the labels off, they leave a hard-to-remove sticky patch. While Bestine®, a rubber cement solvent, can remove the residue from some metals and glass, it is not recommended for use on plastic. Try rubbing a bit of grease, Vaseline®, or shortening on the gummy area. Rub the glue and grease off with a paper towel.

SORTING LOOSE ENDS

Designate a Drawer for Wayward Clippings

—GAIL LEONE, CEDAR, MI

Have you ever noticed that bits of thread tossed toward a wastebasket never seem to land there? Install a small drawer under your sewing worktable, positioned to allow you to quickly toss in errant threads and clippings. When the surface is neat again, the drawer closes away, out of sight. Any add-on drawer from an office-supply store will do the job.

Collect Thread Scraps in a Container

—CAROLINE WALLACE, BARSTOW, CA

If you dislike having to vacuum snippets of thread from the rug every time you sew, place a small container with about $\frac{1}{2}$ in. of water in it beside your sewing machine. An empty margarine tub is just right. Whenever you clip a thread, remove basting, or unpick, just drop the bits of thread into the water. Even if there is a breeze, the thread pieces stay put. You can also place a little water in the thread catcher of your serger, which reduces daily vacuuming drastically.

Make a Thread Catcher

—MARY ALLENSPACH,
WINCHESTER, WI

Here's an easy way to catch threads. Buy the least-expensive wide packing tape you can find. Next, cut a corrugated cardboard rectangle about 8 in. by 12 in. and wrap it, mummy-style, with the tape sticky side out. When sewing, put the taped rectangle to the right of your machine on the floor and either drop the clipped threads onto it or clip the ends just above it. The rectangle is big enough to catch what falls. When both sides are full, cut off the tape and rewrap the cardboard. When machine embroidering, put the taped rectangle to the left of the machine on your cabinet. If you plan to save the thread bits for future use, lessen the tape tackiness by first pressing the rectangle against fabric; it catches the threads, but you can easily remove them from the tape.

Collect Thread in an Empty Tissue Box

—JANET ROGERS,
DORSET, ONTARIO, CANADA

The best place to keep thread ends is in an empty tissue box. Choose the kind with an oval opening covered in plastic film. Tuck threads through the slit in the film: The plastic film lets your fingers in and keeps the thread from coming back out when your fingers are withdrawn. You might also put a bit of double-sided tape on the top at one end of the box. This holds onto the really tiny pieces that result when you rip out a seam. Even if you knock the box over, its contents won't spill.

HOW TO MAKE A HOOK-AND-LOOP-TAPE THREAD MAGNET

I've affixed a 2-in. strip of the hook side of self-adhesive hook-and-loop tape to the left side of my sewing machine (save the loop side of the tape for the following tip). As I sew, I can "wipe" thread clippings onto the tape without even looking. At the end of a sewing session, I just peel off the accumulated threads and toss them in the trash.

—CHANA ZWEIG, PHILADELPHIA, PA

Pick Up Errant Threads

—JOHN J. WORDIN,
SHELLEY, ID

Once a seam has been ripped, bits and pieces of the cut thread remain, which must be removed before resewing. Make those threads disappear quickly and efficiently by taking a loop of sticky (masking or transparent) tape, fitting it over two or three fingers, and rolling it along the old seam. When all thread bits have been picked up, discard the used tape.

Control Stray Threads with Packing Tape

—MICHELLE RODMAN,
AMARILLO, TX

Do you find that when you sew, small thread scraps stick to you, stick to your fabric, or simply litter the floor? Here's a simple trick to keep your area thread-free. Take a piece of clear packaging tape, double it over itself, and press it to the table next to your machine. Then stick any stray threads on the tape as you cut them. Your work area will remain clean, and when you're done, rip off the tape and throw it away for easy cleanup.

PINNING IT DOWN

Eliminate Loose Bobbin Tails

—SAFEYYAH MAR, ST. PAUL, MN

To eliminate long thread tails on your bobbins when you store them, take the tail end of the bobbin thread in one hand and the bobbin in the other. Then pull the tail end against the wound thread to wedge the tail. Clip the remaining tail short enough so that it won't tangle but long enough so that you can release it the next time you use the bobbin.

"Sweep Magnet" Up Your Pins

—HEATHER HAMILTON,
OTTAWA, ONTARIO, CANADA

Here's a great tool you can use to find dropped pins. It's called the Sweep Magnet, and you can find it in the hardware store fairly inexpensively. A long-handled "broom," it ends with a smooth, powerful, 4-in. by 6-in. magnet designed to pick up heavy dropped screws and bolts on construction sites. There's also a smaller magnet on the handle end that can reach into tight spaces. A few swipes of the Sweep Magnet over the floor, and your sewing-room floor will be safe for bare feet again.

Create a Pin-Attracting Dustpan

—DEBRA ROSE,
CRYSTAL BEACH, ONTARIO, CANADA

Attach a self-adhesive magnetic strip to a dustpan to catch all of your pins and needles as you sweep so that you can easily retrieve them.

PART FIVE

working with

PATTERNS
&
TEMPLATES

MARKING

TOOLS AND MATERIALS

Bring New Life to a Marking Pen
—TENLEY ALAIMO, BINGHAMTON, NY

Here's a tip to extend the life of a water-soluble fabric pen: When it goes dry, pop off the blunt end, put six or seven drops of rubbing alcohol into the barrel, and shake.

....

Try Washable Kids' Markers
—BLANCHE REHLING, MILLSTADT, IL

The widely available Crayola® Washable Markers make wonderful fabric markers; the ink washes out instantly in cold water. The package states that normal laundering will remove the marks from cotton, polyester, acrylic, nylon, and their blends. The markers come in colors that work on virtually every shade of fabric except pure black.

....

Mark Fabric with Crayons
—CHRIS WOJDAK, LA MESA, CA

Marks from children's washable jumbo crayons are easily removed from just about anything with only a little water, and they wash out of clothes like a dream. The marks are much easier to see than chalk marks, and they can be used to write information (midriff front, midriff back, and so forth) directly on the pieces so the pattern sheet can be put away. It's always wise to do a test on your fabric before using.

....

Transfer Dots for Smocking
—ELIZABETH MATTFIELD, LONG BEACH, WA

Here's a quick, cheap way to get dots needed to guide the placement of gathering threads for hand smocking. With a water-soluble marker and a yardstick, draw parallel lines on the fabric the required distance apart (usually ¼ in.). Then draw parallel lines the same distance apart at right angles to them. The fabric will look like graph paper.
Use the intersections of these lines for the gathering, just as if they were transfer dots. The lines also make it easier to keep the smocking stitches in the right position.

....

Create Your Own Tailor's Tacks
—EILEEN OLMSTEAD, MADERA, CA

To transfer pattern markings to fabrics, make tailor's tacks with needle and thread. They offer precision, right and wrong sides, and removability. Consider saving those wads of threads wasted when rethreading your serger in a basket next to the serger and later use them for tailor's tacks. This provides an ample supply of precut, usable lengths of threads in every color—for free.

HOW TO PREVENT DISAPPEARING INK FROM VANISHING TOO SOON

I was recently measuring and marking topstitching lines on a bag I was making using an air-soluble marking pen. Time got away from me, and I realized I had to leave my sewing room for an appointment. I didn't want my marks to disappear while I was gone, so I applied a strip of Scotch® Magic™ Tape over each mark, hoping the marks would remain. When I returned to my sewing room the next afternoon, I was thrilled to find every mark as bright as it had been the day before, and the tape pulled off without leaving any residue. It took me much less time to remove the tape than it would have to reconstruct the marks, and I was able to finish the bag in no time!

—NORMA BUCKO, *THREADS* CONTRIBUTOR

Use a Gel Pen to Mark Black Fabric
—DEBRA ARCH, KEWANEE, IL

A silver gel pen works perfectly to mark black fabric. It leaves an easy-to-see traced line, and it doesn't rub off the way a chalk pencil does.

Use Multicolored Flag Tape for Marking
—SUSAN WILLIAMS, LAKEWOOD, CO

Instead of clipping notches in seam allowances or using a special pen to mark specific points, purchase multicolored tape flags at the office-supply store. They are pointed at one end (typically used to point to a signature line on a document), and they are the perfect size for marking notches. Since they come in many different bright colors, they allow for coding notches in places where they will need to be matched (for example, the bodice front and back side seam notches). Place two of them parallel to each other to mark items such as the center-front line. They adhere to the fabric without leaving a residue, they can be reused, and they can be written on with a ballpoint pen if a note is needed.

Use Elastic Tailor's Tacks to Transfer Patterns
—DIANA HILLIARD, OAKVILLE, ONTARIO, CANADA

When it comes to transferring pattern markings to fashion fabric, try elastic tailor's tacks. Using a doubled strand of elastic thread, make a single stitch at each dot or mark on the pattern, leaving 4-in. tails. That's all there is to it. The thread that winds around the elastic's core firmly anchors a tack in place. Plus, because elastic tacks require only one stitch, as opposed to two or three for regular thread tacks, they don't create a major tear in the pattern when removed.

Make Secure Tailor's Tacks

—LAURIE WILCOX, PALM DESERT, CA

Here's a way to make tailor's tacks that hold the threads in place more securely than traditional methods. After cutting each piece, use contrasting unknotted double thread in your hand needle and take a stitch through the pattern tissue and both layers of fabric. Go in and out of the fabric once at each pattern mark, leaving long tails. Then remove the pattern from the fabric, letting the thread ends slip through, and turn the fabric over. With thread of a different color, take another stitch on top of each of the first stitches in the same fashion, again leaving long tails. When pulling the two fabric layers apart, one set of thread stitches is stitched to the top fabric piece, and the other set is stitched to the bottom piece. The two thread colors act as a guide when separating the pieces. Since every mark has been stitched into the fabric, they rarely pull out accidentally. Although this method takes a few more minutes, it's worth spending the extra time for the great results it produces.

MAKING MARKS

Mark Fleece with Correction Fluid and Masking Tape

—ANN STEEVES, BURLINGTON, MA

Polarfleece and sweater knits are difficult to mark using snips, thread tacks, or notches. Instead, put a dot of correction fluid in the seam allowances to mark notches. Or use little clips of masking tape to mark notches and other symbols. The easy-to-spot tape sticks without falling off.

Mark Snap Placement with Chalk

—SHERRI BROWN, BROOKSVILLE, FL

Here's a marking system for sewing snaps onto a garment: Sew the top (male) snap in place first, then rub a little chalk on its tip. Press it against the other side of the garment, transferring the chalk to the exact spot to place its mate.

Use Stabilizer for Hard-to-Mark Fabrics

—PATRICIA S. MILLER, DALLAS, OR

Loosely woven fabric is hard to mark, but here's a way to mark darts on it that works well: Trace the dart shape, including the foldline, onto a piece of tear-away stabilizer. Pin the stabilizer to the wrong side of the fabric at the appropriate dart placement. Fold the fabric and stabilizer together on the foldline, pin to hold, and stitch following the marks. When finished sewing, tear the stabilizer away.

Mark Fabric with a Running Stitch

—SUSANNA PRENTISS,
HEAD OF CHEZZETCOOK,
NOVA SCOTIA, CANADA

When you're machine stitching on the right side of a garment and need to follow pattern markings, mark the wrong side of the fabric with tracing paper and tracing wheel from the pattern. Then hand-sew a running stitch directly over the traced markings with contrasting thread to transfer the markings to the right side of the fabric. Use this thread marking as a guide when machine stitching, and simply pull the hand-sewn threads out when finished. This leaves no unsightly chalk or tracing marks.

Use Pins or an Awl to Mark Darts

—JUDITH NEUKAM,
THREADS CONTRIBUTOR

When cutting out a pattern with darts, consider indicating the markings by clipping into the seam allowance at each marked dart line. Then mark the dart point with a pin or an awl. When ready to sew the dart, fold from the point (keeping the point marker visible) to the seam allowance and adjust the fabric until the two clips align. Then pull a length of thread, twice the length of the dart, through the needle. Start sewing from the seam allowance, take three stitches and stop, lift the presser foot (with the needle down), and pull the long thread from the back to the front (under the presser foot), so it crosses over the point mark. Use the line formed by this thread as the stitching line. When you've stitched to the point, sew off the edge, lift the presser foot, reposition the fabric so the needle will now lower inside the body of the dart, and stitch for about an inch before removing the dart from the machine. Sewing darts this way reproduces the pattern's dart, provides a smooth point, and prevents problems that back tacking or hand tying sometimes cause.

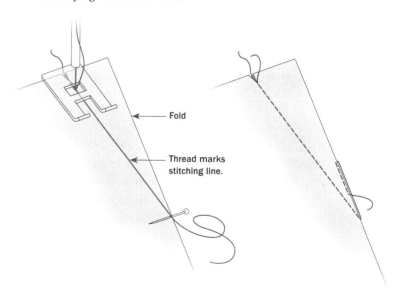

Fold

Thread marks stitching line.

Use Tiny Brass Pins on Sheer Fabrics

—CLAIRE B. SHAEFFER,
THREADS AUTHOR, PALM SPRINGS, CA

Tiny brass safety pins are great tools for quickly transferring garment-construction marks to delicate, sheer fabrics like chiffon. The pins won't mar the fabric or fall out when moved.

....

Use a Tracing Wheel to Mark Seamlines on Slippery Fabrics

—DESIREE ECKERT, LEVITTOWN, NY

Here's a good method for marking seamlines on hard-to-handle, slippery silks and lining fabrics. Use a needle-pointed tracing wheel to mark the seams on these fabrics, but don't use tracing paper. If possible, work on a porous surface so that the tracing wheel will hold the fabric securely in place while tracing the seamline. The tiny holes made by this type of tracing wheel line up easily when it's time to sew the seams. If any holes show on the finished garment (which is rare), work them out with a bit of pressing.

KEEPING MARKS STRAIGHT

Mark the Grainline

—DIANE J. WHIPPIE, KENT, WA

To guarantee a reference point for the grainline on interfacings, put a light grainline down the center of the piece with a yardstick and pencil before cutting into it.

....

Test Machine Embroidery

—DAWN A. JARDINE,
RED HOOK, NY

There are two mistakes to avoid when doing machine embroidery. The first is not making a sample with your actual fabric and threads, only to learn later that everything shrinks at a different rate when pressed, leaving the garment puckered and unwearable. The second mistake is starting to machine-embroider a design, only to realize that the design is not placed exactly where you want it. Here's a way to accurately predict how the embroidery will look and a method to place it on the garment: First, always stitch a test sample on the fashion fabric. Make sure to use the identical stabilizers, tensions, threads, and so on that you'll use in the final product. Press thoroughly, using the same settings and amount of steam. After stitching the design, but before removing the sample from the hoop, use chalk to draw a line around the inside wall of the hoop directly on the sample. Then remove the hoop, and cut out the sample along the chalkline. Now position the sample on the garment, and pin it in place. With chalk, mark along the edge of the sample directly on the garment. When you remove the sample, the remaining chalk circle is a perfect guide for placing the hoop to begin your embroidery, ensuring that the design is where you want it.

SPACING CORRECTLY

Use Punch Holes for Marking

—DAVID MANGELS, WOODINVILLE, WA

Here's an easy way to mark the dots that define a pattern's darts and other key locations. Use a standard paper punch to remove each dot and place a mark directly on the fabric through the hole. First, center a large X over each dot using a ballpoint pen or permanent marker to denote the center of each pattern mark. Use transparent tape over each dot to reinforce the pattern paper, which also allows the punch to work effectively on the thin tissue. Next, fold the pattern in half over the dot's center and punch the half circle. When the pattern piece is unfolded, there will be a reinforced hole where the dot used to be. The ends of the marked X remain on the pattern and will become a guide to the center of the hole when the fabric is marked. If there are two layers of fabric, place a straight pin through the hole's center, flip the fabric and pattern piece, and mark the other side using the pin's point as a guide. Then remove the pin. It's a method that's much easier than other marking options.

Mark Blouse Buttonholes with an Index Card Template

—LUCY THOMPSON, LIVINGSTON, TX

It's easy to place and mark buttonholes on a fitted blouse with a template made from an index card. First, find the fullest part of the bust (a button there will prevent the blouse from gaping), and mark this point on the pattern. Measure from the top buttonhole on the pattern to the new bust-point marking. Divide this measurement in half (or thirds if preferred) to find the distance between buttonholes. On the edge of an index card, cut a notch that distance from one end. Make the point of the notch as deep as the distance from the buttonhole to the edge of the blouse. Starting at the neckline, position the edge of the card on the fold of the blouse opening and make a tiny dot at the notch point to mark one end of the next buttonhole. Then shift the end of the card to that dot to mark the next, and so on. Store the template in a pattern envelope for easy reference.

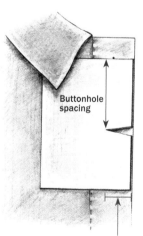

Buttonhole spacing

Distance from edge

Use a Mailing Label to Space Buttonholes

—TERRY GRANT, ASHLAND, OR

Here's a method for making uniform, straight buttonholes. Cut out a rectangle the length and width of the buttonhole from the center of a peel-off mailing label. Stick it on the garment where you need the buttonhole, and stitch inside the rectangle. This template can be reused several times before it loses its adhesives; then simply make another.

Mark Fleece Buttonholes with Tape

—JEANNE HARMON, SEBEC, ME

Marking buttonholes in fleece can be a problem. Here's a remedy. Put a length of masking tape 1 in. from the edge and mark buttonholes on it. The tape will serve as a guide, resulting in smooth, even buttonholes. It works to mark the corresponding button placement on the other half of the garment, too.

Use Elastic to Space Closures

—LINDA BOSTON, *THREADS* CONTRIBUTOR

To position a series of buttons, buttonholes, snaps, or any sewing detail, place equally spaced marks on a piece of elastic. Align the first mark on the elastic with the starting point on the garment and stretch the elastic until the correct number of marks fits the space; then transfer the marks to the garment.

Color-Code Pleat-Marking Lines

—GITA LEVIN, CINNAMINSON, NJ

When making a garment with many parallel pleats, it can be difficult to differentiate between marked foldlines and placement lines. To avoid confusion, mark every pair of lines with tailor's tacks or thread tracing in matching thread; change colors for each additional pleat. Then simply match each pair of lines to fold the pleats into place.

HOW TO TRACE WITH PLASTIC WRAP

When the back of a dress was too intricate to trace using muslin, I hand-pressed a large piece of plastic wrap to the dress back and used a magic marker to trace the seams and other details onto it. After tracing, I removed the wrap from the fabric and placed it on a piece of muslin. To copy the marker lines onto the muslin, I folded the plastic wrap back along each marked line and marked the fabric along the fold with a fabric pen. I then removed the plastic and added a $5/8$-in. seam allowance.

—ELLEN ROSE, DALLAS, TX

CUTTING

TOOLS AND MATERIALS

Use Tape for Crisp Pattern Cutting

—VIRGINIA CAINE, TUSCALOOSA, AL

With patterns that routinely require alterations, here's a way to cut new, crisp patterns. First, draw new cutting lines on the pattern, adding additional tissue paper, if necessary; then center a strip of transparent frosted tape along the entire length of each line. Use several small pieces of tape around curved edges. The tape is see-through, so it's easy to make cuts; each cut edge is crisp, stable, and easy to handle without tearing. The tape makes additional alterations easier, if they are needed. It also helps to preserve patterns throughout the cutting process. Once the patterns are perfectly altered, they'll be in good shape to use again and again.

Cut Patterns without Pinning

—MARJORIE DEQUINCY, SACRAMENTO, CA

To eliminate the distortion that pins cause when securing paper patterns to layered fabrics, especially on small pattern pieces, try using self-adhesive reinforcing rings from a stationery store instead. Position each ring half on the pattern and half on the fabric wherever they need to be secured together. Since the rings are paper, they can be cut through, and since they're low-tack, they'll pull off the fabric or the pattern without leaving residue. It isn't always necessary to remove them because the fabric they're sticking to is scrap, and they won't hurt the pattern. Consider also using the rings to keep track of the different size needles needed for a single project. Write the number on a ring and use it to stick each needle on the front of the machine temporarily.

Use a Gingham Tablecloth as "Graph Paper"

—GWEN JONES, NIAGARA FALLS, ONTARIO, CANADA

Here's a trick for cutting fabric: Use a gingham vinyl tablecloth. The gingham squares can help you accurately place your fabric on grain, and the tablecloth makes it so much easier to square the fabric. As a bonus, your pins won't scratch your table.

PATTERNS

TRACING PATTERNS

Use Freezer Paper to Trace Pattern Pieces

—REBECCA LOWELL,
SANTA ROSA, CA

Use a permanent marker to trace through pattern tissue onto freezer paper. Lay the pattern tissue over the dull side of the paper, smooth the pattern on the paper, and trace and transfer all appropriate markings onto the tissue. The marks bleed onto the freezer paper and will produce a perfect copy. When finished, mark the company, pattern number, and other pertinent information on your new pattern pieces, creating an easy-to-alter copy of the original pattern, which can be placed (coated side down) and ironed onto fabric. It peels right off without leaving a residue (to be safe, test first using a fabric scrap), and it can be ironed on a couple of times before it no longer sticks. This is especially helpful for small pieces, like facings, that tend to shift during pinning.

HOW TO CREATE A WINDOW LIGHT BOX

As a mother of six, I try to get as much mileage as possible out of my sewing patterns, especially my children's clothing patterns. Tracing multiple sizes from a single pattern had been a headache for me until I discovered that I could use my kitchen window as a light box. I tape the pattern pieces to the window and then tape pieces of kraft paper over them. The outdoor light makes the pattern edges easy to see, and working at eye level is much easier on my back. What's even better—my children can trace over their own pattern pieces, which they really enjoy. The kraft paper we use comes in a roll, so it doesn't have any creases and lies nicely against the window during tracing. It's so easy for me to duplicate multiple pattern sizes without altering the original.

—MARY ANNE BREDEMANN, KANSAS CITY, MO

Use Post-it Notes to Help Trace

—TERI STERN, CHAPEL HILL, NC

Following the correct lines can be a challenge when tracing patterns from complicated, multisize pattern sheets like those from Ottobre Design and Burda®. Start by finding the correct piece on the sheet and tracing it with a finger to get a "feel" for the shape. Then place little Post-it® Notes or flags at critical junctures, corners, and other turning points. The bright colors will show up nicely underneath the tracing paper and guide the tracing, and the Post-it Notes can be reused many times.

Follow Body Curves with a Flexible Ruler

—DIANA VAN DER SLUYS, CALGARY, ALBERTA, CANADA

A flexible ruler is not only helpful when making a pattern from a finished garment, it's also useful for pattern drafting and altering commercial patterns. With a flexible ruler, it's possible to duplicate the idiosyncrasies of a subject's body easily by adjusting the curves on the pattern. Just shape the flexible curve to hip, armhole, desired neckline, or crotch curve, and transfer body shape to the pattern. It's also possible to change the shape of style lines by bending the curve into desired shapes and transferring them onto a pattern. When using this method, be sure to allow for sufficient ease in the finished garment.

Mark Pattern Outlines with a Highlighter

—RITA JACOBSON, FOUNTAIN VALLEY, CA

Tracing tissue patterns onto stiffer paper with a pencil or pen often means losing the thin lines when the pattern is cut out. To create a more visible outline, place the stiff paper pattern over a sheet of scrap paper and go over the edges with a broad-tip highlighter or felt-tip pen.

Make Easy Dart and Transfer Marks

—ALICE TOWNSEND, VERO BEACH, FL

Try backing patterns with nonwoven fusible interfacing. This adds body to the tissue and keeps it from getting tattered. If shaped darts are added to garments, exact marks are crucial. Here's how to transfer the dart markings from reinforced patterns to fabric without punching holes in the patterns: Cut the pattern along one side of the shaped dart and fold back the dart along its center line. Use a marker to trace the outline of the open area onto the fabric. When sewing the dart, fold the fabric on the marked center line and sew along the other traced line. There's no need to draw the whole dart since only one side will be visible while sewing.

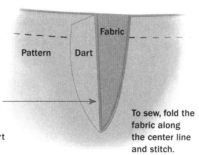

This is an easy way to mark and sew perfectly symmetrical darts—even when they're curved.

Cut one side of the dart and fold on the center line. Use the void to mark the dart on the fabric.

Pattern

Dart

Fabric

To sew, fold the fabric along the center line and stitch.

Trace and Mark Patterns from Magazines

—CHARLENE PAWLUCK, CHARLOTTETOWN, PRINCE EDWARD ISLAND, CANADA

To copy pattern pieces from magazines without damaging the sheets, trace the pieces onto a large sheet of rigid plastic (the type used with overhead projectors) with a water-soluble marker. Then trace the pieces onto blank newsprint or tissue paper. Static electricity holds the plastic to the paper, but in case it does shift, always start tracing at a corner so you can realign things. The plastic can be used repeatedly.

Consider adding a seam allowance to the pattern, after making adjustments, rather than adding it to the fabric. Collect a compass and a piece of thin cardboard. Set the compass to draw a circle with a radius of ⅝ in. or whatever seam allowance is preferred. Then draw this circle on the cardboard. Cut out the circle and poke a hole in its center. Put a pen tip through the snug-fitting hole, and make sure that the perimeter of the circle touches the pattern's edge exactly while drawing around the pattern piece. At corners, extend the line past the pattern piece, keeping the same curvature. Mark the corner with a hole in the pattern, and remember to transfer the mark to the fabric. Try using a ruler to add large allowances, such as hems. After marking darts, notches, and interior points, write the name of the garment, the name of the piece, and the number of times to cut it out on each piece.

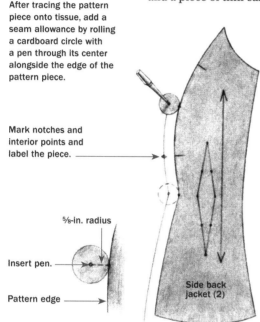

After tracing the pattern piece onto tissue, add a seam allowance by rolling a cardboard circle with a pen through its center alongside the edge of the pattern piece.

Mark notches and interior points and label the piece.

⅝-in. radius

Insert pen.

Pattern edge

Side back jacket (2)

Copy Patterns Quickly

—JANE MCCARTIN, BRUSH PRAIRIE, WA

I like to use stiff pattern paper when I'm cutting fabric. It does not fly around like tissue paper, and my pattern weights (cans of cat food) are more effective on it. And the occasional cat that leaps up to see what I'm doing is less likely to cause irreparable damage to the paper. To copy my favorite patterns onto the heavier paper, I tape the tissue pattern to the paper using removable tape. Instead of tracing the pattern, I merely cut it out as I would fashion fabric. I also cut out the notches and use a paper punch to mark pattern dots. If I use gridded paper, I line up the grainlines with the grid; otherwise, I draw a grainline before taping and match the pattern's grainline to the one drawn. This quick technique gives me a cleaner pattern that's more suitable for my needs.

HOW TO USE ALTERNATIVES TO PATTERN PAPER

Pattern paper is wonderful, but experiment with other materials, too.

Plastic Tablecloths

Consider tracing pattern pieces onto thin white plastic, available by the roll from banquet caterers and discount stores. It's easy to see through the thin plastic for tracing, and it's easy to cut. The plastic doesn't hold creases, so it doesn't require ironing, and it's durable and waterproof. It's also possible to see the fashion-fabric design through the plastic for pattern placement. This works especially well for pin fitting because it hangs more like fabric than tissue. Either pin or staple the seams together to find the perfect fit before cutting the fabric.

—SHERYL VANDUSEN,
KAMLOOPS, BRITISH COLUMBIA, CANADA

Interfacing

Lightweight, nonwoven, sew-in interfacing is a good substitute for tissue paper or shelf paper when tracing or correcting a pattern or making an original pattern by flat pattern drafting. Interfacing is sturdier and lasts longer than tissue paper, but it's still transparent; stores well folded; irons out nicely with a warm, dry iron; and resists tearing, even when traced over with a tracing wheel. It isn't necessary to use the best quality, so get it in bulk at a discount fabric store.

—FREDRICKA HOUSMAN, NAPLES, FL

Oilcloth

Patterns cut from oilcloth last for ages, their edges never tatter, and they are easy to store.

—TATIANA KOSOVA, MONTREAL, QUEBEC, CANADA

Kraft Paper

If planning to use a tissue pattern several times, cut a permanent pattern out of kraft paper (brown wrapping paper), sold in stationery stores. These strong paper patterns can be rolled and stored in the used tubes from paper towel rolls.

—GRACE B. WEINSTEIN, LOS ANGELES, CA

Freezer Paper

After constructing several garments from the same pattern, tissue pieces may end up in tatters. In order to make them durable again, try ironing each piece and seal the largest tears with tape. Then iron freezer paper to the back side of each piece, overlapping sheets for especially large pattern pieces. The freezer paper sticks to the tissue without adhesive and makes flimsy tissue patterns nearly indestructible. They remain lightweight enough to fold and store—without the hassle of tracing each piece. With a new pattern, consider ironing freezer paper to the back of the pattern sheet before cutting out the pieces. It's a quick and easy step that will keep patterns in great shape for many years and many garments.

—WYLIE BECKERT, SANTA BARBARA, CA

Place Odd-Shaped Patterns on Grain

—PHYLLIS RETTKE,
BELLEVUE, WA

Looking for a simple trick for placing pattern pieces (even irregular ones, like pants or facings) on grain? Try using a piece of lined notebook paper, two pins, and a straightedge. Position one of the lines on the paper over the grainline on the pattern piece. Then, find one of the outer lines on the notebook paper that is at or outside the widest part of the pattern piece. Highlight that line, and use it to align the grainline. This trick establishes a grainline to refer to, and eliminates unnecessary measuring, pinning, and unpinning.

Transfer Patterns

—SHARON SPRADLIN-BARRETT,
RICHMOND, VA

It is easy to transfer an embroidery or quilt pattern by using the transparent quality of tulle. Cover the line drawing with tulle. Trace the pattern with either a water-soluble marker or pencil onto the tulle. Place the tulle on the right side of the fabric surface. Trace again over the first tracing. Then remove the tulle, and the pattern is ready to be quilted or stitched.

HOW TO PUNCH IN PATTERN MARKS

At a local craft store, I purchased four different paper punches, which I use to punch out the marks on my patterns.

I use punches of various shapes and sizes to distinguish the marks: A ¼-in. round punch removes the large black circles; a ⅛-in. round punch removes the small circles; a tiny square punch removes the square marks; and a tiny, narrow rectangular punch removes the ends of lines and notches. If I can't reach the pattern mark to punch it, I just fold the pattern through the center of the mark, which allows me to punch it easily. Once the pattern has been placed on my fabric, I can use a fabric-marking pencil to mark directly on the fabric right through the holes in the pattern. Tailor's tacks are easier, too, because the stitches don't have to go through the pattern paper or the top fabric (marked with a pencil).

If I need to mark a critical stitching line, as in the topstitching for a zipper fly, I punch a series of ⅛-in. holes at ½-in. intervals along the line. I make chalk dots through the holes, remove the pattern, and then connect the dots. It takes a little time to prepare the pattern pieces, but makes the marking process much easier. It is especially wonderful for patterns I plan to use again.

—KAY WAGNER, GOLDEN VALLEY, MN

USING PATTERNS

Work with Multisize Patterns
—SHIRLEY ZAK, MONTARA, CA

Here's how to use multisize patterns over and over in different sizes. Before laying the pattern tissue on the fabric, clip the curved areas of the pattern tissue perpendicular to the cutting line and just up to the smallest size, as if clipping curves in a sewn garment. Where there is a sharp curve, such as in the neck area, make six to eight clips. For a raglan or drop-shoulder sleeve, only three or four clips suffice.

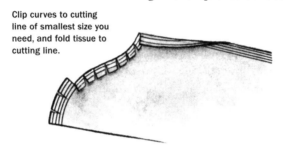

Clip curves to cutting line of smallest size you need, and fold tissue to cutting line.

Fold the tissue along the proper cutting line and cut out the fabric. When it's necessary to use the pattern for a larger size, all that's needed is to refold the pattern along the cutting line for that size. This method also works for patterns where the garment requires more than one size to fit properly.

Use Block Fusing
—ANNE SMOCK, EAST NORITON, PA

Block fusing is a great method for fusing interfacings to facings. Simply cut a piece of fabric and fusible ½ in. larger than the pattern piece all the way around. To save time, don't follow the exact shape of the facing; instead, cut a rough rectangle or whatever shape best suits the pattern piece. Then fuse the interfacing to the fabric and cut the facing piece using the pattern. This will provide the same shape as the pattern piece, without distorting the grainline.

Make Tailor's Tacks through Pattern Tissue
—MRS. LEE PECORA, MASSAPEQUA PARK, NY

Use the tip of a needle to make a little slit in the pattern tissue before making a tailor's tack. When the pattern is removed, the tailor's tack slips neatly through the slit without tearing the pattern.

Use Waxed Paper to Alter Patterns
—BARBARA BURNETT, FORT WORTH, TX

Rather than cutting and taping pattern pieces to make necessary alterations, consider drawing new ones using inexpensive waxed paper. Tear off a strip of waxed paper long enough to cover the altered pattern piece. If the waxed paper needs to be wider, tear off two strips, overlap them lengthwise 3 in. to 4 in., and bond them by pressing the overlapped area with a hot iron and a press cloth. Lay the waxed paper over the pattern piece and trace the altered piece, using a permanent marking pen.

Mend Sewing Patterns

—FRANKIE LEVERETT, ATLANTA, GA

Instead of using adhesive tape to mend tears in sewing patterns, try using a strip of Stitch Witchery sandwiched between the pattern and a piece of the cutaway edge of pattern tissue. The repaired pattern will withstand pressing better than with tape, and it won't get gummy over time.

Keep Style Number Visible when Folding

—ELIZABETH RYDMAN-HARRIS, SANTA FE, NM

Here's a simple idea that saves a lot of time and shuffling when looking for pattern parts: Just make sure each pattern piece is folded so that the style number and the name or number of the piece are visible. This makes it easy to pull out just a collar or pocket when experimenting with combined patterns, without having to unfold each piece.

Create the Perfect Pants Crease

—STEPHANIE GAJEWSKI, ST. THOMAS, ONTARIO, CANADA

When you know a pants pattern fits perfectly and won't need any adjustments, cut out the pattern pieces and set the crease in the front of the pants before you sew any seams. When you finish sewing the pants, lay them on the ironing board with the front crease already in place—it will be a breeze to crease the back of the pants.

Make a Permanent In-Seam Pocket Pattern

—PATRICIA ANN VAN MAANEN, FRIDAY HARBOR, WA

To avoid having to search through all your patterns for a good in-seam pocket pattern piece, use a nonwoven tracing material (such as Red Dot Tracer by HTC) to make a permanent in-seam pocket pattern, and keep it handy in your sewing notions drawer.

Match Patterns on Pockets

—JUDY RAND, COCONUT CREEK, FL

Here's a great trick for matching pocket fabric when cutting out a print shirt: Position the pocket pattern piece on top of the cutout front piece, align the placement marks using a purple disappearing marker, and trace the outline of the dominant print onto the tissue pattern. When the pocket fabric is cut, it will be easy to see exactly where to match the design, and the purple marks disappear by the next time the pattern is used.

Seal Pattern Seams Securely

—DOROTHY MADIAS, HAMPTON, SC

Because waxed paper only comes in narrow widths, here's how to join two or more widths together to trace larger pattern pieces. Overlap the pieces slightly and attach them using a glue stick. Then iron the seam. This process keeps the joint secure through the entire pinning-cutting process, and it remains tight even after being stored.

HOW TO COPY GATHERED-GARMENT DETAILS

I devised a simple method to calculate the flat width of gathered fabric contained in the seam on a garment. I wanted to duplicate a dress with a bodice that was lightly gathered into a deep waist yoke, and the skirt below the yoke was also gathered.

Since I was using the dress to create new pattern pieces, I needed to determine the bodice width at the waist seamline and the skirt width without dismantling the original dress. I hand-stitched along the gathered bodice fabric as close to the waist seamline as possible, using small running stitches. Beginning with a knot in the thread at the center front and taking care to stitch only through a single thickness of fabric, I stitched along each gather. When I reached the side seam, I cut the thread ⅝ in. longer to account for the seam allowance. Then

I pulled it out and measured from the knot to calculate the waist seam on that pattern piece. I continued in this manner to measure the length of each gathered piece composing the bodice. Then I could accurately draw the bodice waist seam and complete copying the bodice pattern pieces using more traditional methods. I duplicated the skirt pattern in the same manner. With this technique, the copied dress looked and fit exactly the same way the original did.

—JOY MASTERS, FAIRFAX, VA

Use Sticker Labels for Pattern Pieces

—MARY SULLIVAN, FRAMINGHAM, MA

Recently, I worked on a sewing project that had many pattern pieces. The jacket required fashion fabric, interfacing, and lining, and I knew it would be hard to keep track of which pattern pieces required which fabric. I had a stash of "reward" stickers from my teaching days, so I decided to use them to keep me organized. I affixed a pink sticker to the tissue pattern pieces that required fashion fabric, a yellow sticker to pieces that needed lining fabric, and a blue sticker to pieces that required interfacing. The colorful stickers were quick and easy visual reminders that helped to make the cutting and sewing process go smoothly. Now, reward stickers are an important part of my sewing supplies.

"Stretch" Your Favorite Patterns

—CYNTHIA DUNN, NEDERLAND, CO

Have favorite patterns gotten a little snug? Solve this problem by stitching with ¼-in. seam allowances instead of the usual ⅝-in. indicated on the pattern on the side seams, which is usually enough to do the trick (remember to use a ¼-in. seam on any underarm sleeve seam, too). This will create the extra room needed without making any pattern alterations.

HOLDING PATTERNS IN PLACE

Mend Patterns with Paper Tape
—L. D. PACE, TOLEDO, OR

Paper surgical tape (such as Micropore™ from 3M, sold in most drugstores) can be used to mend torn tissue paper patterns. The lightweight, flexible tape holds paper securely but removes easily.

....

Reinforce Pattern Holes with Paper Reinforcers
—SHERRI BROWN, BROOKSVILLE, FL

The first time a pattern is used, make holes at the ends of the darts, and at any other internal point that needs to be marked (like pocket ends), then reinforce the holes with those little round stick-on reinforcements designed for the paper in loose-leaf binders (available at stationery stores). Each time the pattern is used, it's possible to safely and easily mark through the holes with chalk.

....

Use Cellophane Tape to Reinforce Patterns
—SUZAN L. WIENER, SPRING HILL, FL

Before cutting out a new pattern, tape around all the sharp curves, corners, and along long straight seams with clear cellophane tape. This will prevent these areas from ripping and will keep the edges stiff so they're easy to follow while cutting or tracing around the pattern.

....

Use Scrap Fusible as Tape
—MARY B. GIBBONS, GLENBURNIE, ONTARIO, CANADA

A quick and easy method to shorten patterns permanently is to use leftover scraps of fusible interfacing instead of tape. Place the fusible between the overlapped pattern pieces and press lightly. Pressing bonds the fold of the overlap and eliminates the use of tape, which can stick to the sole of the iron if the pattern has to be pressed.

....

Reuse a Blouse Pattern
—DARLENE MCDONALD, BLACK CREEK, BRITISH COLUMBIA, CANADA

Here are some tips for using the same blouse pattern again and again. If a small pattern piece is cut on the fold (yoke, etc.), copy the pattern on tissue paper, but make it full size so it doesn't have to be placed on the fold. Now the pattern piece that makes the most sense can be used, given the pattern layout on the fabric. Make interfacing patterns $\frac{1}{2}$ in. smaller than the pattern piece to have the properly sized interfacing piece ready without trimming and without waste. Cut a piece of cardboard to make a template of the buttonhole positions on a finished blouse that buttons perfectly to your liking. Keep this template in the pattern envelope. It saves a lot of time, and the buttons will always be in the right place.

SAVING TIME

Use Mini Patterns to Visualize Design

—MAUREEN TAYSE MILLER,
NEW CARLISLE, OH

Having trouble following the directions on a new designer pattern? Try photocopying the pattern layouts from the instruction sheets and enlarging the pattern pieces. Then cut the main pattern pieces out of lightweight fabric and sew the miniature pieces together, which shows how the design should be sewn. Practicing will help you successfully cut and sew the pattern from expensive fabric and save agony, doubt, and possibly money.

Pin-Tuck More Quickly

—KATHY BLINCO,
DOYLESTOWN, OH

Want to save time when cutting out a garment that you plan to pin-tuck? Rather than estimating the amount of fabric the tucks will use and altering the pattern, try sewing the tucks on the fabric first, then place the pattern on it and cut it out.

Start with a rectangle of fabric slightly larger than the pattern piece. Sew the tucks, and then place the pattern piece over the tucked fabric, so the tucks fall where you want. Use a fabric marker or chalk to mark the outline of the pattern piece. Using a short stitch, sew around the pattern shape, just inside the marked line. This secures the tucks and prevents them from coming unstitched. Then cut out the garment section just beyond the stitched line.

Mend Pattern Tears Fast

—MERRILIE BROWN,
CHAPEL HILL, NC

Mend tears in frequently used tissue-paper patterns by ironing patches of waxed paper onto the underside of the pattern. First, tack the patch in place with the tip of the iron. Then cover the patch with a piece of paper and firmly iron on the patch. Waxed paper does not distort the pattern like cellophane or masking tape, and it can be removed and adjusted easily. Plus it's inexpensive.

Experiment with Extra Patterns

—DOTTIE SHELDON,
WINTER PARK, FL

Whenever possible, buy extra copies of patterns used, especially if the finished garment is flattering and fits well. Fine-tune the patterns to improve the fit, or map out creative embellishment or alteration techniques. The extra copies help in experimenting with changing darts, adding or removing pleats, moving hemlines, and other alterations without damaging the original pattern. Keep an eye out for fabric-store pattern sales as well as garage sales to stock up and fuel creativity.

TEMPLATES

DESIGNING TEMPLATES

Photocopy Lace to Make Quick Designs

—CAROL ASHENDORF, NORTON SHORES, MI

You don't have to cut up precious lace to check design ideas. Instead, photocopy the lace repeats. Cutting and pasting designs from the copies allows you to choose the design that is best suited for the garment. Before copying, protect the lace with clear plastic and lay it on medium gray construction paper or a similar neutral background for contrast. Make as many copies as there are repeats.

Make Fast Design Size Changes

—MRS. JOHN BATES, CLEARWATER, FL

Have a perfect appliqué design, in the wrong size? Enlarge or reduce the design quickly on a photocopier to get the size you want.

Make Post-it Note Templates

—MIMI ANDERSON, TACOMA, WA

To help ensure all machine-made buttonholes come out the same size, try using a template made from a Post-it Note. First, draw a line on the note parallel to the sticky edge the distance you want your buttonholes to be from the edge of the buttonhole band. This marks your buttonhole line when you stick the template on the fold of the fabric. Then cut two lines on the adhesive edge of the note the same distance apart as the length of the buttonhole and deeper than the buttonhole placement line. Fold back the middle section, stick the note onto the garment at the mark for the first buttonhole, and stitch between the unfolded flaps of the note.

HOW TO SCAN A DESIGN

When I come across a design element I want to remember—a motif I want to embroider, a quilt patch I admire, or a garment closure I find interesting—I copy it using a scanner. The scanner reproduces the design in its original size. If I want to enlarge or reduce it, I can also do that with the scanner. If the design involves overlapping, intersecting, or seamed pieces, I make as many copies as needed to be able to cut a complete pattern for each element (and add seam allowance if needed); they fit back together perfectly.

—EFFAT MAHER, VICTORIA, BRITISH COLUMBIA, CANADA

CREATING TEMPLATES

Gauge Length Guide for Buttonholes

—PAM HOBSON, ANACORTES, WA

To measure buttonholes accurately when using an automatic buttonholer on your zigzag machine, use a strip of see-through graph paper, found in architectural or office-supply stores. Place the button on the grid and mark the number of squares required for the buttonhole. After marking the buttonholes on the fabric, lay the graph-paper template over the buttonhole line. Sew each buttonhole the length of the template. Simply tear away the paper when finished.

Make a Template for a Stitching Box

—PHYLLIS DAVIS, LAKEWOOD, CO

Here's an easy way to mark the stitching boxes needed to sew around placket and welt-pocket openings. Cut a template (rotary cutting is the most accurate way) of just the stitching box from white flannel. The flannel clings to the fashion fabric and is easy to stitch around—no marking required. Store the template with the pattern so it can be reused.

HOW TO USE FREEZER PAPER FOR APPLIQUÉ TEMPLATES

If you create designs on the computer, you can print them on freezer paper, which makes an ideal appliqué template. When ironed, the waxy side of freezer paper is tacky and adheres to fabric. A dot matrix printer set to accept sheet feed, not continuous feed paper, will accept freezer paper. Make a printout of the image you want to appliqué on continuous feed paper first to serve as a guide. Cut freezer paper to the length of the printout plus 12 in. to allow for the beginning and end of the feed. Direct the program to print the design in reverse, and feed the freezer paper into the printer, unwaxed side down. If you can't print in reverse, iron the image onto lightweight cardboard and cut around the image. Use the cardboard cutout as a template.

—CAROL STONER, DENVER, CO

I use freezer paper to trace elaborate pattern pieces, especially multisize children's smocking patterns. When ironed to the fabric, the freezer paper is securely held, allowing me to thread-trace the intricate smocking markings easily. I also use it to trace smaller pattern pieces next to one another, which are easier to reposition and cut out. These patterns usually remain tacky through three pressings.

—JOLEE NAIL HORN, CHARLOTTESVILLE, VA

HOW TO MAKE DURABLE APPLIQUÉ TEMPLATES

I cut frequently used appliqué template shapes from clean, large, ridgeless tin cans or from thin tin, aluminum, or brass sheets sold in hobby shops. These long-lasting metal templates are good for creasing sharp appliqué seamlines.

To make the template, I first draw the design without seam allowances on the metal with a permanent marker and roughly cut the template with tin snips, staying outside the marked line. (If you are making the templates from tin cans, you'll need to flatten the tin with a wooden mallet before you can use it. Be sure to wear gloves; the metal edges are sharp.) Next, I carefully cut inside the marked line. I file burrs and rough or sharp edges, then remove any traces of the marker with nail polish remover.

A major advantage of a metal template is that the seam allowances of the appliqué fabric can be pressed very sharply over it without harming the template. Spray the wrong side of your appliqué piece lightly with starch, center the template on it, and iron the seam allowances over the template, coaxing them as needed. The starch tacks the appliqué to the template so the fabric won't slip and slide. On points (see drawing above), first press the fabric

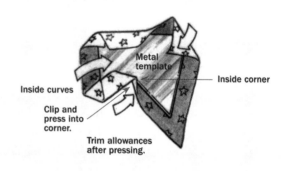

Inside curves

Metal template

Inside corner

Clip and press into corner.

Trim allowances after pressing.

up and over the corners, then fold and press the side seams. Clip into inside corners, then push the point of the iron into each corner while pulling allowances over the template. On curves, pull the fabric snugly around the template with one hand while pressing with the other. Press until the fabric is completely dry and the seam allowances stay flat. Allow the metal to cool, then gently remove the template. Touch up the appliqué as needed.

—CAROL STONER, DENVER, CO

Use T-Shirt Cardboard for Templates
—NATALIE GARRITY, BALTIMORE, MD

The lightweight, white cardboard used in packaging T-shirts and other clothing is great for making templates for pockets, flaps, collars, or design details such as scallops. Because it's white, it can be pressed over without damaging fabric. When finished, slip the template into the pattern envelope, ready to use the next time.

Reinforce Cardboard Templates

—SHERRI BROWN, BROOKSVILLE, FL

Cardboard templates, especially the kind you make yourself, wear with repeated use and lose some of their accuracy as marking and cutting guides. To give your templates a longer life, apply clear plastic tape, like Scotch Magic Tape, around the perimeter of each new template to keep its edges from disintegrating.

....

Create Permanent Template for Appliqué

—MRS. O. W. OLSON, MILL BAY, BRITISH COLUMBIA, CANADA

If lots of identical or mirror-image appliqués are being called for, a template made from a lightweight sheet of copper (sold in craft shops for metal tooling) will give precise results and will last a lifetime with reasonable care. Cut one into the exact finished shape with old scissors, then smooth the cut edge with an emery board. Use the template as the pattern, adding the appropriate seam allowance. Center the template on the facedown fabric, and press the seam allowances over the template, clipping corners and curves as necessary. A pin or tweezers protects fingers while helping to shape the fabric.

USING TEMPLATES

Hold Templates with Basting Tape

—DARLEEN A. CLEMENTS, SEATTLE, WA

Too often when working with templates, the template shifts and in turn spoils the perfect lines being cut or stitched. Basting tape (available through notions catalogs or in sewing stores) holds the template firmly in place. Apply two long strips lengthwise to the back of each template, leaving the waxy, protective outer layer in place until it's time to use. Then peel off this layer carefully so it can later be re-adhered to the basting tape when the template is stored. The tape lasts quite a long time this way, but when it starts to lose its tack, peel it off and add a fresh strip. The tape's ability to grab a fabric surface is the reason this works so well.

USE TEMPLATES FOR MANY TASKS

Whenever I need strips of fabric cut to a specific width (for bias trim, fabric tubes, and the like), or I need to cut a hem allowance to a certain width, I reach for a set of templates I created from oak tag or manila file folders in widths ranging from ⅛ in. to 4 in. I store these templates in a large zip-top bag, vertically stitched into compartments, as shown below, and labeled. My trims and hems are always even now, thanks to these simple tools, and the bag ensures quick access.

—ROCHELLE P. KENNY, NEW YORK, NY

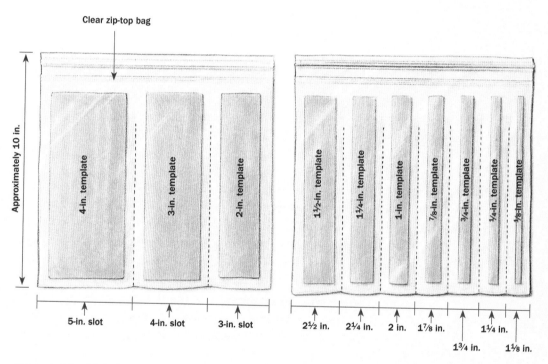

Clear zip-top bag

Approximately 10 in.

4-in. template | 3-in. template | 2-in. template

1½-in. template | 1¼-in. template | 1-in. template | ⅞-in. template | ¾-in. template | ¼-in. template | ⅛-in. template

5-in. slot | 4-in. slot | 3-in. slot

2½ in. | 2¼ in. | 2 in. | 1⅞ in. | 1¾ in. | 1¼ in. | 1⅛ in.

Bias tapes, trims, fabric tubes, and hems will be perfectly even when you use templates as cutting guides. Cut a set of templates in various widths from oak tag, then label and store them in a channel-stitched zip-top bag as shown.

Each slot stores one template. Machine-stitch channels about 1 in. wider than the template.

Make Great Darts

—LINDA HENRY, FAIR OAKS, CA

Here's an easy way to get perfectly shaped darts without marking, clipping, or thread tracing. After cutting fabric, fold the pattern piece along the dart fold and align the fold with the straight edge of a piece of freezer paper. Trace the stitching line of the dart onto the paper, and then cut out and discard the dart. Use the remaining shape as an iron-on template: Fold the fabric, right sides together, to match the folded pattern. Align the freezer paper template, shiny side down, to correspond to the dart placement; iron gently. Then, stitch along the edge of the template to make the dart, peel off the freezer paper, and use it for a corresponding dart. Save the template for future use with the same pattern.

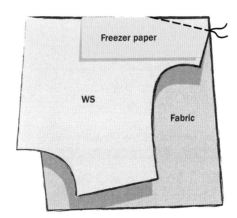

TAKE A TODDLER'S MEASUREMENTS

Last summer I needed to make a dress for my 2-year-old to wear in a wedding, but she couldn't stay still long enough for me to take her measurements. I was finally able to take accurate chest and waist measurements while she was asleep, but getting her length measurements was still troublesome. I purchased a roll of butcher paper and asked her to lie down on it. After I traced her she decorated her silhouette, which I used to measure. And I have a nice memento of her at two years of age.

—JENNIFER LARSON, FREDERICK, MD

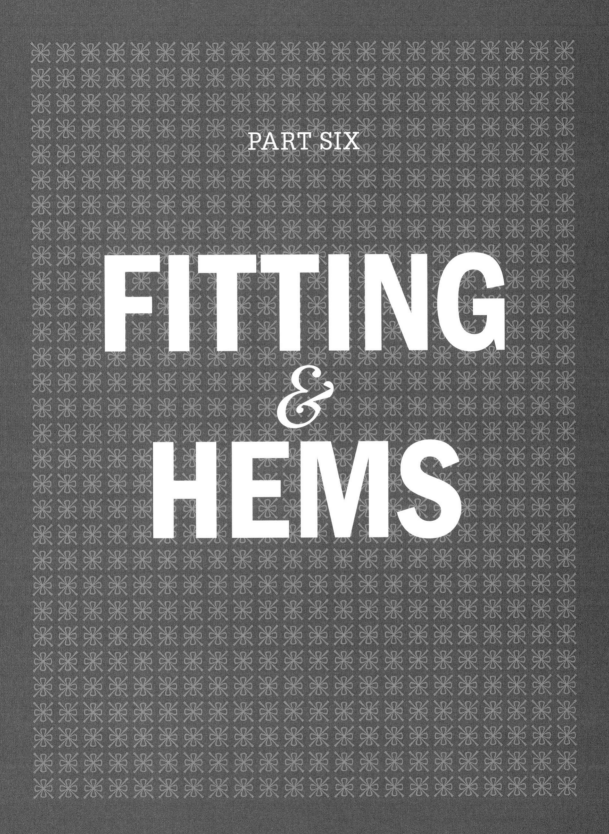

PART SIX

FITTING
&
HEMS

FITTING

VISUAL RECORD OF FITTING

Make a Digital
Design Record

—CLAUDIE CHAN,
GREEN VALLEY, AZ

Use a digital camera to record and compare design ideas after completing the fitting muslin for a garment. Then review the photos using the camera itself or print the photos to compare them side by side. This method can also be used to compare sleeve designs or pocket placement at the muslin stage and button choices as the final garment is being constructed. It's almost as good as having two finished garments to work with!

TAKE PHOTOS TO CHECK FIT

I asked my husband to take photos of the progress of a fitting shell (sloper) I recently drafted and stitched as a muslin. I downloaded the photos onto my computer, which allowed me to view the muslin from various angles. It's amazing what the photos showed. I saw things that I missed in the mirror and could also see my back view clearly. I could focus on wrinkles and fitting issues, such as shoulder seams that were too far back, one shoulder sloping more than the other, and armscye problems. If you're a sewer striving for a perfect fit, I highly recommend taking lots of photos, particularly for tailored and fitted garments.

—CHRISTINE SUTHERLAND, PERTH, WESTERN AUSTRALIA, AUSTRALIA

MARKING AND PINNING

Use Colored Markers to
Track Fitting Order

—BARBARA SNYDER,
SEBASTOPOL, CA

When adjusting and fitting patterns, many of us make an adjustment, test it, and then make several more adjustments. To keep track of which marking line is the most current one, try marking them in rainbow order (red, orange, green, blue, indigo, and violet—skip yellow because it's too hard to see). Use a red pen the first time, then mark the new line in orange, then green, and so forth. It will show at a glance which adjustment line reflects the most recent change.

HOW TO PIN-FIT ADJUSTMENTS ON A GARMENT

Here is a simple way to pin-fit adjustments on a garment with the seam allowances to the inside while the garment is right side out and on a dress form (or on a person). Doing this lets you analyze adjustments more accurately and preview the finished garment. And, because the pins do the marking, you never have to worry about damaging the fabric with your pencil or chalk.

Start with the garment fully basted, including darts, except for the side seams or the seam you want to adjust. With the garment on the dress form or person, fold under the back-seam allowance; lap it over the flat, unfolded front-seam allowance, and make the fitting adjustment by sliding one section over the other. You may need to alter the depth of the seam allowances on both sections, thus establishing a correctly placed stitching line.

Pin through all three layers to secure them. If you're fitting a person, point the pins down. Next, pin in a continuous line to mark the new front seamline. Do the same on the back seamline, pinning through only one layer on the fold. Now take out the original pins holding the seam together, releasing the two sections. Voilà—pin-marked stitching lines for your new seam.

To sew the new seam, match pin lines right sides together, pinning perpendicular through both layers, with each pin entering the fabric on the matched seamline. Use lots of pins. Now remove the other pins marking the seamlines, and stitch the final seamline from one pin-entry point to the next. To check the fit before stitching, push in the pins all the way to their heads, fold the seam allowance to the back, and put the garment on the dress form or person.

—BARBARA E. LIES, RIVERSIDE, IL

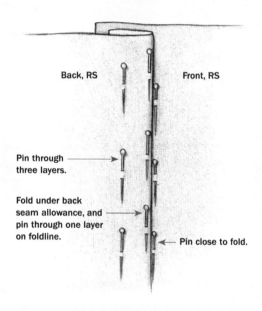

Back, RS

Front, RS

Pin through three layers.

Fold under back seam allowance, and pin through one layer on foldline.

← Pin close to fold.

This method enables you to see how a garment will really look when fitting vertical seams and eliminates chalk or pencil marks that can mar special fabrics.

Secure Pins with the Back of an Earring

—BEVERLY STONE,
ENCINITAS, CA

To avoid the "ouch!" and keep pins from escaping when fitting, slip a spare barrel-type pierced earring stud back (the "butterfly" type won't cover the point) over the points of the pins in the most critical places during fitting. Most bead shops will sell a handful of backs (called "barrel ear nuts").

Pin-Fit with Interfacing

—RETHA MENEGHINI,
ESCONDIDO, CA

When buying a new pattern, cut out the pattern pieces and press lightly; then affix lightweight interfacing to the pattern pieces with an iron that is just hot enough to adhere the interfacing. Pin-fitting is easy with this method because the pattern pieces have body and bend without risk of ripping. Make seam adjustments directly on the pattern while fitting by trimming the seam allowance or adding to it, whichever is appropriate. When finished, store the pattern in a large zip-top bag to use again. Despite folding the pattern pieces once or twice, they're easy to smooth flat for the next project.

Use Basting Tape for "Pinning" Leather

—SUE JOHNSON, VALDOSTA, GA

Because leather pieces cannot be pinned in place (pinholes mar the leather), try using two-sided thin basting tape to hold the pieces together. This tape sticks well but can be repositioned, and it's easy to remove when the stitching is complete. Consider also trying to join the leather pieces with long clips typically used in hair salons. These clips are much longer than clothespins, so they hold better, but because the gripping area is spread over a larger area, they don't leave pinch marks.

Try Masking Tape When Hemming Heavy Fabric

—MARJORIE DEBENEDICTIS,
AGAT, GUAM

When tacking a hem on fabrics that buckle if pinned, apply small pieces of masking tape instead. Many machines sew through the tape without difficulty, and the tape can be removed easily without distorting the fabric. It won't leave a residue as long as it's removed within a reasonable amount of time.

PERSONALIZING A DRESS FORM

Pad a Dress Form

—DAWN JARDINE,
RED HOOK, NY

To pad a dress form to mimic your unique curves, dress the form in one of your well-fitting bras, using scraps of polyester batting to fill the cups. For "hips," cut off the top of an old pair of tights, pull these onto the form's hips, and pad in the same way.

Make a Dress Form

—SANDY MOECKEL, LOS GATOS, CA

Having reviewed all the dress forms and mannequins on the market, I deduced they were extremely expensive and wouldn't fit my body perfectly. (I'm 5 ft. 9 in. tall and wear a size 8.) I decided to make my own. It cost considerably less than made-to-order dress forms, and it only took about two hours to modify so that it replicates my shape.

I refer to my dress form as Madeline. I bought a bridal mannequin and a nylon body shaper (a bra with an integrated body-hugging slip, ending midthigh) plus a larger-size body shaper because I wanted it to be snug-tight, but not girdle-tight.

Madeline came with a nicely weighted, iron rolling stand and was constructed of linen over a fiberglass form. I lengthened the bottom half of the torso by wrapping it with poster board and secured it with wide painter's tape. I also added some strategically placed padding—½-in. quilt batting—to duplicate my measurements. Then, I slipped the skin-colored body shaper over it all. I adjusted the padding as necessary, took a few stitches through the padding to hold everything in place, and took a few stitches to secure the body shaper to the form. Now I can create skirts or drape dresses with perfect fit.

Madeline can easily be adapted as needed. My daughter is getting married, and she bought a beautiful dress that needs alteration. In a few minutes, Madeline received a new shape that now matches my daughter. I know her dress will look and fit like a million bucks with Madeline's able assistance.

MODIFY A DRESS FORM

Adjustable dress forms have modification limitations, and sometimes it takes some creativity to fine-tune them to produce a body double. Here are some ways I used to get my form close to my shape.

First, I adjusted my dress form to reflect my measurements as closely as possible, choosing a smaller setting if the form wasn't exact. Second, with a friend's help, I made a "cover" for my dress form that perfectly duplicated my every curve. Then I stuffed the empty spaces between the cover and my form—the areas where the form's dialing mechanism wasn't able to accurately duplicate my curves. To make the cover, I wore my typical foundation garments and put on an oversize T-shirt. Then my friend cut away the excess fabric under the arms and at the sides, and cut the sleeves so that only small caps remained. Using strips of duct tape, she taped the T-shirt to me, overlapping the tape as she worked. She taped every square inch of my torso until the duct tape securely covered and molded my entire upper body to form a shell. The T-shirt underneath the duct tape protected my body from the tape.

Next, my friend cut a slit up the back of the duct-tape/T-shirt shell. I carefully slipped out of it and placed it on my dress form. Using short pieces of duct tape, I reattached the cut back of the shell as if it had never been cut. If the cut edges weren't able to abut, I reduced the size of the dress form in that location to allow the edges to meet. Then I slid old plastic grocery bags under the shell to pad the shell areas that were larger than my dress form (batting would have worked as well). Once the shell was completely stuffed where needed, I measured the standard areas of bust, waist, and so forth again and adjusted the duct tape along the back seam as necessary to tweak the measurements.

The dress form is now a perfect representation of my body, and if I should gain or lose weight, I'll just invite my friend over for lunch and re-pad my dress form to resemble the new me.

—ANNE K. BRENZ, CADILLAC, MI

FITTING BLOUSES AND SHIRTS

Ease in Caps of Set-In Sleeves
—JANET EARNHARDT, UTICA, PA

Here's a good way to ease in the cap of a set-in sleeve, which eliminates the puckers that are often associated with the use of machine gathering stitches.

Using a regular stitch length, begin to machine-stitch slowly from one notch in the sleeve along the seamline to the other notch. To ease the cap as you stitch, use the eraser end of a pencil in one hand and

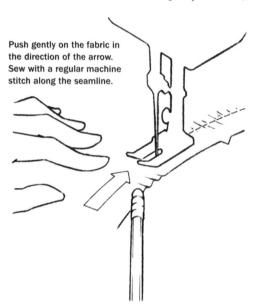

Push gently on the fabric in the direction of the arrow. Sew with a regular machine stitch along the seamline.

the fingertips of your other hand to gently push the fabric toward the back of the presser foot on both sides, as shown in the drawing at left. Start pushing about ½ in. to ¾ in. in front of the needle. Stop when the fabric is a little beyond the needle, reposition the pencil, push again, and repeat until you reach the other notch. Sometimes I stretch the fabric outward while pushing back, which eases even more. The result will be a sleeve with a nice cap and no puckers in the seamline.

If more or less ease is needed, simply push more or less as you stitch. You can also pull on the thread or clip it to adjust the gathers while inserting the sleeve in the armhole.

Trim Sleeve and Armhole Seams Correctly
—JANN JASPER, NEW YORK, NY

Improve both the fit and comfort of sleeves by trimming the seam allowances of the bodice and sleeves correctly. Trim the sleeve seam allowance, but not the garment seam allowance, above the notches (the section that goes over the shoulder). This lessens bulk and forces the seam allowances to fall toward the sleeve and stay there. The result is a smooth sleeve cap and shoulder area. Below the notches, trim both seam allowances, then finish the edges to prevent raveling. This keeps the armhole from being tight and feeling uncomfortable.

FITTING PANTS AND SKIRTS

Fix the Hem on "Aged" Jeans

—KYRIA LOSCALZO, HEMLOCK SHORES, CT

Since today's jeans are sold already worn and faded, shortening them leaves a telltale new hem. To avoid the contrast between the hem and the jeans, try aging the hems. After hemming the jeans, loosen the tension knob on your machine and stitch two rows of gathering stitches in the hem. Rub the exposed outer edges with an emery board until the fabric begins to lighten and fray. Lightly dab exposed areas with a one-to-one solution of bleach and water. Dry with an iron or hair dryer to prevent the bleach from spreading. Wash and dry the jeans to remove all traces of the bleach before pulling out the gathers.

Loosen a Pair of Beloved Jeans

—ELIZABETH RYMER, HURRICANE MILLS, TN

Here's how to make jeans that have become snug around the hips wearable again: Find an old pair of jeans whose color closely matches that of the snug pair. Cut a gusset-shaped piece from the old denim about 4 in. deep by 12 in. long. Then, with a seam ripper, open the inseam of the tight jeans from the crotch down each leg 4 in. to 5 in. Use a bit of tape to tack the gusset on the inside, right side to wrong side, with the gusset's long side extending down each inseam. Now put on the jeans. Adjust the fit and pin or tape the gusset firmly in place; then take off the jeans.

Next, fold under the original seam allowance on the opening, and, with the zipper open, edge-stitch the gusset to the crotch on the right side. Trim off the excess denim and serge-finish the seam allowances (or use a machine-zigzag stitch). The gusset doesn't show when worn, and your jeans will be a lot more comfortable.

Make Pants Hems Match

—MRS. LEO KOELLNER, SAN BRUNO, CA

When fitting pants hems, try fitting only one leg and then mark the back of both legs the same distance from the floor. Holding those marks together, mark and trim both legs at the same time. Many people have different-length legs or hips, but this way, the length of both legs comes out even.

Fit Full, High Hips

—SUSAN HUTCHINS,
SAGAMORE BEACH, MA

If you've generally followed the method of blending to a smaller size at the waist from the full hip on multisize patterns, but never got a good fitting result, here's another solution. Cut the pattern the same size from hip to waist at the side seam, then add a second dart at the waist. The result may be a much smoother and better-fitting garment.

....

Create a "Suspension" Skirt to Fit Round Tummies

—SARAH VEBLEN,
SPARKS, MD

For ladies with a tummy whose skirts tend to ride up in front, here's a solution: Make the skirt to fit the abdomen and hips, but instead of completing the skirt with a waistband, sew a lightweight camisole of silk or other slippery fabric to the top of the skirt. Now the skirt hangs from the shoulders instead of the waist, and is comfortable for the wearer while hanging straight. Since a top can't be tucked in with this system, an overblouse is needed to finish the ensemble. Using the length of the top as a guide, place the camisole/skirt waist at a line that won't show under the top. Lower the neck of the camisole an inch or conceal it under the top. To allow the camisole to fit comfortably without adding a lot of fabric to bunch or distort the lines of the skirt, add side bust darts to the camisole. Next, sew a zipper in the side seam, which runs right down into the skirt. Finally, drop the armscye of the camisole $1/4$ in. to $1/2$ in. May stylish comfort be yours.

HEMS

MARKING HEMS

Use the Presser Foot to Mark a Hem

—DONNA DUNANN,
CANYON LAKE, CA

Simplify the process of marking and measuring a long, straight hemline by using the presser foot on your sewing machine and a mark on the needle plate as guides. Measure the distance needed from the inside edge of the foot to the needle plate, marking that distance with a preexisting line on the plate or a Post-it Note. Slide the fabric under the raised foot, keeping the raw edge against the mark on the plate, and mark the hemline with a marker held against the edge of the presser foot while sliding the fabric along.

Mark for Hem Folding

—ANTONIO PATTERSON,
BROOKLYN, NY

If marking the hem foldline on either side of the fabric seems inconvenient, don't mark the foldline. Instead, mark the "fold-to" line. Measure twice the hem allowance above the turned-under edge and mark it on the inside of a garment, then fold the turned-under edge up to it.

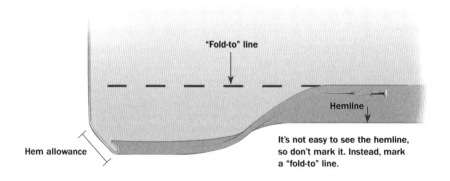

"Fold-to" line

Hemline

Hem allowance

It's not easy to see the hemline, so don't mark it. Instead, mark a "fold-to" line.

Try Washaway Tape to Help with Narrow Hems

—CYNTHIA YOUNG,
FRESHAM, OR

To make an even, double-folded, ¼-in. hem on hard-to-press fabrics, try using ¼-in.-wide Wash Away Wonder Tape (available at many fabric stores). Lay a strip of tape along the raw edge of the fabric, on the wrong side. Fold the fabric up, using the edge of the tape as a guide, and stick it in place. The tape holds the first fold in place while making and stitching the second fold, and it negates having to measure, pin, or baste.

HAND HEMMING

Hand-Roll Hems

—TRICIA KLEM,
SAN LUIS OBISPO, CA

Here's a hand-rolled hem technique with hidden stitches. Machine-stitch ¼ in. from the raw edge of the fabric, and trim the edge to within ¹⁄₁₆ in. of the stitching. Fold about 1 in. to 2 in. of the stitching to the wrong side, with the crease just inside the stitches, finger pressing as you go. Insert the needle into the turned edge, bringing the thread out on the crease. Now insert the needle into the single layer of fabric directly opposite, picking up one to two threads about ³⁄₁₆ in. from the machine stitches. The stitches must be perpendicular to the edge of the hem, not slanted. Reinsert the needle through the creased edge, and let it travel inside ¼ in. before coming out again to repeat the process. After taking four to five stitches, bring the needle out at the edge of the crease and pull the thread gently to tighten and enclose the row of stitches. The result will be a tightly rolled hem with all the stitches inside.

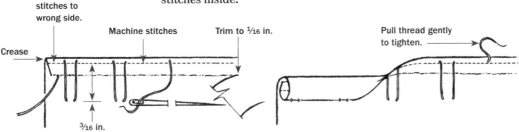

Fold machine stitches to wrong side.

Crease

Machine stitches

Trim to ¹⁄₁₆ in.

Pull thread gently to tighten.

³⁄₁₆ in.

Use Multiple Colors of Thread for Hand-Hemming Prints

—EVELYN BLAKE,
ROANOKE, VA

For truly invisible hemstitching on multicolored fabrics such as prints and plaids that have sharply contrasting colors, sometimes it's worth the trouble to hem with two or more different colors of thread. Thread as many needles as there are colors to use, start them all, then stitch the unused colors only into the hem allowance until it's time to switch. Use the appropriate color to make the hem stitches.

MACHINE HEMMING

Machine-Baste for Narrow Hems

—NAN REBER,
EL SEGUNDO, CA

To turn under a fabric edge to press it (particularly a narrow width), it's much easier to first baste a line of stitches just outside the foldline. If the pattern advises turning the edge under ¼ in. and then pressing, first machine-baste at slightly less than ¼ in. from the cut edge. The stitch plate's seam guide makes this a snap. The stitching provides a guideline to finger-press and results in a neat, consistent edge.

Use a Hemming Wedge

—DIANE SCHULTZ,
ST. PAUL, MN

When sewing over bulky jean seams or appliquéing over heavy braid, a simple wedge will prevent skipped stitches and a stalled sewing machine. One can be cut from a scrap of corrugated cardboard ¾ in. wide by 5 in. long. To use it, stitch up to the rise in the fabric, lift the presser foot, and insert the cardboard under the rear of the foot. Lower the foot and proceed to sew. When the foot has traveled forward off the wedge, raise the foot with the needle down and put the cardboard under the front of the foot). Turn the wheel by hand and take a few stitches; raise the foot and repeat as necessary until the foot is completely off the rise and is level.

LENGTHENING HEMS

Make Pants Longer at the Back

—BECKY JOHNSON,
CHILLIWACK, BRITISH COLUMBIA, CANADA

To get a dress-pants hem to be longer at the back than the front, the trick to getting the slanted hemline to fold smoothly is to make a ½-in. snip at the center front of the hem allowance.

Make Pants Longer without Leaving a Line

—BECKY JOHNSON,
CHILLIWACK, BRITISH COLUMBIA, CANADA

When a pair of pants shrinks, the hem usually leaves a permanent fold mark that becomes a challenge when trying to lengthen the pants. Here's a quick remedy to disguise the unsightly perma-fold. Open the hem and extend each pant leg to the desired new hem length, then stitch the hem in place with invisible hand stitches. As a final detail, stitch two rows of embroidery thread in a similar color, with the first row exactly over the original foldline and a second parallel row of stitching above or below the first row. The result looks much like the stitched hem usually found on jeans and nicely hides the old hem edge. This method works particularly well on linen and chino pants.

MAKING QUICK HEMS

Use a Serger to Create an Instant Hem
—GEORGIANE L. BISHOP, SAN FRANCISCO, CA

Use the rolled-hem feature on your serger to quickly and easily hem the lining on skirts and dresses. This is also great for repairing fraying hems.

Make an Easy, Fast, and Bulkless Hem
—B. RANDY JOHNSTONE, LA LUZ, NM

Here's a hem that works on all kinds of clothing for all ages and both sexes. Turn the garment to be hemmed inside out, and turn up a hem, with the fold about ½ in. longer than desired for the finished length. Fold over the same size hem once more, straightening the edges carefully, and press the bottom edge. The hem will now be three layers thick. Stitch ¼ in. away from the edge, catching all three layers, then turn the garment right side out and unfold the hem. This will create a neat hem with a decorative tuck that looks like a cuff. Adjust the size of the cuff by adjusting the size of the folds made; the length taken up in the tuck is twice the width of the seam sewn.

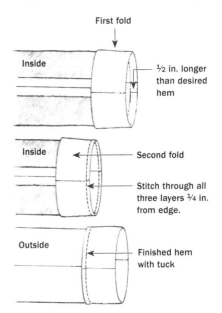

First fold

Inside

½ in. longer than desired hem

Inside

Second fold

Stitch through all three layers ¼ in. from edge.

Outside

Finished hem with tuck

Create Bulkless Hems
—B. RANDY JOHNSTONE, LA LUZ, NM

For quick, durable, bulkless hems, zigzag the raw edge with a close stitch—twice if the fabric is ravelly. Fold the hem inside to the desired length and press. Sew two or three evenly spaced rows of straight stitches to secure it: Two rows 1¼ in. from the bottom and ¼ in. apart look good on slacks; two or three rows ¼ in. to ½ in. from the bottom and ⅛ in. apart are good for skirts.

MAKING NEATER HEMS

Use Fusible Thread on Shirt or Blouse Hems

—JEANNE HARMON,
DOVER-FOXCROFT, ME

When making neat, narrow hems is an issue, here's a method that gets perfect results every time. Fill the bobbin with fusible thread (available from mail-order notions catalogs), a thread that fuses when pressed. Stitch ¼ in. from the bottom edge, with the fusible thread on the wrong side of the shirt. Press approximately ⅜ in. from the edge so that the line of stitches falls on the hem allowance. Trim very close to the stitching, fold over, and press again, forming a narrow hem. Then stitch the hem. Presto: a smooth, pucker-free hem.

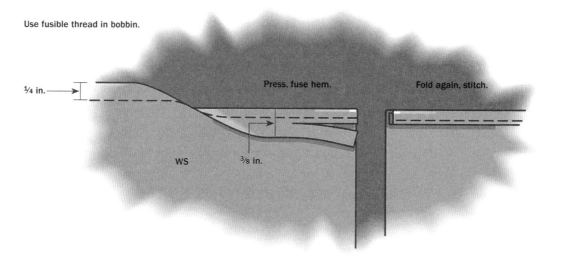

Use fusible thread in bobbin.

¼ in.

Press, fuse hem.

Fold again, stitch.

WS

⅜ in.

Use a Pillow to Create Tidy Hems

—ELLEN MAURER,
BOULDER, CO

Hem stitching that is too tight will cause puckers, and stitching that is too loose will cause sags. To make neat hand-sewn hems, fold the hem to the appropriate length, and pin and press it. Then pin the fabric to a small pillow. Hand-stitch toward yourself, keeping the fabric taut. This will keep stitches even.

MAKING SPECIAL HEMS

Use a Zigzag Stitch for Ruffled Hems
—MARIANNA KRAJEWSKA, BEVERLY HILLS, CA

Here's a timesaving solution for hand-rolling ruffle hems. Draw the ruffles on the fabric, zigzag in a very fine stitch along the drawn lines, and cut out the ruffles as close to the machine-stitched hems as possible. There'll be no stretching, no puckering, and no fabric getting caught in the machine.

Make an Even A-Line Hem
—RUTH S. GALPIN, SOUTHPORT, CT

To evenly adjust the fullness of the hem on an A-line skirt, first pin the hem. Then cut a length of seam binding that is long enough to travel around the top of the hem and overlap slightly where the two ends of the binding meet. Pin the seam binding to the hem while easing the fullness to the skirt fabric. Machine-stitch the seam binding to the hem, stretching the binding between the pins. While stretching, hold the binding in front of, and behind, the needle to avoid putting pressure on the needle. After it's stitched, the binding will resume its normal length and gather in the fullness of the hem as it does so. On a very wide A-line skirt, run a basting thread in the hem and gather the hem slightly to take up the ease first.

Create a Slimming Pegged Hem
—ANN TAECKER, WATERTOWN, SD

Get a more flattering silhouette with a "pegged hem," a hem in which the circumference is 1 in. to 2 in. narrower than the widest point of the body. It creates a more feminine shape and visually trims the hips. Wrap a length of fabric around yourself as a straight skirt. Then, pin in the hem just a bit (1 in. to 2 in. is the standard) and take another look. It will visually take off about 10 pounds.

Make a French Tack
—BRENDA BOLIN-SANDAGE, BATESVILLE, AK

A French tack or swing tack holds two parts of a garment together, such as the two hems of a lined garment. It is usually placed at the bottom end of the side seams on the inside. Here's an easy way to make these. After serge-finishing the hem edge of the garment fabric before stitching the side seams, leave about a 5-in. to 6-in. tail of serging at the end of the edge. After finishing the final hem on both the garment and the lining, thread the serged tail through the eye of a large tapestry needle and sew it to the top edge of the lining hem in a 1-in. to 2-in. tack (depending on the width of the hem). This process is so much faster and easier than making a hand-chain-stitched loop, and it looks and functions wonderfully.

WORKING WITH SPECIAL MATERIALS

Hand-Hem Silk

—MARSHA M. KITT,
TWO HILLS, ALBERTA, CANADA

Hand-hemming silk is a little easier this way: Apply water mixed with a bit of liquid starch to the fabric edges first, then fold the edges several times to the wrong side using narrow folds. Let the silk dry without disturbing the folded edges. When they're dry, they will be easier to hem, because the silk stays folded while stitching.

Hem Sheer Fabric

—GAIL MANNING,
NORTH YORK, ONTARIO, CANADA

Filmy chiffon, transparent gauze, and fine silk are all a challenge to hem. After all, the hem must be delicate, yet it must look good on both the inside and outside. Here's an amazingly simple technique that produces flawless hems for sheers. Instead of a typical stitched look, this method produces a hem with no visible stitches on the garment's right side and creates the effect of a tiny piped edge. It even works with French seams (which are often used with sheer fabrics).

First, along the raw edge to be hemmed, fold ¼ in. up on the right side of the garment and press. Fold this edge up once again, press, and machine-stitch along the center of this double fold. Finally, "flip" this stitched fold back under to the wrong side of the garment to get the effect of a "piped" edge. Press carefully along the seamline to hold the hem in place.

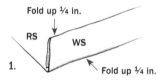

Fold up ¼ in.

RS   WS

1.   Fold up ¼ in.

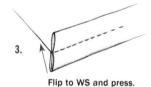

3.

Flip to WS and press.

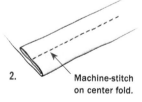

2.   Machine-stitch
on center fold.

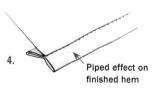

4.   Piped effect on
finished hem

Add Lace to a Hem

—ALYCE JULIEN SMITH-ROBINSON, DONALDSONVILLE, LA

When altering or constructing lined skirts or dresses, consider adding lace (either ½ in. or ¾ in. wide) to the bottom edge of the lining instead of finishing it with a machine hem. Use lace that either matches or complements the lining color. This way, the lining has the look of a slip if it happens to be seen.

....

Attach Lace Edging to Fine Fabrics

—GAIL MANNING, NORTH YORK, ONTARIO, CANADA

This technique is perfect for finishing fine lingerie and linings. Position the lace edging facedown on the right side of the fabric, about ⅛ in. from the raw edge. With the needle centered and set to zigzag, adjust the stitch width so that the needle catches the lace heading on the left and clears the fabric on the right. Set stitch length to a near satin stitch, then increase the needle-thread tension.

Starting at the left, insert the needle into the lace heading, lower the presser foot, and begin stitching slowly and evenly. The tension on the needle thread will roll the fabric up and over, and the zigzag will enclose the raw edge. Press the lace and fabric open. If the lace is gathered, it works best to straight-stitch the lace down first, then zigzag over the straight stitching and off the edge as described.

HOW TO ADD STRETCH TO FRINGE

I wanted to add ready-made fringe to the bottom edge of a Latin ballroom dance dress I recently made. The dress was made of stretch fabric, but the bound edge of the fringe had no stretch at all, and I didn't want the fringe to affect the stretchiness of the hem.

Despite many experiments, I was unable to tame the flyaway fringe well enough to neatly affix it, until I discovered that attaching masking tape on each side of the fringe prevented it from flopping around and made it more workable. Then to give the fringe stretch, I folded the raw hem edge over the finished woven (nonstretchy) fringe edge with the right side of the fringe facing the right side of the fabric and the wrong side of the dress hem edge on top. I stitched along the inside edge of the fringe binding using a three-thread stretch serger seam. I made sure that the cutter removed the woven edge of the fringe and the stitch length was short enough to catch all of the fringe threads to create a new, stretchy fringe edge (a setting of 1.7 was perfect with my machine).

When I opened out the fringe, it hung beautifully, and the hem edge had plenty of stretch.

—ANN EHRLICH, NORTH COLLINS, NY

Serge to Keep Web Under Control

—MARY BLAKESLEE
BURLINGTON, VT

Do you like bonding using web (such as Stitch Witchery) for hemming trousers, but have trouble with it creeping out of the hem and sticking where you didn't want it? Serge the web to the wrong side of the pants leg, which finishes the edge and holds the web securely in place.

....

Add Strips of Leather to Jeans Hems

—JIM RYERSON, VICTORIA, BRITISH
COLUMBIA, CANADA

The double row of stitching in jeans hems are traditionally narrow to match the flat-fell seam's double row of stitching on the rest of the pants. The problem is folding up the flat-fell seam at the hem's side and inseam—twice. The accumulated bulk makes for difficult stitching. Avoid the problem by sewing a thin strip of leather on the inside of the hem. (Seek out leather scraps from local leather stores.)

Cut a narrow leather strip about ½ in. wide by several inches more than the circumference of the jeans hem. With the jeans right side out, fold and pin the pant-leg bottom to the desired length.

Using a jeans needle and heavy polyester jeans thread, edgestitch the leather to the pant inside the pant leg and flush with the hem foldline. Overlap the leather ends by a few stitches, then cut off the excess leather. Fold out the leather strip and trim the denim hem allowance to ½ in. from the edgestitching. Fold under the pant bottom and stitch the leather ½ in. from the hemline, concealing the denim's raw edge. You'll have fewer layers to sew at the side and inseams, and a clean finish.

To add a design element to your jeans, stitch the leather so it turns to the right side or extends below the hem. Or even make fringe from the extension.

A narrow strip of thin leather (sheepskin is perfect) makes a durable hem facing that avoids bulk at side seams and inseams.

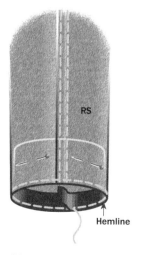

Stitch leather flush with hemline.

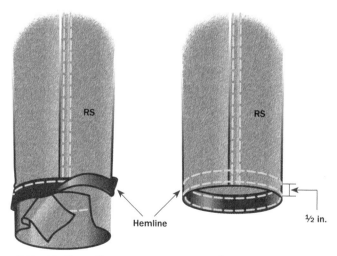

Fold out leather; pull down hem allowance and trim to ⅛ in.

Stitch ½ in. above hemline to finish.

HEMMING TRICKS

Avoid Leaving Hem Impressions
—SUZAN L. WIENER, SPRING HILL, FL

A strip of brown paper placed between the fabric layers of a hem before pressing them prevents the hemline from leaving a press line on the right side of the garment.

Prevent Burned Fingers When Pressing ¼-in. Hems
—JUDITH NEUKAM, THREADS CONTRIBUTOR

Here's an easy, safe way to press ¼-in. hem allowances for straight or shaped edges: Cut an oak tag template to match the shape of the desired edge (a curve for a veil or a patch pocket, for example). On an ironing board, lay out a fine press cloth or paper (try silk organza). Overlap cut fabric facedown on top, leaving at least 4 in. of the press cloth extending beyond the hem edge. Then align the template on the fabric so the exact hem allowance shows around the edge. Place a straight pin or two through the template into your ironing board to hold the template in place. With one hand, lift the press cloth over the template, folding the hem allowance neatly over the template edge. It is now safe to press the hem with the other hand without getting fingers near the iron.

Secure a Hem from Unraveling
—BETTY BOLDEN, NEWPORT, TN

When hemming pants or a skirt made from heavy or midweight fabrics, knot the thread three or four times while stitching around the hem every 5 in. or 6 in. If the thread breaks along the hemline in the months or years ahead, the entire hem won't come out; only the section between the knots will be able to loosen. Don't use this method on sheer or lightweight fabrics, however, where the knot might be noticeable on the right side.

Use No-Melt Hem-Pressing Templates for Hems
—ELAINE DUNCAN, PURDIN, MO

Try no-melt Mylar® templates, often used for making quilting templates, to press hems. Cut strips in various widths from this heat-resistant plastic, marking the width of each with a permanent marker. To press a hem, select the template of the desired hem width and align one long edge with the raw edge of the fabric on the wrong side. Fold the template and fabric up, and press the crease that forms along the enclosed edge of the template.

PART SEVEN

CARE
&
REPAIR

CARE

REINFORCING GARMENTS

Keep Facing from Stretching

—ELIZABETH MARTIN, SEATTLE, WA

Stretching a curved neck or armhole facing beyond repair when applying the fusible interfacing is easy to do, especially when working with lightweight fabrics like rayon or challis. And when the shape no longer matches the pattern piece, it's not easy to get the facing to fit in the garment without buckling. Here's a solution to prevent the problem from happening in the first place: Arrange the tissue pattern piece facedown on the ironing board and position the fabric pattern piece facedown over it, adjusting the fabric facing to exactly match the shape of the pattern piece. Carefully position the fusible interfacing piece sticky-side down on top of the fabric and press, keeping all three layers aligned. Now when sewing a facing to a bodice, the shapes will be accurate and the neckline or armhole will be smooth and even.

Use Fusible Nylon Tricot to Stop Slippage

—LAUREN HUNT, EAST LANSING, MI

Rayons and other slippery, loose fabrics that tend to slip or shred at the seamline can be supported without significant bulk with ½-in.-wide bias bands of fusible nylon tricot. Apply the bands about ⅜ in. in from each cutting line before sewing so the seamline (assuming ⅝-in. seam allowances) is centered under the bands. Alternative interfacings include a combination of fusible web and a seam binding such as Seams Great™, or a lightweight fusible such as Easy-Knit or Sew Sheer.

Use a Tape Closure to Create a Flexible Waistband

—VIRGINIA KOTECKI, SCOTTS VALLEY, CA

To make sure waistbands remain comfortable even as weight fluctuates, instead of using a button and buttonhole or other closure, use hook-and-loop tape slightly narrower than the waistband. Put the soft side facing the body on the overlap, and put the other side facing out. Use 2 in. to 3 in. of the tape, depending upon the garment. Whether weight is lost or gained, the waistband will still be comfortable, especially nice to temporarily make a little more breathing room following a big meal.

Reinforce Sleeve Seams

—LAURA PROUDFOOT,
PALOS HEIGHTS, IL

When sewing a blouse or top, attach the sleeves before you stitch the side seams. Use the following method to sew the side seam to keep it perfectly aligned and give extra strength under the arm: To pin the side seam, start at the underarm and pin toward the bodice hem edge. Then pin the sleeve seam, starting at the underarm and working toward the sleeve hem edge. Sew the seams in the same direction—from the underarm to the hem edges—with one change. Instead of sewing from the underarm, begin stitching about an inch before the underarm seam. Stitch across the underarm and down toward the hem edge. Stitch in a similar fashion for the sleeve seam. Pinning and stitching in this manner helps prevent "fabric creep" and reinforces the underarm seam with double stitching 1 in. on either side of the underarm seam.

Protect Delicate Fabrics from Brooches and Pins

—SUSAN DELANEY MECH,
PLANO, TX

When pinning a heavy brooch to a fine fabric like silk, adapt a technique used by the British Royal Family to pin the crown jewels to delicate evening clothes. Cut a piece of white felt the size of the brooch and place it underneath the fine fabric where the pin will go. The felt supports the brooch and protects the garment from tearing.

SECURING BUTTONS

Reinforce Buttons on Silk

—BARBARA NACHTIGALL,
ROSLINDALE, MA

If a silk jacquard or crepe de chine blouse or dress pattern requires a button placement with only fabric to support the button, try using heavyweight, nonfusible interfacing rather than a backing button. For small buttons, cut out a tiny circle with a paper hole punch. For larger buttons, use the top or bottom of a thimble or a thread spool to draw a circle on the interfacing scrap and then cut it out with small, sharp scissors. This reinforcement is strong, flexible, comfortable, and washable.

Save Scraps to Fix Covered Buttons

—KAREN ROTH WOLFF,
ALISO VIEJO, CA

Always keep some fabric scraps when using self-covered buttons. On occasion, a covered button pops apart, especially when the garment is frequently washed, and the fabric is lost or not reusable, or the button falls off the garment and is lost. It's great to be able to replace the special button and keep the garment looking perfect.

Make Handy Button Protectors

—MARVIS LUTZ,
PORTLAND, OR

Protect special buttons from chipping and scratching from washing or dry cleaning in this ingenious way. Cover them with hook-and-loop button protectors, which can be made for just a few cents apiece. Here's how: Buy a 1½-in.-wide hook-and-loop tape like Velcro® (make certain that it's not the self-stick variety) and cut it into pieces 1½ in. long, which will be large enough to cover most buttons. On the stiff hook side, cut a slit from one edge to the center. Slide the cut side under the button and seal with the soft loop cover. Keep a supply of these protectors handy in a jar near the washing machine—just pop them over your buttons and wash without worry.

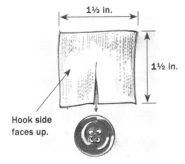

1½ in.

1½ in.

Hook side faces up.

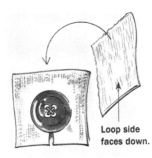

Loop side faces down.

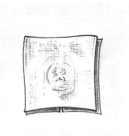

Protect Exotic Buttons

—HEATHER HAMILTON,
OTTAWA, ONTARIO, CANADA

Here's a great way to protect exotic, decorative buttons from getting damaged in the wash or at the cleaners. Attach the decorative button to a plain men's shirt button, making a button "cuff link." Place a toothpick or stiletto (depending upon the thickness of the shirt fabric you're using) between the buttons as they are sewn together, which will ensure ample space to accommodate the thickness of the shirt plackets. Then sew buttonholes on both sides of the tops, the outside buttonhole sized for the decorative button, and the inside for the men's button. Button the double button through both sides of the blouse, decorative button out. As a bonus, the shirt button on the inside offers extra support for a heavy or irregularly shaped decorative button on the outside. You can button and unbutton the shirt normally for wear, but can easily remove the buttons for laundering, or just to change the buttons to enjoy a different look with the same top.

Create a Fake Buttonhole Closure

—EVELYN BLAKE, ROANOKE, VA

Buttonholes in delicate or gauzy fabrics are nice, but they wear quickly. To save them, make fake buttonholes. Work the buttonholes, but don't cut them open. Sew a button on the top of each buttonhole and sew silk-covered snaps underneath. This also works well with fancy silk or antique buttons that are too fragile to button and unbutton.

Keep Buttons On

—SUZAN WIENER, SPRING HILL, FL

Here's a great way to keep the buttons on clothes. First, make a habit of using four-hole buttons. Sew the buttons in place by running the needle and thread a few times through two of the holes, then break and knot the thread. Insert the needle again and repeat the process for the other two holes, creating two sets of stitches to hold one button in place. If one set of stitches tears loose, the other set will still hold the button on the garment. Works great!

Safeguard and Change Buttons

—JOSEPHINE HARKNESS, TOPEKA, KS

Looking to use fragile or nonwashable buttons on a vest, blouse, or jacket, but don't want to remove and resew them before and after each washing? First make the buttonholes (large enough to accommodate the buttons you have selected) on both sides of the vest. Then cut a strip of fashion fabric that's 1½ in. wide by the length of the buttonhole area, plus a few inches. Cut and fuse a piece of interfacing to the fabric's wrong side. Fold right sides together, and seam the long edge and ends. Turn inside out, press, and sew the buttons on this strip, spaced to match the garment's buttonholes. When you wear the vest, you can't tell from the right side that the buttons aren't attached in the conventional manner. The strip is removable, of course, when laundering the garment, so it's possible to use fragile or nonwashable buttons, such as ceramic, glass, or antique, with this method. Consider changing the look of a vest or jacket by making several button strips.

WARDING OFF WEAR

Reinforce Patch-Pocket Corners
—SARAH NOCK, MARIETTA, GA

Here's how to reinforce corners of patch pockets. In addition to stitching a small triangle at the upper corners of a pocket, it also helps to put a small scrap of interfacing against the wrong side of the main garment, behind the pocket's corners. This provides added support for the garment itself and keeps the pocket from pulling at the fabric with repeated washing and wearing.

Prevent Corduroy Abrasion
—ARLENE FOX
BURNABY, BRITISH COLUMBIA, CANADA

Corduroy pants sometimes wear badly on the inner leg long before the rest of the garment is ready to be tossed. Lining the pants can help, but lined pants are not always ideal. Try this instead. Add a piece of stretchy press-on interfacing from the crotch down through the thigh just along the chief area of wear. It's amazing how effective this is to prevent extra wear. If the pants are made in stretch corduroy, it is especially important to use stretchy interfacing. If the edges of the interfacing need securing, it is easy to run a straight stitch invisibly between the corduroy's ridges.

Childproof Pants Knees
—CAROLYN BOTTOMLY,
FORT MEADE, MD

When you make pants for children, always make a pair of iron-on knee patches to match. Lay a purchased patch on the fabric along with the pattern and cut a ¼-in. seam allowance around it. Centering the right side of the purchased patch on the wrong side of the one cut, fold the seam allowances to the patch's sticky side and fuse them using the point and side of your iron. Fold the corners in and secure the edge with stitching. When the inevitable holes in the knees appear, these patches will be handy, and are twice as thick as the original pants.

Fabric, RS

Patch, WS

2 pleats

Prevent Snags
—TISHA THORNE,
WASHINGTON, DC

Sometimes delicate fabrics snag when they brush against a wooden ham holder. To prevent this from happening, wrap the ham stand in Polarfleece. It helps the ham stay in place and gives fabric a soft surface as it gets moved around for pressing.

REPAIR

FIXING FASHION

Get Ultimate Moth Insurance

—JANE CONLON,
EUGENE, OR

Here's a great way to repair insect damage in wool garments. Save a large scrap of leftover fabric in a mothproof container. If insect damage occurs in the garment, take the garment with its scrap to be rewoven to a tailor's shop, where they can make the repair from the scrap, instead of having to filch fabric from a facing or hem. A skilled reweaving job is barely detectable from the fabric's original surface, and this method sure beats darning!

Patch Ripped Jeans

—PAM LELAND,
JAMESTOWN, CO

It's possible to patch worn-out or ripped jeans or pants easily and quickly without having to feed the entire pant leg under the presser foot. Simply rip out a section of the inseam, which is usually not topstitched, from a little above to a little below the area you want to patch. After applying the patch, restitch the seam. This method allows you to reach even the narrowest areas of a pant leg easily.

Find Extra Fabric for Alterations

—MARIANNE DIETRICH,
CHATHAM, ONTARIO, CANADA

When waistbands are too tight, here's a way to add 1½ in. for comfort: Find extra fabric by releasing darts, seams, tucks, or gathers to expand the section of a garment that's too snug. If the waistband doesn't have hidden fabric, try expanding it with the belt loops, sewn together, side by side, overlapped (exactly as they came off the garment). Remove the waistband stitches from the center front, in both directions, until you can release enough fabric from the darts, tucks, and seams. Then cut the waistband at the center front and insert your topstitched belt loop extension.

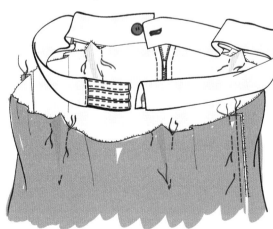

Use the belt loops to enlarge a waistband.

If the topstitching doesn't look like a design element, topstitch the entire waistband to match it. If the fabric is too thick for this treatment or the waistband is too wide for the number of belt loops, open the loops before stitching them together and use an appropriate fusible interfacing as backing. The loss of the belt loops is a small price to pay to save a favorite skirt or pair of pants.

Taper Tuck for Missing Shoulder Pads

—LUANNE B. REDWOOD, CHICAGO, IL

Some garments, like those with raglan sleeves, don't always hang well with the shoulder pads removed. Here's how to fix that. A tapered tuck in the shoulder seam of the garment, starting at the neck edge and widening to about ½ in. at the shoulder curve (the standard height of most shoulder pads), will remove the excess fabric allowance. The tuck will vary in length depending on the original shoulder seam and your shoulder. Baste the tuck first and try the garment on for fit; the proportions of the tuck may have to be adjusted. The seam allowances may need to be clipped and trimmed.

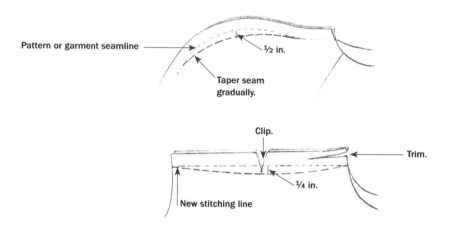

Pattern or garment seamline

½ in.

Taper seam gradually.

Clip.

Trim.

New stitching line

¼ in.

Reduce Your Jeans' Waistband

—PATRICIA FERRITO, ANGOLA, NY

When taking in jeans, sometimes it is difficult to ease the denim fabric to fit a smaller waistband without creating bulk. It's possible to take apart the center-back seam through the seat and remove some of the fullness. Remove the stitching at the center back from the waist down to just below the back yoke seam. Slide one side of the center-back seam allowance over the other and pin in place. The overlap acts like a dart to take in the jeans. Use thread that matches the color of the original topstitching, and set your machine's stitch to match the length of the original topstitching. Resew the center-back topstitching without opening the original folded seam allowances. The seam won't be a flat-fell seam—but it will look like it is, and the jeans will fit better.

Lengthen Sleeves

—BARBARA CONTE GAUGEL,
NORTH SYRACUSE, NY

Here's a neat method for lengthening sleeves. Let down the hem (assuming it's already been sewn), open the seam about 8 in. to 10 in., and press out the crease line. Using fashion fabric, cut a sleeve extension the same width as the sleeve and about 5 in. long. Sew the extension, right sides together, to the sleeve that's too short (if the crease didn't press out completely, use the crease line as the stitching line to hide it). Open and press the seam, and on the outside of the sleeve, topstitch ⅛ in. on both sides of the seam. Resew the sleeve seam, and hem the sleeve to the length needed.

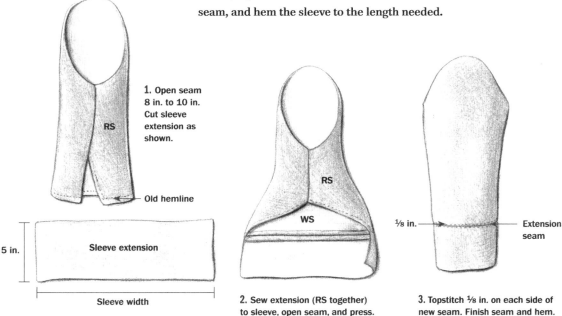

1. Open seam 8 in. to 10 in. Cut sleeve extension as shown.

RS

Old hemline

5 in.

Sleeve extension

Sleeve width

RS

WS

2. Sew extension (RS together) to sleeve, open seam, and press.

⅛ in.

Extension seam

3. Topstitch ⅛ in. on each side of new seam. Finish seam and hem.

Repair Ripped Skirt Vents

—PAT LOWTHER,
AUGUSTA, ME

If the top of a kick pleat becomes torn or stressed on a skirt, repair it with Ultrasuede (try any nonraveling fabric or glove-weight leather). First remake the bottom of the seam where the top of the pleat has torn. To end the seam in solid, unfrayed fabric, try shortening the pleat by ½ in. Place a piece of Ultrasuede over the seam allowances. Pin-baste through the center of the seam and the middle of the Ultrasuede. Stitch the Ultrasuede to the seam allowances as close as possible to the seamline. Restitch the topstitching on the right side of the skirt through the seam allowances and Ultrasuede, securing the three layers.

HOW TO REPAIR A TURTLENECK

My husband had several long-sleeved knit turtleneck shirts that wore out along the cuff and neck edges, but the rest of the turtlenecks' sleeves and bodies were in good shape. I cut off the cuffs and neck ribbing and removed the original stitching. Then, I cut the neck ribbing fabric in half along the full length of its crease, removing the threadbare edge, and cut one of these long strips in half to make two shorter pieces. That gave me one long ribbing strip to fold over and stitch onto the neck, creating a mock turtleneck, and two shorter strips that were the perfect length for new cuffs. I followed standard methods to apply the neck and cuff ribbing. The shirts look new again, and I've saved money by not having to buy new ones. Hopefully, I won't have to replace the shirts for at least another year.

—PEGGY D. YACKEL, PLYMOUTH, MN

TOOLS AND MATERIALS

Rescue Waistband Elastic

—SHERRI BROWN, BROOKSVILLE, FL

Here's a quick fix for a waistband that wears out before the garment: Baste cord elastic through the worn elastic. Gather the cord up to the waist's original size, keeping it relaxed and not stretched. Tie it off, and the garment is rejuvenated.

Fix a Warped Cutting Mat

—LYNETTE DAMIAN, MILFORD, MI

Here's a way to successfully flatten a warped cutting mat. Lay the mat on the floor and cover it with a thin terry-cloth towel. With your iron set to the hottest steam setting, press over the towel until the mat becomes warm and flexible. Then flip the mat over and press the same section. Next, leaving the towel in place, stack three of the thickest books and catalogs available on top of the softened area; put the books in a bag so they don't get damaged. Leave the books until the mat cools completely, then progress around the mat, ironing one section at a time. It takes some patience, and some spots may need to be ironed more than once, but it will save the mat.

Repair a Cracked Ruler
—CRYSTAL GRIFFITHS,
BAKER, FL

Many of the rulers and templates used in sewing are made of acrylic. They're pretty sturdy, but they can get cracked or broken. If one breaks, try fixing it with the glue sold for affixing acrylic nails. Hold the pieces together for a couple of minutes until they are well bonded.

Remove Water-Soluble Marks
—JEAN K. SPERO,
COLUMBUS, OH

Looking for a great way to get rid of marks made by water-soluble markers without a major wash? Try using a pen-shaped, sponge-tipped envelope moistener to apply water to the mark and a paper towel to absorb the extra moisture. Touching the sponge to the mark and giving it a gentle squeeze releases just enough water to do the trick.

FIXING ZIPPERS

Get a New Slider
—SUSAN POTTAGE,
COLORADO SPRINGS, CO

Often when a zipper isn't working properly, all that's needed is to replace the slider. Instead of buying an expensive zipper-repair kit, buy a zipper in the appropriate color, remove the slider, and replace the old one. If the new slider doesn't fix the problem, you already have a new zipper to replace the original zipper.

Replace a Zipper Pull
—PAULA RAK,
WRANGELL, AK

If the zipper on an outerwear jacket front doesn't work properly but appears to be intact, the zipper pull might be the problem. Luckily, it's easier to replace the pull than the zipper; it takes only minutes, and costs pennies.

For zippers with teeth, start at the zipper's top and force the pull off between two teeth. Then, likewise force the new pull on. Coil-type zippers take more time. Open the seam holding the zipper's top in place, slide off the old pull, slide on a new one, then close the seam. If there's a zipper stop at top, remove it with wire snippers. Zip the old pull off the end of the zipper, zip the new one on, and install a new stop with pliers. (Pulls and stops are available by mail from outerwear sewing suppliers.) If zipper teeth are missing, replace the zipper.

HOW TO REPAIR A ZIPPER

I often replace zippers on which the slider has jumped the tracks. But recently, reluctant to replace a decorative zipper in a slot pocket because it matched the decorative zipper on the other side, I decided to repair the zipper itself. I removed the bottom stop with small pliers and slid the slider off the end. Then I was able to reengage the zipper by feeding both sides together back into the slider. I replaced the stop, using a hammer to bend the prongs, and greased the coil with Thread Heaven®. The zipper works great! If your broken zipper has one spot that's not working but is otherwise perfect, you may be able to bypass the problem area by resetting the stop above it. Or if the zipper is unsalvageable, try placing the decorative pull on the slider of a new zipper so it still matches its mate. I guess this is how zipper-by-the-yard works. But I suspect many people are unaware of how easy this is to do.

—DAWN JARDINE, RED HOOK, NY

MAKING THE BEST OF MISTAKES

Fix an Embroidery Error
—K. M. LAING, CAPITOLA, CA

To get rid of stitch mistakes, thread a blunt needle with scrap yarn. This keeps it from getting lost. Insert the needle under the wrong stitches, keeping it flat against the right side of the embroidered fabric. Push the mistake loops to the center of the needle. Holding scissors flat on the work with the open blades under the trapped needle, shear off the mistake, freeing the needle. Now it's possible to tweeze the cut loops away from the underside. Use the needle to undo a few stitches on each side of the error and anchor the tails. Then rework the bald spot.

Remove Embroidery Stitches
—JUDY LEE, SHREVEPORT, LA

Here's a quick, easy way to remove embroidery stitches. Run a long glass-head straight pin through the embroidery thread about 20 stitches at a time. Then using a single-edged razor blade, carefully cut the thread along the top of the pin. All of the embroidery will be removed without any damage in minimal time, with little effort and great results.

Remove Buttonhole
Stitching

—JULIETTE CURTISS,
LEEMING, WESTERN AUSTRALIA

Nobody likes to remove stitches, and taking out faulty buttonholes must be the worst type of stitch ripping possible, but here's a quick and easy way to do it. Use a seam ripper to cut through all the buttonhole stitches on the back of the garment, including the bar tacks at the top and bottom. On the front of the garment, use the seam ripper to gently pull out the top thread (it should pull off in one piece), taking most of the bottom stitches with it. If the top thread doesn't pull off completely, make sure all the stitches under the buttonhole have been cut. After the top thread is removed, use tweezers or masking tape to pull any remaining stitches.

HOW TO TURN A BLOOPER INTO A DESIGN ELEMENT

Sometimes disasters have a good ending. I planned to make a patterned silk charmeuse, long-sleeve blouse during some personal sewing time. I had carefully redrafted the cuff for my thin wrists and changed the sleeve pleating. The sleeve vent was sewn using standard men's tailoring techniques. The vents were inserted without a hitch, until I tried on the blouse.

I have been sewing for nearly 60 years, but I had accidentally reversed the sleeves, and the cuff closure and vent sat prominently on the top of each wrist. The charmeuse sleeve would have been impossible to rip out, as it was sewn and topstitched along the armscye. The fabric was simply too delicate to do that much ripping. I walked away from the sewing machine hoping I would come up with a solution.

About two hours later I had the "aha" moment. Since the left and right sides of each sleeve cap were essentially identical, I decided to leave the armscyes stitched, but cut off the bottom half of both sleeves. I switched the left and right sleeve bottoms, which put the plackets where they belonged. Then I reattached them and embellished the seams with a decorative stitch. I chose the area slightly below the elbow as the most appropriate location for my cut. The sleeves were a tad long, so I knew the added narrow seam allowance would have little impact on the fit of the repaired sleeves. I pressed the seam allowances open after reattaching each sleeve bottom and used a decorative herringbone stitch over the seamline, catching the seam allowances as I stitched. The stitch held each side of the seam allowance in place, broke up the strong horizontal line, and disguised the seam as if it had been planned as a decorative embellishment.

If I have learned anything in my years of sewing, it is to be flexible and think outside the box. I'm thrilled with my blouse and its unexpected adornment.

—PEGGY CODNER, WHITINSVILLE, MA

PART EIGHT

GO GREEN!

reduce, reuse, repurpose

RECYCLING CLOTHING

REIMAGINING APPAREL

Turtleneck Sweater as Dickey
—SUZAN L. WIENER, SPRING HILL, FL

Try making a dickey from a cast-off turtleneck sweater that has set-in or drop-shoulder sleeves. Remove the sleeves, then shape the body in a graceful curve and hem the raw edges.

Shirt as Bodysuit
—NANNETTE KONSTANT, FLOURTOWN, PA

Here's a trick for converting any shirt into a bodysuit. Take out the hem of the shirt, and sew it to a pair of underpants. Then cut horizontally through the crotch, reinforce the cut edges with ¾-in. cotton twill tape, and add three snaps (hook-and-loop tape is a good alternative to snaps). The result is a bodysuit that fits perfectly.

Footies as Footless Pajamas
—KATY DILL, JACKSONVILLE, FL

Here's an easy way to keep wearing footed pajamas when they're in great shape—but have become outgrown at the foot. Cut off the feet at the ankle seam and use ribbed knit fabric to add a 3-in. cuff in a matching or contrasting color. Measure the leg opening after it's trimmed and simply cut a rectangle for each leg 7 in. wide and as long as the leg opening. For a more snug fit around the ankle, reduce the leg opening measurement by ½ in. Fold each rectangle in half matching the short sides, right sides together, and stitch along the edge using a ½-in. seam allowance. Fold the tube in half lengthwise, wrong sides together, and pin the long raw edges to the cut pajama leg, matching the leg inseam with the ribbed fabric seam. Stretch the ribbed knit, and pin it evenly around the ankle. Stitch around the entire ankle. You can add a longer cuff to the sleeves as well.

Large-Size Garments as T-Shirts
—LUISA ROJAS, WASHINGTON, DC

If you can't find the fabric you want to use to make T-shirts or other tops in fabric stores, recycle fabric from large-size garments found in department store bargain basements, designer outlets, or even secondhand stores at markdown prices. Detach the sleeves, then cut front and back pattern pieces aligned with the finished hem of the garment. Stitch the front and back together, add a collar, and reattach the sleeves. The result is a professional-looking garment with professionally finished hems.

Worn Socks as Seam Roll

—MARY MCGUIRE,
HOUSTON, TX

Take a pair of long woolen socks and halve each sock by pulling the top edge down until the top is even with the toe. Push one folded sock inside the other, and presto!—a seam roll that works as well as those specially made for pressing. When finished, simply return the socks to the sock drawer.

Necktie as Trim

—BETTY DORFAN,
HOUSTON, TX

Silk neckties can help create an elegant finishing touch for necklines and armholes and, already cut on the bias, make great bias trim. Check closets for good-looking ties that are no longer worn (or try thrift shops or outlet stores). Select a tie that works well with the project's fashion fabric, remove all the stitches, open it up, and cut strips from the bias fabric. Stretch and sew it onto the neckline or armholes for a nice look that's easy to accomplish.

Convert Seams to Darts to Maximize Fabric

—YELENA YANTOVSKAYA BARTH,
CENTERVILLE, VA

When there isn't enough fabric for a jacket, vest, or blouse, try eliminating some of the seam allowances by converting the seams into darts. The more seams that you convert (including princess seams), the more economic the fabric use—just pay attention to the grain. It's also possible to convert button or snap closures into zipper closures to conserve fabric, which saves 2 in. to 3 in. of fabric on each side. This technique can be adapted for skirts and dresses, too.

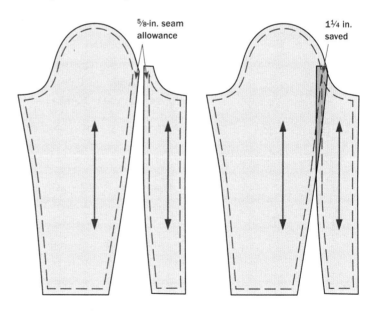

Fray Denim for a Retro Look

—ARLENE ZAJICEK,
MEMPHIS, TN

For a really fluffy faux chenille stitch-and-slash jacket or vest, try recycling denim. Though denim can be heavy, it naturally frays beautifully. And because it's a twill weave, one layer of denim will fray into two shades of thread, so it will look like two layers of fabric. Using recycled denim jeans for this technique also offers a lot of bulky flat-fell seams to work with as design elements. A retro-sixties vest can be made using the legs from two pairs of faded blue jeans. The flat-fell seams placed strategically down the vest's fronts and back and channel stitching between them makes for a cool design.

Make Over Used Clothing

—JANE SWANSON,
LUCCA, ITALY

Take advantage of resale/consignment stores for getting material you need to create pretty new clothes. You can even salvage used men's shirts. It doesn't matter if they have frayed collars and cuffs, just as long as they have good, solid bodies. At home, cut off the collars, cuffs, and sleeves, open the side seam, and then press everything flat. Lay out a basic blouse pattern over the remaining shirt in such a way as to take full advantage of existing button plackets and even hems. Consider making a scoop-neck blouse, adapting the scoop as necessary to make the best use of the original button placement. Cut short sleeves from the original sleeves, and you'll have enough fabric left to cut a new self-facing for the neckline. Depending on how the original shirt fits, perhaps keep the original shoulders and yoke and just adapt the neck, arms, and length.

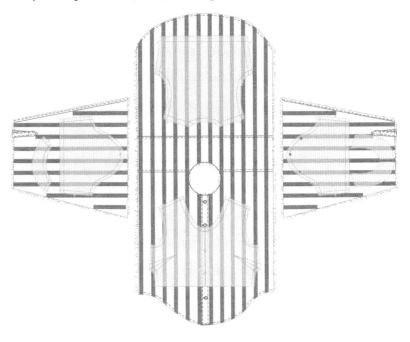

Use Belts as Tote-Bag Handles

—SANDI SCHMITT, GASTON, OR

I recently came across some fabulous embroidered corduroy and knew it would be perfect for a large tote. I added a wide "waistband" to the top front of the bag and a separate band on the top back so I could insert two sturdy belts to form the handles—much like I would insert elastic in a garment's waistband. I eased one belt through the front channel and a second belt through the back channel and buckled them to finish. I can change the length of the handles by adjusting the buckles, and I can change the handles if I want to give the bag a different look—or if I want to wear one of the belts! Besides being pleased with the tote, I'm thrilled that my belts have found a new purpose.

Recycle a Bridal Gown

—JANE VANBEMDEN, OVIEDO, FL

I was married in 1957 in a long gown of embroidered tulle, which my three sisters also wore at their weddings. While cleaning closets this year, I found the dress. My sisters and I decided to recycle it. Here are a few projects made from our gown that will perhaps inspire others to honor special garments:

- a stole, appliquéd with embroidered floral sprays and the neckline bound with the gown's satin
- an evening purse, embellished with silk-ribbon embroidery
- a ring bearer's pillow and wedding hankies
- a bridal doll's gown
- a framed shadow box containing small items from the wedding
- a christening dress featuring the gown's appliqués for my future great-grandchild

Search Thrift-Store Clothing for Pretty Notions

—SUSAN KLEMENT, TUCSON, AZ

Thrift shops are a good potential source of inexpensive, hard-to-find fabrics, trims, and buttons. Mother-of-pearl buttons can be found on garments that cost less than what the buttons alone might cost in retail stores. Remove the buttons and sew on replacements, then donate the clothes back to the shop. Other hard-to-find notions to look for in thrift shops include necktie interfacings, bra underwires, fur trims, interesting belt buckles, and more.

REWORKING GARMENT PIECES

Reuse an Old Belt Buckle

—MARY RINO, BOUNTIFUL, UT

I recently made a dress that had a matching narrow belt. When I went to the fabric store to purchase a belt buckle, I couldn't find the size I needed. As a last resort, I took a measuring tape to the thrift store and found an old belt that had a buckle that looked like new and was the size I needed. The cost was $1. I cut the buckle off the old belt and sewed it to my fabric belt. The buckle was distinctive and unique and was the perfect complement to my dress—and so much cheaper than ordering from an online specialty store!

HOW TO DISSECT RECYCLED CLOTHES FOR STUDYING CONSTRUCTION

I enjoy making one-of-a-kind clothes that look like they were purchased from a high-end boutique. In order to understand ready-to-wear more, I go to resale shops and look for interesting styles. Most of the time the fabric is outdated or looks worn out, but I try on the garment for fit. If all is well, I purchase it, take it home, and take it apart. By doing this, I learn so much about pattern pieces, linings, interfacings, and construction. It's an education from the design shops of ready-to-wear. I take notes, iron each piece to the back of freezer paper, and use it later as a pattern. I photograph the garment before disassembling it, give it a name, and label my pattern pieces. I tape the photo to the main pattern piece for future reference.

—MICHELLE CURETON, HACKETT, AZ

REPURPOSING FABRIC

RECYCLING TEXTILES

Cloth Napkins for Sewing Projects
—MRS. CAROL GILFILLAN, BETHEL PARK, PA

Charming old linen napkins may not be in regular use for meals, but they can be used in sewing projects. Sometimes found secondhand at yard sales or estate sales, they often come in sets and have lovely edge treatments or embroidery. Sew five or six napkins together to create a table runner, curtain tie-back, pillowcase trim, or scarf. Sew several sets together to use as a border trim on a linen tablecloth. Matched handkerchiefs make for nice smaller trims, but it's also fun to mix and match assorted delicate hankies.

Worn Bedsheets as Muslin
—NANCY L. GOULD, HOCKWOLD, THETFORD, UNITED KINGDOM

A tip for the frugal-minded: Use worn bedsheets for muslin. Even new ones are pretty cheap (if purchased at an outlet store on sale) as compared to the cost of regular muslin.

Craft-Panel Fabric for "Couture" Clothing
—CATHIE MARANO, LAKE HOPATCONG, NJ

Ever seen printed craft panels in stores? These are the odd fabrics (waiting to be sewn and stuffed into dolls, bears, and pillows) with their cutting lines, seam allowances, and sewing instructions printed smack in the middle of the yardage. It's possible to have lots of fun making "fashion" garments out of these fabrics. To make a shirt or vest from craft-panel fabric, buy three panels per garment, which allows sufficient room to work with and showcase the choicest whimsical details. Consider featuring the craft panel's finished sketch (there's always a sketch) on a front pocket, center the panel's decorative title bar ("Fedora the Sewing Doll" or "The Wild West Pillow") across the back, or run the printed instruction panel right up a shirt sleeve. After deciding how to show off this unusual fabric, cut and sew the garment the same way you would any fabric.

Leftover Muslin for Embroidery Samples
—KAREN WOLFF, LAGUNA HILLS, CA

Cut unused muslin into pieces suitable for various size hoops for stitching out machine-embroidery samples. Other fabrics or interfacings may be suitable for this use as well. When tracing patterns onto tissue, use the large pieces of excess tissue in layers for stabilizing machine-embroidery samples—it's similar to the commercial tissue-weight stabilizers that are sold just for this purpose.

Old Flannel Sheets as Support

—SHERI RAND, EUGENE, OR

Used flannel sheets provide just the right backing for many sewing projects. One sheet can supply various weights from the worn center section to the thicker edges. Use them for underlining, interfacing, and lightweight, soft backing for heirloom sewing. When the flannel interfacings or underlinings are pressed to the fashion fabric, they hold together long enough to be sewn in place. As an underlining, the flannel lends a soft, supple drape to the garment. Of course, any printed design on the sheet will show through a lightweight fabric, so be sure to test fabrics first.

REUSING SCRAPS AND SWATCHES

Fabric Samples for Garment Details

—DOROTHY CARDI, COMMACK, NY

Check local fabric stores for outdated sample books they may be giving away or will consider selling inexpensively instead of throwing away. Even though the swatches will be small—sometimes only 18 in. square or smaller—there's enough to add intriguing detail on many projects, like a decorative striped piping edge on a vest or an appliquéd floral motif on a wool beret.

Make Bags Out of Fabric Scraps

—JULIETTE KIMES, DRIPPING SPRINGS, TX

I save leftover scraps of fine fabrics, like silk, to make small zippered bags as gifts. I quilt the fabric to thin polyester batting, but while digging through my stash, I came across some wool/cashmere coating fabric that was the perfect thickness and had more body than the batting. I quilted as usual with a walking foot and lined the bag with silk charmeuse, so no one ever sees the "insides." After I've used up the coating in my stash, I plan to visit the local charity shop to find a used coat for my next batch of bags.

Leftover Fabric as Gift Wrap

—JEAN SMILING COYOTE, CHICAGO, IL

If sewing and quiltmaking were as common as they should be, nearly every gift (including the big ones) could be wrapped in a piece of fabric usable by the recipient in some project, instead of paper, which gets discarded.

Reuse Stuffed-Toy Scraps

—BETTY SAGER, SPRING VALLEY, CA

When making a stuffed toy, sew scraps of the material being used for the outside, and for any costume being made, inside the toy along with the stuffing. Future repairs will be easier with the appropriate materials right at hand.

Leftover Fusibles as Zipper Seam Allowances or Stay Tape
—KEITH FARMER, NEWARK, NJ

Thin strips of fusible can be used to stabilize zipper seam allowances. Also, a thin strip, cut on the nonstretch grain, can substitute for stay tape around the waist of a bias-cut skirt. Small curved pieces can be used to reinforce fabric areas that must be clipped, such as sleeve curves, princess lines, and portions of seam allowances that fray.

Selvage as Trim
—LOIS JUNGAS, CANTON, CT

Here's a clever trim that always perfectly matches any garment, is often unusual and quite beautiful in its own right, and is right there on the edge of the fashion fabric: the selvage! Here's how to use it. Fuse a strip of ⅝-in. double-faced fusible tape to a length of selvage. Using the edge of the tape as a guide, carefully cut the selvage off the fabric (a rotary cutter makes easy work of this). Next, fuse this trim to the garment (along the edge of a lapel, at a cuff, and so on). Zigzag-stitch along each edge of the trim to hold it in place permanently and ravel-proof the trim at the same time.

Elastic as Hair Bands or Accessories
—SAMANTHA BURGIN, WARWICK, RI

Use leftover fabric and elastic from the waistband of pants or skirts to make hair bands as cute accessories to match the clothing. If fabric allows, try to make fabric-covered scrunchies or adorable matching purses embellished with extra buttons or trims. They're always a huge hit.

Interfacing Scraps for Buttons and Zippers
—CAROL WALLACE, WALDORF, MD

When using fusible interfacing in making a garment, does it seem like there's always a pile of small, oddly shaped leftovers that are too big to throw out and too small to save for other large projects? Save them anyway—they're the perfect size for interfacing bound buttonholes or zippers and for sewing on buttons.

Interfacing Scraps as Stabilizer
—LOUISE WONNOCOTT, ROCKHAMPTON, QUEENSLAND, AUSTRALIA

Save fusible interfacing scraps and cut them into strips with a rotary cutter and cutting board, about ½ in. to ¾ in. wide. Keep them handy for stabilizing areas, such as shoulder or neckline seams. Saving these scraps will mean there's always a ready supply of fusible strips that are just the right size.

REUSING
MATERIALS

REPURPOSING THREAD, SEWING TOOLS & NOTIONS

Use Leather Needles on Other Heavy Fabrics
—LAUREN KRAMAR, EAST LANSING, MI

Leather needles pierce heavy fabrics well, even over thick seams, and can solve the problem with skipped stitches when sewing through heavy fabrics. This needle is equally effective for sewing through hook-and-loop tapes.

Donate Thread Clippings for Bird Nests
—LILY YOST, DES MOINES, IA

Want to help feathered friends with their homemaking? Drop thread clippings into a disposable mesh bag—the kind that some bulk vegetables come in. Then, in the spring, move the bag to a tree where the birds can pluck out bits of thread and clippings to use as building materials for their nests.

Use the Entire Bobbin
—FRECIA KELLY, RENTON, WA

I make a lot of freestanding lace on my embroidery machine. The lace almost always takes more than one bobbin of matching embroidery thread, but usually not two. This leaves me with many bobbins partially filled with embroidery thread, and as a frugal person, I want to use every bit of the thread. I tried using it as the bobbin thread for other embroidery stitch-outs, but the bobbin thread used in lace making is stiffer than the bobbin thread used in regular embroidery. I discovered, however, that I could place the bobbin on my thread stand and use it in place of a regular thread spool. Although it's a stiffer thread, it works beautifully as the top thread in regular embroidery stitch-outs.

Sewing-Machine Needle for Turning Small Tubes
—BEVERLY WHITE, LONGMONT, CO

If a small tube needs to be turned without using a set of turners, enlist the aid of a sewing-machine needle. Pass a double strand of thread through the eye of the machine needle (needles with large eyes are easier to thread). Then pass the doubled thread—now four strands—through a hand needle, and sew the thread to one end of the tube. Remove the hand needle, tie a knot at one end of the double thread, and feed the blunt end of the machine needle through the tube, pulling the thread and tube easily to the right side.

HOW TO KEEP TRACK OF SLIGHTLY USED NEEDLES

I do lots of alterations at my business and frequently change machine needles, but I don't want to throw any out after just one short use. So I simply put them back into the original clear plastic slide case and mark it with a china marker. (This pencil has a soft waxy "lead" and is wrapped in a paper spiral, which is pulled away with a string. You can buy china markers at an office- or art-supply store.) I place one mark on the case on top of each specific needle every time I use it. After a needle has several marks (sort of like a thermometer rising), I discard it.

—DAWN JARDINE, RED HOOK, NY

Sleeve Board as
Ham Holder

—JULIETTE KIMES,
DRIPPING SPRINGS, TX

It isn't necessary to have a base to use a tailor's ham. To ease a jacket sleeve, lay a sleeve board on its side and set the tailor's ham between the two sides. It will hold the ham securely enough to free up both hands for pressing, without having an additional notion to store.

Crochet Hook for
Removing Basting

—NORMA TAYLOR,
ORO VALLEY, AZ

A size I/9 crochet hook works great to remove basting threads, to remove ease-stitching threads, and to open seams. Use the rounded point to push under the stitch and the hook to remove the thread. This eliminates the danger of snagging the fabric's threads or accidentally cutting a hole in the fabric, both of which can happen with a seam ripper.

RECYCLING HEALTH AND BEAUTY ITEMS

Dental-Floss Threaders
as Weaving Tools

—BETH KARJALA,
MUNICE, IN

Dental-floss threaders, found in packets of 20 in drugstores, are useful weaving tools. Use them to thread embellishments such as beads, buttons, and shells. They are also handy to hemstitch or overcast loosely woven fabric.

Nail Polish for Brightening Buttons

—KRISTINE KADLEC, LOS ANGELES, CA

How can you fix discolored buttons? You can try cleaning them by soaking them in bleach overnight, but that will only serve to whiten some of them. Try instead painting the yellowed buttons with nail polish. The nail polish will hide the discoloration nicely and also create some very interesting results. Just note: While the buttons may fare well in the washer, the heat of the dryer can affect the nail polish and cause the buttons to stick to the fabric. For that reason, it's recommended that you air-dry garments sewn with this type of button.

Nail Polish to Make Machine Needles More Visible

—EVELYN BLAKE, ROANOKE, VA

When threading your sewing machine needle front to back, make the needle eye more visible and easier to thread by painting the presser foot directly behind the needle with white nail polish or correction fluid such as Liquid Paper®. The white background will reflect light.

Baby Nail Clipper for Trimming Short Threads

—MANAL KHALIFE, WINDSOR, ONTARIO, CANADA

To get rid of short threads sticking out on projects, try using a baby nail clipper (which is much smaller than a standard nail clipper) to cut the stray threads right up against the fabric. The result will be a nice finished garment without the worry of accidentally snipping the fabric with large scissors.

TWO WAYS TO CUT THREAD USING A FLOSS CONTAINER

On an Airplane

Time spent traveling on airplanes is ideal for us dedicated/addicted needle artists, especially with early arrivals and two-hour waits. Here's a fine substitute for scissors if you're nervous about bringing yours onboard: the tiny blade on your dental-floss container. It cuts threads smoothly and evenly, including the thick embroidery flosses I use for my personal addiction, sashiko handwork. Dental-floss containers come in all sizes and shapes, so it's easy to find one to fit perfectly in your project bag. And you don't need to empty the floss container to use it as a thread cutter.

—NANCY SHRIBER, SPRINGFIELD, VA

On a Sewing Machine

Remove the metal floss cutter from an empty dental-floss package and tape it to the tiny metal cutter on your sewing machine to cut thread. It works great.

—DEBRA ARCH, KEWANEE, IL

Antiperspirant Bottle as Pressing Tool

—LOUISE KAMMER, PLEASANT HILL, CA

Here's a good tool for pressing seams. Take an empty roller-type antiperspirant bottle, wash it well, and fill it with water. The roller nicely moistens only the small areas that need pressing and simplifies the task significantly.

Hair Clips as Straight Pins

—C. EMMA BROWN, ST. JOHN'S, NEWFOUNDLAND, CANADA

Here are some helpful alternatives to straight pins: bobby pins and bend-to-close hair clips. These hold two or more layers of fabric together securely, are easy to apply and remove, and spare tender fingertips.

Hair Elastics as Closures

—MARGARET JAMES, KINGSWOOD, SOUTH AUSTRALIA

Hair elastics make excellent button loops, and they're perfect for many other embellishments as well. The elastics give a professional finish to a garment, and they come in an extraordinary array of colors, patterns, and finishes. They can be sandwiched between the facing and the fashion fabric or added as an embellishment on the outside. Use them intact, or cut them for smaller loops. Loop one over a button on one side of a jacket opening, and twist, stitch, or knot it in the middle. Then loop it over a button on the other side so that the elastic holds the two sides together without having to bother with buttonholes. Use thicker elastics to fasten handbags and totes using a plain, chunky, or oddly shaped button to complete the closure. Be careful not to sew over the crimped or glued section of the elastic. Also, thinner elastics are much easier to work with when stitching by machine, so keep a variety of elastics on hand to incorporate in your sewing projects.

Hair Elastics for Securing Bobbin Threads

—BETTY BOLDEN, BOLTON, CT

If tail threads on bobbins often unwind and become tangled, secure them with small ponytail elastics, which can be picked up inexpensively at a dollar store. They come in a variety of colors in an extremely stretchy knit, so they snug up against all bobbins—the ones that are full as well as the ones that are almost empty. Choose a band that most closely matches the thread color, which will help when searching for a particular bobbin color.

Earring Backings for Securing Smocking Gathers

—ROBERTA CROSBY, BURNABY, BRITISH COLUMBIA, CANADA

When arranging the gathers for smocking, wind the groups of gathered threads around a pin to hold them. Secure each pin in the fabric with a butterfly back from stud-type pierced earrings. Packages of butterflies (or the newer style of rubber-lined holders) are inexpensive and can be bought at many department-store costume-jewelry counters.

Makeup Brushes for Painting on Fray Blocker

—CINDI STOWELL,
ROUND ROCK, TX

Try using inexpensive makeup brushes to paint on fray blocker. When carefully painted on your fabric, fray blocker doesn't run, and it's easy to control exactly where it's intended to go. Use just a small amount on the edge of the fabric, and the fabric will be less likely to discolor. The makeup brushes can be washed in warm water and used again and again.

Home-Permanent Wraps as Stabilizers

—CANDICE E. WILLIAMS,
ROCKY MOUNT, NC

Some people use scraps of fabric or stabilizer to start sewing fabric that tends to catch in the throat plate at the beginning and end of seams, but that means tediously cutting lots of little squares of fabric or stabilizer. Instead, try using the jumbo end wraps typically used for wet-setting hair from any beauty-supply store. Jumbo end wraps are precut into $2\frac{1}{2}$-in. by 4-in. rectangles, and are packaged in an easy-to-use dispenser. To support the whole seam, just butt the wraps together. End wraps are designed to be used wet, so they are strong, but they tear away without distorting the fabric or stitches.

Nail Salon Push-Bottle Aids for Moisturizing Fingertips

—DOROTHY R. MARTIN,
ROCKVILLE, MD

Sewers often moisten their fingertips to grip fabric, turn a fine hem, or line up cut edges. Why not try the type of handy "push" bottle a manicurist uses to dispense polish remover to moisten fingers? A push on the bottle's top releases a small amount of liquid—a perfect solution! Available at beauty-supply stores, the bottle top twists to lock for safety, conveniently flips up when in use, and provides moisture in a simple, yet sanitary manner.

RETHINKING HOUSEHOLD GOODS

Pliers for Saving Beads

—DOROTHY SMALL,
POUGHKEEPSIE, NY

When sewing seams in beaded fabrics, try using small needle-nose pliers to crush or shatter the beads within the seam allowances instead of clipping the threads. Wear safety glasses, hold the fabric over a wastepaper basket, and take care not to catch the fabric in the pliers. Because you're not cutting the threads that hold the beads on, the remainder of the beads won't fall off, and the threads under the crushed beads will still be there in case it becomes necessary to go back and fill in the beaded pattern. Always save a few intact beads for replacements.

Pliers as Seam Rippers

—RUTH GALPIN,
SOUTHPORT, CT

Needle-nose pliers are useful for ripping seams. Pull out the threads from side to side with the pliers, while holding the cloth near the seamline so it isn't distorted. This eliminates the bits of cut thread that have to be picked out if you just rip the seam. But if you prefer ripping, the pliers are great for getting those tiny bits!

Pliers for Hemming Jeans

—SUE JOHNSON,
VALDOSTA, GA

Hemming jeans can be a challenge even if a Dritz® Jean-a-ma-jig™ (or a Hump Jumper) is used to adjust the presser foot so it accommodates the height of the seam thickness. Try first flattening those extremely thick seams with a pair of Rubbermaid ⅜-in.-wide grooved pliers. Turn up the hem, flatten the seams with the pliers, and proceed as usual, using the Jean-a-ma-jig to adjust your presser foot. The pliers make all the difference in the world to help ease the needle through all of the thicknesses!

Empty Film Canisters as Weights

—NANCY SHRIBER,
SPRINGFIELD, VA

Here's a terrific use for those plastic 35-mm film containers that may still be lying around from your film camera days. Fill the empty canisters with sand. With the cap secured, they make great pattern-cutting weights. When extra-heavy weights are called for, try filling the canisters with fishing sinkers, and pattern and fabric will stay put.

Dryer Sheets as Press Cloths

—BARBARA NACHTIGALL,
ROSLINDALE, MA

Recycle nonwoven fabric-softener sheets such as Bounce® or Snuggle® as press cloths for small craft projects. These nearly transparent sheets can withstand the high heat settings needed to set fabric paint or double-fuse materials such as Wonder-Under. Place one or two sheets under and over designs before pressing. The softener sheets protect both the iron and ironing surface; should any glitter or iridescent particles from the paint or fusible materials adhere to the sheets, just throw the sheets away.

Baking Parchment as Press Cloth

—NANCY MACAULAY,
MICANOPY, FL

Parchment paper, typically used to line cookie sheets, makes a great press cloth. It's especially useful when pressing fusibles, appliqués, and the like. It's inexpensive, highly heatproof, and transparent, and any excess adhesive stays on the parchment paper. It's impenetrable, however, so it's not good when a task requires steam.

Plastic Tablecloth as Waterproof Lining

—EDITH FRANKEL, HANNAWA FALLS, NY

Do you need waterproof fabric to line a cosmetic bag or slipper soles? Try a flannel-backed plastic tablecloth. These tablecloths come in various patterns and colors, including neutral tones. They are inexpensive, easy to sew through, and contain enough yardage for several small projects.

Plastic Grocery Bags for Smoother Sewing

—BETTY BOLDEN, BOLTON, CT

Here's a simple solution for taming fabrics that are difficult to sew, such as batting, bulky or loose-weave fabrics, faux fur, or Velcro. If they don't glide smoothly over the machine plate or get stuck in the machine foot while sewing, use a plastic grocery or other store bag to help. Cut the bag to make it one layer; if you have a lot of seams to sew, cut the bag into strips about 2 in. to 3 in. wide. Place the plastic on top of or beneath the fabric and sew normally, stitching through the plastic. The plastic helps the fabric slide smoothly as the stitches are made, and a simple tug easily removes the plastic after the seam is complete.

Contact Paper for Preventing Beads from Rolling

—JEAN FENGLER, SHEBOYGAN, WI

It's difficult to prevent individual beads from rolling away, especially when working with large quantities for a project. Here's a terrific solution that prevents the beads from wandering, while allowing them to be easily selected and removed for use. Line a tray with contact paper (sticky side up) or Sulky Sticky+™ self-adhesive tear-away stabilizer. The beads do not slide at all, yet they can be removed easily one at a time. This also prevents accidental bead spills.

Paper for Threading Needles

—MURIEL WAITS, MT. ORAB, OH

Here's an easy way to thread a needle: Cut a thin strip of paper about 1 in. long and only as wide as the needle's eye. Fold it in half, slip the fold through the needle's eye, and then insert the thread into the fold. Pull the paper strip through the eye, and the needle is threaded.

Rubber Bands for Gripping Needles

—ELIZABETH SHELTON, CEDAR RAPIDS, IA

For hand sewing, a useful device for pulling the needle through thick fabric is a rubber band. Fold the band over the needle and grip on top of it. It will turn a difficult task into an easy one without any special tools.

Spice Jars for Needle Disposal

—SUSAN INFANTE, LISLE, IL

An empty 4-in.-high spice jar (with the shaker top still attached) presents a good way to safely dispose of used, bent, or broken needles and pins. The holes in the shaker top are large enough to easily add pins and needles, but small enough to keep them in the jar should it get knocked over. As a side benefit, the jar can add a subtle fragrant aroma to your sewing room.

Bubble Wand as Cone Thread Adapter

—PATRICIA "T. C." FERRITO, ANGOLA, NY

Make an instant cone thread adapter for a regular sewing machine. To route thread to feed smoothly from cone to machine, tape the wand from a jar of kid's soap bubbles to the thread spool holder so that it projects horizontally to the back. Now put the thread cone behind the machine on a piece of foam to keep it stable, and guide the thread through the wand. The thread will feed snarl-free to the tension disk.

Rubber Band Stitching Guide

—NANCY CAMPERUD, WATSONVILLE, CA

Put a rubber band around the free arm on your sewing machine to make a stitching guide for deep hems or curtain-rod pocket allowances. Since magnetic seam guides are not recommended for electronic machines, a rubber band is ideal. It won't slip, doesn't mess up the machine, and costs nothing.

Post-it Note Sewing Guide

—GINETTA HUNTRESS, NOVATO, CA

For wide topstitching, try rigging up a temporary sewing guide using a single Post-it Note (up to 3 in. wide). Cut off the gummed portion on the back and place this sticky piece on the machine's strike plate where glue is needed. Guide the edge of the fabric along the Post-it paper line while sewing for a consistently even row of stitching. This guide can be easily repositioned or removed: Just lift it off.

Silicone Pot Holder as a Hem Guide

—CHRISTIANNE DEHART, CHICO, CA

If metal hem guides become too hot when pressing a hem, use a strip of silicone pot holder instead. Cut the pot holder into hem guides of different sizes. The iron won't harm these templates, and they always remain cool to the touch.

Eyeglass Case as Rotary Cutter Carrier

—SHELLY SCORESBY, HANSEN, ID

Here's a way to prevent accidental rotary cuts to the fingers. When transporting a rotary cutter, make it a habit to place the cutter in an eyeglass case. Many economical case styles are available at optical shops, with closures featuring hook-and-loop tape, snaps, or sliding mechanisms.

Hangers as Dress Form

—LENA M. WARDELL,
BURLINGTON, ONTARIO, CANADA

Enjoy the many benefits of having a dress form with a few simple tricks for hanging your garments-in-progress.

Skirts that need to hang overnight before being hemmed can be suspended from a plain coat hanger on which four or five large spring clips have been placed. These will support the entire waistband more uniformly and more flexibly than a regular pant or skirt hanger.

Flared or circular skirts do better hung in the round; an inflated beach ball inserted inside will do the trick, hung by a piece of string from the blow-up valve.

Consider installing a ceiling hook, of the sort used to hang plants, in a convenient area. Hang from it a length of twill tape, knotted at intervals into loops. This will make it possible to hang garments at various heights from the loops and turn them easily to work on or view.

Eyeglass Repair Tools as Sewing Aids

—CYNTHIA DUNN, NEDERLAND, CO

One of the handiest tools to have for a sewing machine is an eyeglass repair kit. The screwdriver is perfect for bobbin setting, and the magnifying glass is great for seeing needle sizes.

Jewelry Box for Storing Notions

—LINDA COBB,
LEXINGTON, KY

Consider using a jewelry box to stock sewing supplies. The smaller compartments are ideal for feet and other small items, and the larger compartments are perfect for other notions. It can hold everything needed and can be kept close to your sewing machine for easy access. It's also portable. To take your notions box on the go, place some polyester batting on each shelf of the box to keep things from shifting. Close the box, and put a Velcro "carry handle" around it. This will keep notions in place as well as organized and easy to find while in transit.

Empty Aluminum-Foil Boxes for Storing Stabilizer

—PATRICIA JINKENS, OXFORD, OH

Repurpose empty aluminum-foil boxes (wax paper and plastic-wrap boxes also work) by using them to store stabilizer. Roll stabilizer around the empty cardboard tube and store it in the box. The rolls stay neat and clean, and the container acts as a third hand because it holds the roll when "dispensing" the needed amount of stabilizer.

Wrapping Paper for Making Patterns

—ALISON HYDE,
ST. LOUIS, MO

Consider using leftover Christmas wrapping paper for pattern making. Sometimes this paper will be printed on the back side with a grid pattern—perfect for aligning bias edges, marking fabric grainlines, and drawing straight lines. To stock up, make it a point to shop for wrapping paper the week after Christmas when the paper is greatly reduced in price.

HOW TO STORE BOBBINS IN SPIRAL BINDING

When my husband cleaned out some of his paperwork, a notebook with a plastic, spiral-looking closure was unearthed. When I examined the closure more closely, I realized it was not a spiral at all; each section of the binding was a separate plastic tab that curled back around itself to hold the pages in place. The binding was easy to remove from the paperwork, and I found that I could use it to store my bobbins and hold their loose threads in place. Simply insert a filled bobbin into one of the tabs, and then wrap the binding around the bobbin. Turn the bobbin to secure the thread tail. There are up to 25 tabs on each binder strip, and they're easy to store with my notions. I can leave the tabs connected and store my bobbins in one strip, or I can use scissors to cut the tabs apart.

—ELIZABETH MARTIN, BRANTFORD, ONTARIO, CANADA

Oven Mitt as a Pressing Aid
—SHARON CIRRITO, NIAGARA FALLS, NY

Here's a great tool for pressing open seams in hard-to-reach areas: an oven mitt. Start with a mitt covered with silvered fabric if possible, for the greatest protection from steam. Cover the mitt with three or four layers of cotton terry toweling, cut and sewn in the shape of the original mitt, each mitt layer about ¼ in. larger than the previous layer. After the last mitt layer has been put on, your hand should just be able to squeeze into the mitt, and you should still be able to manipulate your hand so you can support almost any small, awkward shape while you press with the other hand. The thumb is particularly handy, especially for children's clothes and when you want to use just the tip or edge of the iron on delicate fabrics. If your mitt has silver on one side only, be sure to mark that side of the new mitt so you can use that side when you're steam pressing.

Wooden Rulers and Handles as Pressing Aids
—VAL BARBARO, PITTSFIELD, MA

When pressing small areas—seam allowances on collars, inside turned tubes, and so forth—standard pressing tools aren't very helpful. Here are some nifty solutions. Wooden rulers and the handles of wooden spoons work well for tubes: Slide one inside the tube, finger-press the seam allowances open, and press with the iron. For collars, try a pencil. Look for unpainted ones, and use them either unsharpened or sharpened with the graphite point snapped off.

Plastic Lid as an Embroidery Hoop

—SUSAN KNIGHT, BAY VILLAGE, OH

Improvise a small embroidery hoop from a plastic container with a snap lid, such as a frozen whipped-topping bowl. Using ordinary kitchen shears, cut off the bowl ¼ in. or ½ in. below the lip. Cut out the inner circle on the lid. Snap the two together and an instant hoop is made.

Plastic Lids as Circle Guides

—JUDITH LONG, CRANBERRY TOWNSHIP, PA

Sewing a perfect circle is tricky, but here's a way to simplify the process. Find a shallow, round object that is about ½ in. smaller in diameter than the size of the circle to be sewn. Depending on size, the top of a vitamin bottle often fits the bill, as do flat-topped lids or mint tins. Next, cut a circular piece of fine sandpaper to fit the tin and attach it with double-sided tape. Position the fabric with the needle on the circumference where sewing will begin. Lower the presser foot, hold the tin (sandpaper side down) against the outer edge of the presser foot, and start sewing. The tin acts as a template, and the sandpaper holds the tin to the fabric, causing it to rotate as you sew a nice circle. Sew slowly and stop with the needle down and lift the presser foot to ease the fabric if it begins to pucker.

Plastic Lids and Caps as Mini Buttons

—LOUISE HAMPTON, LITHONIA, GA, WITH EVELYN BLAKE, ROANOKE, VA

Because small buttons are difficult to find in some colors, why not make your own? Using recycled plastic containers, such as margarine tubs and toothpaste tubes, take a hole punch and cut out "chads." Then pierce with a strong needle to create a button. Craft stores carry punches in various sizes—a couple of sets of homemade punched "buttons" pays for the tool.

Soda-Can Tab as a Bodkin

—SUSAN DELANEY MECH, PLANO, TX

To thread elastic into a casing, reach for a soda can—not for a drink, but for the metal tab on top. Snap the tab off the can and get a perfect two-hole handle for attaching the elastic and pulling it through. The smaller hole, which was attached to the can, is slightly jagged, so it's the better one to attach to the elastic to. Slip the elastic through the hole and tack it near the end. The larger hole is an ideal size and thickness for pulling through gathers.

Toe Separator for Transporting Bobbins

—GAYLE WOLFE, VICTORIA, BRITISH COLUMBIA, CANADA

The spongy toe separator that's typically used during a pedicure is a great way to easily transport bobbins. It's lightweight and keeps the thread ends in place so they don't unwind, yet it doesn't take up much space, so it's easy to carry around.

KITCHEN MATS AS SEWING TOOLS

Cutting Mats

Pliable kitchen cutting mats are useful when preparing food but can also be extremely helpful when sewing. They work great when using a rotary cutter, especially if there isn't space (or the need for) a larger cutting area. Consider cutting them with a mat knife to make a smaller size.

—SHEILA CLARK, ORINDA, CA

Surface Protectors

Flexible plastic kitchen cutting mats make terrific sewing tools, which can be used in several ways: to create a smooth, hard surface for pinning or hand hemming projects on an ironing board (which increases your workspace); to protect furniture from damage that might result from pinning or basting fabric on it; and to protect laps and make a firm surface when hand-stitching projects.

—TIA ABELL, VANCOUVER, BRITISH COLUMBIA, CANADA

Door Stops for Preventing Neck Strain
—CAROLINE ZIMMERMANN, LANCASTER, CA

If you have neck pain when you sew for prolonged periods, you can buy specialized small, flat trays designed to place under the back of your sewing machine to tilt the machine forward, which will allow you to see better and to relieve neck and back strain. They are expensive, however. An inexpensive alternative is to use rubber door stops. They are available in different sizes at superstores and home stores. Put a couple of them under the back of your machine, one on the right and one on the left side. They tilt the machine forward, and make it easier to see without having to bend your head down too far.

Floral Net Sheaths as Spool Covers
—CHRISTINE HAMMILL, MANCHESTER, WA

Net sheaths used to transport flowers make great covers for thread spools. They work especially well with cone thread, but can be cut to fit any size spool. They prevent the thread from unwinding in storage and help keep the spools and cones clean.

Chip Clips for Attaching Fabric to Table
—STEPHANIE WHITE, SCHAUMBURG, IL

Use "chip clips" (the clips used to close potato chip bags) and large clothespins to clip fabric to the side of the table while working. The clips keep the fabric secure while cutting and can also be used to help lift the fabric that drapes over the table and clip it to the table.

Book Light for Threading Serger
—TINDY MACBAIN, ANN ARBOR, MI

Use a travel book light for help in threading a serger. It has a small but intense light that's easily directed, and can rest securely on a sewing table while stitching.

Oven Liner as Ironing Board Cover
—DEBRA ARCH, KEWANEE, IL

Keep a nonstick oven liner near your ironing board for use when you adhere fusible web to appliqué pieces or press fusible interfacing onto garment pattern pieces. Place the liner on top of your ironing board and under the item you are fusing. Any traces of fusible adhesive will rub off the nonstick surface, protecting your ironing board cover. The mat is heat resistant up to 500°F, so it's not affected by the iron's heat or steam, and it also does not crease, making a smooth pressing/fusing surface.

Shopping Bag Handles as Cording
—KARIN BUUS, ELLINGTON, CT

Here's an alternative for cording. Many shopping bags use cording for their handles. The bags' handles aren't very long, but they can do in a pinch, and save a trip to the fabric store.

Straws for Making Tiny Ties
—ELIZABETH SHELTON, CEDAR RAPIDS, IA

When making tiny fabric ties or straps, try using a plastic drinking straw to aid in turning the bias tube right side out. Sew the tube with right sides together and insert the straw into the tube. Push a long, metal turning hook through the straw to catch one end of the fabric and pull the fabric down through the straw. With hardly any effort, the strap or tie turns right side out as it comes out of the end of the straw.

Spoon for Ironing Small Puffed Sleeves
—MARINA RODRIGUEZ PALACIOS, BUENOS AIRES, ARGENTINA

Here's an easy, old-fashioned method for ironing very small puffed sleeves, such as those on baby dresses. Heat a metal ladle over a stove burner. Once the spoon is evenly heated, insert it into the sleeve and iron it from the inside by sliding the bowl of the spoon along the tiny sleeve. Add steam by placing a damp press cloth over the bowl and holding the cloth ends to the spoon's handle while pressing.

Shelf-Hanging Tool for Straight Lines
—THERESA FLYNN, LONGUEUIL, QUEBEC, CANADA

Try using a Laser Straight (found in building-supply stores) shelf-hanging tool to transfer or make straight lines on fabric. Every time you press the tool's button, a line of light appears that can be used to mark the placement of buttonholes and pockets, and ensure a pattern is accurately placed on the grainline.

Tissue Paper for Sewing Delicate Fabrics
—JUDITH FLATLEY,
STERLING, VA

Always have strips of tissue paper ready to use in the event there are delicate or sheer fabrics that need to be sewn. Using tissue prevents the feed dogs from "eating" sheer fabrics like chiffon, organza, and nylon knit, and it protects specialty or delicate fabrics from feed dog abrasion. Take a new pack of ordinary white gift-wrapping tissue and cut the entire stack into 2-in.-wide strips. By preparing tissue paper in bulk, it's easier to store than large sheets of tissue, and it's always ready when you need it.

When you sew lightweight fabrics, use a piece of tissue under and even on top of your seams as you stitch.

X-Acto Knives for Buttonholes
—GEORGE A. BOLTON,
NORWALK, CT

Here's a great alternative to using a wood block and chisel to cut buttonholes. X-Acto® knives sometimes come with assorted blades, including chisel blades. The chisel blades aren't slanted like the common X-Acto blades; rather, they are straight across, similar to a regular chisel. They are simple to use, thin, easy to replace, and less expensive than a wood block and chisel. As with all sharp blades, it's important to use extreme caution when using this method.

Wooden Dowel as Point Turner
—TERRY GRANT,
ASHLAND, OR

Here's a great make-it-yourself tool for turning points and opening seams. Starting with a ¼-in. hardwood dowel cut 14 in. long, use a craft knife to shape the end into a flattened oval. After being smoothed with fine sandpaper, the tip is wonderful for turning collar points, and the flattened edge presses the seam open for a crisp, sharp edge.

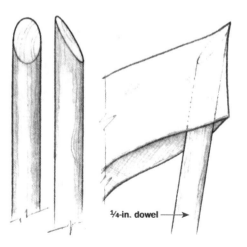

¼-in. dowel

Toilet Paper for a Tailor's Ham

—MYRA MAE MCFARLAND, FORT WAYNE, IN

Here's an inexpensive substitute for a tailor's ham, using one roll of toilet paper, one large safety pin, and an 18-in. square of prewashed muslin.

Center the roll on the fabric. Wrap the fabric snugly around the roll, and fasten it with the safety pin with the "seam allowance" on the outside. Place the seam allowances over the pin so that it's concealed. Tuck the loose ends of the fabric into the toilet paper tube, thus holding the seam allowance in place over the pin.

This improvised tool offers an advantage over a real ham because it rolls along with the fabric as you press, which is especially useful when shaping a sleeve cap or pressing a long hem.

Compass for Marking Seam Allowances

—BRANDY ANDERS, BIGGS, CA

To mark perfect seam allowances on commercial patterns that don't include them, use a drafting compass (the kind with a pencil on one side and a pointer on the other). Open the compass so that the distance between pencil point and compass point is ⅝ in. (or whatever the seam allowance happens to be), then tighten the adjustment screw to lock the measurement. If necessary, cover the pointed end with tape to soften the sharp point. Drag the pointer gently along all of your cutting lines, causing the pencil to mark seamlines on the pattern. It is fast, turns out true to the curves and straight lines, and there is no measuring involved. Just make sure to use a gentle hand.

REIMAGINING HARDWARE & SPECIALTY EQUIPMENT

Washers as Pattern Weights

—PATTY DUNN, CORPUS CHRISTI, TX

I like to use large, heavy washers (typically used in woodworking) as pattern weights, but first I wrap them in beautiful fabrics to make them look attractive and to coordinate with my sewing-room décor. I use pinking sheers to cut a fabric circle three to five times the diameter of the weight. I place one or more washers in the center of the circle, pull all the fabric edges to the top, and hand-gather them. I use a tiny rubber band (brightly colored rubber bands are especially nice) to hold the edges together, twist the rubber band until it is tight, and push it down close to the weight. The gathered fabric tops make the weights easy to move as I work, and they look lovely on my shelf when not in use.

Rubber Grippers for Grabbing
—HELEN THORKELSEN, BONNYLAKE, WA

Often it's a lot easier to push a needle into something than it is to pull it through. To get a good grip on the needle, try using a miniature version of the rubber disk grippers made to help loosen jar tops—a silver-dollar-size circle cut from the back of an old rubber glove. When hand sewing or quilting, wear the finger and thumb cut from the same old glove to prevent having to keep picking up the disk.

Hemostats for Shaping and Piping
—DALE JENSSEN, TAOS, NM

Surgeon's clamps (aka hemostats, which can be bought at a local surgical-supply store) have rounded ends, which make them excellent for shaping collar points. They're also handy to use with piping. After sewing piping in a seam, use hemostats to hold the piping to trim the cord out of the seam allowance. To protect the piping from the serrated jaws, put a scrap of fabric between them and the piping. Clamp the piping tightly $2\frac{1}{2}$ in. from the garment's edge to secure the cord, then slide the fabric back and trim $\frac{5}{8}$ in. from the cord. When you press the seam open, there's no cord to add bulk.

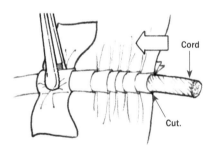

Cord

Cut.

Soldering Iron for Hemming
—CARRIE BLACK, HENDERSON, NV

Save lots of time on a sheer layered garment by hemming layers with a soldering iron. (Note: This works only on synthetics.)

Cut the sheer layer about 3 in. longer than necessary. Hem the skirt fabric as desired and then cut the sheer to the desired length with a knife blade on a light-duty soldering iron. Any "feathers" can be smoothed out with the barrel of the soldering iron, which is a little hotter than the knife blade. (Also try using a curling iron for last-minute repairs.) For a more permanent and more noticeable "hem," use a fine-point tip instead of the knife blade.

Experiment on fabric remnants to get used to handling the soldering iron and to find the best look.

Shop Vise to Flatten Jean Seams for Hemming

—JANE E. HILL, LONGMONT, CO

Using a hammer to flatten jean seams is not ideal, as the hammer pounding can damage a countertop or break a tile. Instead of using a hammer, try crushing those difficult thick seams with a shop vise.

Cover the two flat jaws of the vise with a scrap of fabric. The vise crushes the threads evenly and leaves no hammer-head marks—without the risk of harming fingers or the surface being worked on! Using the vise will allow maneuverability for any area of the garment between the vise jaw plates while holding the bulk of the garment under your arm. Turn the vise tightly to accommodate a double-rolled hem of many layers because the vise flattens even the thickest of hems. A jeans needle will penetrate these seams without difficulty, which makes hemming a snap.

Football Tee as a Ham Holder

—MARTHA ALLEN, HAMILTON, ONTARIO, CANADA, AND BARBARA WICKHAM, CARMICHAEL, CA

Use a football tee (the stand that football players use to hold the ball in place so that it can be kicked) to hold a tailor's ham in position for delicate ironing tasks such as steaming a sleeve cap. There are many varieties, ranging in price, so it's best to visit a local sporting-goods store and try them with your ham first.

HOW TO FIND SEWING TOOLS IN ART- AND OFFICE-SUPPLY STORES

On my latest forays to art- and office-supply stores, I found some useful marking and cleaning tools. While a lot of sewers know the virtues of drafting tape—it's inexpensive, can be removed from paper, and can be written on—they may not know about drafting dots. These adhesive dots, 7/8 in. diameter, come on a continuous tape in a box of 500. They pull out easily with a pull tab, are a little quicker to use than drafting tape, and are handy for marking anything small (notches, dots, directional arrows, etc.).

Another useful item I found is a handheld, battery-operated air blower. This blower makes a nice addition to your cleaning and dusting equipment. It isn't quite as powerful as canned air, but it won't harm the most delicate machine innards, doesn't blow cold air, and won't add cans to landfills.

—LONNIE PIPOSZAR, PITTSBURGH, PA

Hard Plastic Ball as a Stitching Aid

—MARIE REBELLO,
MISSISSAUGA, ONTARIO, CANADA

When stitching a small, difficult-to-reach area or darning a small hole, slide a hard plastic ball under the area to be stitched. It will provide a firm base to sew on, plus it makes it easier to stretch the fabric while stitching. These plastic balls are available in most dollar stores and some toy departments.

Hose Nozzle as a Thread Adapter

—CAROL MCNEAL,
NEW ORLEANS, LA

An inexpensive plastic hose nozzle (typically used in the garden) makes a fine cone thread adapter for a regular sewing machine that has a vertical thread spindle. Simply put the nozzle on the spindle and place the cone over it. It keeps the cone upright and steady while sewing.

Bolt Retriever for Picking Up Pins

—SHEILA CLARK,
ORINDA, CA

Here's an original tool for picking up loose pins: a telescoping magnetic bolt retriever. It's designed for retrieving nuts, bolts, and other small metal items that might fall into car engines during repair, and it also makes a great tool for finding a dropped needle or picking up spilled pins. And since it has a telescoping handle, there is no need to even bend over.

Postage-Stamp Moistener as a Sewing Dauber

—LINDA COBB, LEXINGTON, KY

A postage-stamp moistener makes a great sewing notion. Keep one to use as a "dauber" when pressing wool and another to "erase" the blue marks from water-soluble disappearing-ink markers. They are inexpensive and extremely useful.

Wood Vise for Installing Hardware

—CHRIS HAYNES,
SEATTLE, WA

Have trouble setting grommets, eyelets, and snaps? Perhaps pliers feel uncomfortable to squeeze, and hammering in the hardware is awkward and inaccurate? Try using a wood vise for installing hardware. Simply tape the hardware bits together so that they don't fall apart, place them in the vise, and gently squeeze the assembly together. If sharing a vise with a woodworker, cover the vise dogs (the blocks of steel that squeeze together) with some scrap fabric or plastic to protect your project from shop dirt.

Wallpaper Scissors for Cutting Fabric

—LINDA COBB, LEXINGTON, KY

Try using wallpaper scissors with long blades to cut out fabric. The weight and length of the blades make for easier, more comfortable cutting than with regular scissors. Purchase these shears at home-improvement stores for a reasonable price and sharpen them at home with a stone sharpener.

HOW TO MAKE COLOR-COORDINATED BONING

While making a fabric tote, I became frustrated in my attempt to stabilize the tote opening with boning due to the boning's natural curl. To straighten the boning, I soaked it in hot water, clamped it to a board, and waited for it to dry. Unfortunately, it didn't help one bit. A trip to my local home-improvement store yielded the solution. I can now make my own flexible boning for handbags and other projects using multipurpose cable ties and bias tape. The ties (also called duct fasteners) come in a variety of lengths and widths to fit any project. It's easy to use standard bias tape or quilt binding tape to encase them, which allows me to color-coordinate the project, alleviating any color show-through problems. But the most exciting result is that my totes no longer sag at the top (where they open) when I carry them.

—SALLY GELBAUGH, GEORGETOWN, TX

Wired Ribbon as Trim
—BRENDA BOUDREAU, HALIFAX, NOVA SCOTIA, CANADA

Use wired ribbon as trim for pillows and other sewing projects. To add ruffles to the edges of a rectangular pillow, cut a length of ribbon twice the pillow's perimeter and remove the wire from one ribbon edge to show on the outside of the pillow. Do not remove the wire from the ribbon edge that's inserted in the pillow. This wire makes gathering the ribbon easy. You simply slide the ribbon's fabric along the wire to gather it without having to use basting stitches, and the wire is hidden in the seam allowance when the pillow is complete. Or, if desired, the wire can be removed after the ruffle is stitched.

Use Paint to Create Matching Buttons
—F. WILLIAM VOETBERG, GRAND RAPIDS, MI

I scoured the Internet looking for loden-colored, leather-knot buttons, but I could only find them in natural, brown, black, and gray. So I ordered natural buttons and applied Fiebing's® Deglazer to remove the finish. Then I was able to obtain the desired result with acrylic craft paint, matte finish, and shoe polish. I applied the paint to the buttons, sprayed a protective matte finish over them, and then applied black shoe cream, which I buffed with a shoe-shine brush. The result is exactly what I had hoped for.

SEWING WITH VETERINARY TOOLS

Stitch Scissors

Over the years, I have used embroidery scissors, needlecraft scissors, razor blades (ouch!), and the faithful seam ripper to rip seams. But the best unpickers I currently own are the "stitch scissors" given to me by a veterinarian who also likes to quilt. The scissors are intended for removing sutures, but I find they are especially sharp and have a fine hooked point on one side that works to pick up that one thread that you need to cut. The blades are thin enough to get into small areas, yet are sharp enough to use like a razor blade. They are available at medical-supply stores, and are reasonably priced.

—ROBIN WARD, POULSBO, WA

Needle Holders

I used to use forceps in the sewing room, but after watching the veterinarians where I work use "needle holders," I asked them to order a pair for me. A "needle holder" is a pair of locking forceps with blunt tips and a small cutting edge. They are great for pulling needles through tough fabric and for cutting threads when you are finished. They are also really handy for turning collar corners and other tasks. Most veterinary-supply shops should carry them.

—MATTIE WELCH, ALNA, ME

Kaleidoscope for Choosing a Palette

—CAROLYN REHBAUM, ALTAMONTE SPRINGS, FL

Combining aesthetically pleasing fabric colors and prints for a quilt or color-blocked garment takes a special eye, and a child's kaleidoscope is a great tool to use for choosing harmonious colors and establishing a pleasing palette. Find a kaleidoscope in a toy store—they're often stocked in the children's party favor section. Arrange three or four different fabrics so they touch or overlap. (More than four can take away from your ability to really see the collection.) View the fabrics through the kaleidoscope by moving it slowly across your selections until the mirrors reflect all of the fabrics. Rotate the scope and observe the color combinations through the eyehole. Through the kaleidoscope, you can discern the dominant color(s), evaluate the contrast, and choose the ratio of one color to another. By adding and subtracting fabrics, a suitable balance between contrast, tone, color, and pattern will arise.

Chisel for Welting Corners

—MARY JANE McCLELLAND, DIAMOND BAR, CA

When making welt pockets, bound buttonholes, and anything else that requires clipping all the way into a stitched corner, it's often difficult to clip safely as far as needed with the tips of scissors. A better tool is a buttonhole chisel (which comes with its little companion block of wood), available at most notions counters and by mail from the major notions catalogs. Of course, the chisel is perfect for clean, precise openings in buttonholes, but the end of the chisel blade can also be easily positioned exactly at the corner needed to clip into. Push it through the fabric, and the clipping will be perfect. If the blade is too wide for the hole or clipping being made, just position the cutting area over the edge of the wooden block. The chisel will only cut as far as the block extends.

Use Clamps to Avoid Pin Pricks

—DAVID DOREN, MINNEAPOLIS, MN

Try using mini construction clamps for alterations. They work much like clothespins, but they have a tighter grip, and they are readily available at home-improvement and hardware stores. The clamps hold the fabric together tightly without any danger of pin pricks to either you or whomever you are fitting. They are metal with slightly tapered, rubberized tips that protect the fabric, and they come in a variety of sizes.

HOW TO FASHION A CLEVER FABRIC PRESS BOARD

My sewing space is limited, so I made a handy press board that I can easily store when not in use. I covered a fabric core—the cardboard that flat bolts of fabric are wrapped on—with an old bath towel (to prevent lint). Most fabric stores will give you the empty ones at no charge. I secured the towel with safety pins along the edges, making sure one edge was pin-free so that it could also be used for pressing. The safety pins allow me to remove the cover easily when it needs to be washed.

—NORA ROARK, FORTUNA, CA

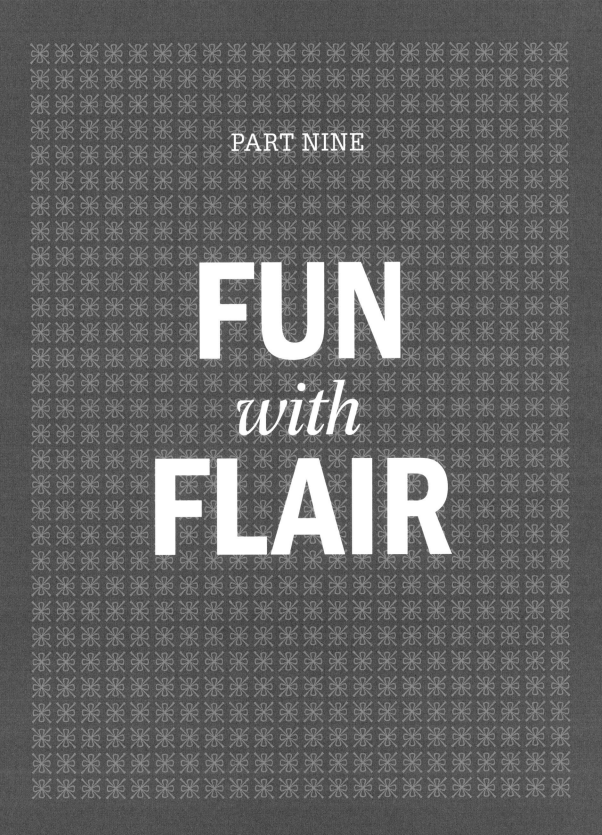

PART NINE

FUN
with
FLAIR

LINING & EMBROIDERY

LINING

Make a Detachable Lining
—DIANE STARKEY,
CEDAR RAPIDS, IA

To make a detachable lining for wool pants, start by finishing the pants as if they were unlined. To attach the lining, sew small, flat buttons on the waistband facing on each side of the zipper and a few inches apart along the rest of the facing. Then make and hem the lining, finish the waistband and zipper opening with a strip of bias self-fabric binding, and place corresponding buttonholes at the waist.

Line Patch Pockets
—JEANETTE BERNSTEIN,
CRANSTON, RI

Perfect patch pockets are easier to sew when they are lined. Lined pockets create fine finished edges and eliminate hand finishing. Cut the pocket in fashion fabric with a hem allowance and the lining in a lightweight fabric without a hem allowance. Interface the pocket fabric with a fusible. Press the hem allowance on the pocket to the right side. Place the lining on top of the pocket, right sides together, and align all edges. Stitch three sides of the pocket, leaving the top open. Trim seam allowances and turn the pocket right side out, folding the hem allowance over the lining; press. Hand-stitch the hem to the lining or topstitch the layers together.

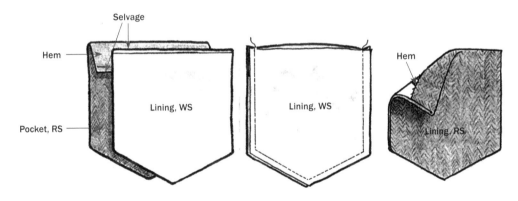

Line Handmade Camisoles
—DIANNE BOATE,
SAN FRANCISCO, CA

To line knit or crocheted cotton camisoles, cut out bias triangular pieces of voile or any light lining material in a skin tone, allow a 1/2-in. turn under, and slipstitch the pieces in place at the bust area. The little triangles will eliminate the need for a full lining or cumbersome underwear.

HOW TO LINE PATCH POCKETS

To make an easy and professional-looking patch pocket, line it. It will look good and feel nice to the touch.

Fold 1 in. or more of the top of the pocket to the wrong side to make a self-facing. To make the lining, cut a small piece of fabric, compatible with the garment fabric, to the shape of the folded pocket, leaving ¼ in. at the top for the seam allowance.

With right sides together, stitch the self-facing to the lining with a ¼-in. seam allowance. Press the seam open.

Next, fold the pocket at the foldline of the self-facing. Pin or baste the lining and pocket together about 1 in. from the raw edges.

Stitch around the pocket, leaving a 2-in. opening at the bottom. Turn the pocket right side out. Baste the lining and pocket, including the 2-in. opening. Press the pocket smooth, place it on the garment, and topstitch, securing the beginning and ending stitches.

The pocket and lining can sometimes be made of the same fabric, depending on the fabric weights. Cut the pocket and lining as one piece, fold it at the center, right sides together, and baste it. Close the pocket and attach it as described above.

—SHIRLEY KATES, NEWTOWN, CT

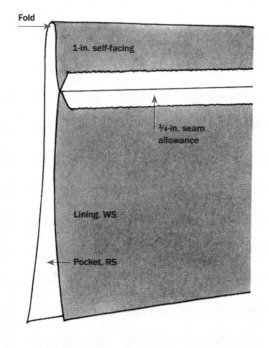

EMBROIDERY

Mirror-Image an Embroidery Chart
—ANN M. PROCHOWICZ, TREMPEALEAU, WI

I was working on a complicated counted cross-stitch project recently that had a double border and a floral wreath with many colors. The pattern included only half the border and wreath and instructed me to work the other half in reverse. When I tried transcribing the pattern onto graph paper, I found the process very tedious and frustrating. Since I needed a mirror image, I photocopied the pattern onto a sheet of tissue paper (it could also be traced). I could then read the pattern through the reversed tissue.

Use Embroidery to Guide Beadwork
—DEBRA HIRAKI, BURIEN, WA

To embellish a project with beads stitched in a pattern, use one of the decorative stitches built into your sewing machine to create the design. Stitch the design using monofilament thread, and then use the stitching lines to guide hand-stitched beads right on top of the machine stitching. It's easy to follow the thread design and produce a perfectly stitched beaded pattern.

Use Cross-Stitch Charts
—EMMY STORHOLM, HERON, MT

Try marking pattern graphs with alternating red and black lines at 20-count intervals both vertically and horizontally. Ignore the printed guidelines when they don't intersect in the center, and start marking at midpoint. Then run corresponding red and black threads through the evenweave fabric at the same 20-count intervals. These long basting threads are easy to remove when the graph is finished, before the backstitching begins.

BUTTONS, SNAPS & ZIPPERS

BUTTONS

Make Buttons from Unusual Materials

—ANN HENRY,
NORTH HIGHLANDS, CA

Ever considered making buttons from unusual materials, like deer antlers? Use a lapidary trim saw or a hacksaw (meant for cutting metal). A fine metal blade with 24 teeth to the inch makes a smooth cut. Sand the cut pieces, varnish them, and drill buttonholes. Black walnut shells can also be cut into slices and made into buttons.

Dye Buttons

—CATHERINE NEFF,
MUSCODA, WA

Can't find the colored buttons you want? Try dyeing white, porous plastic buttons in Tintex™ or Rit® dye (found in the supermarket). Since each button takes color differently, do two or three sets of buttons at once to have enough of the same shade. Stir the buttons in the dye bath and remove them when they are a shade darker than desired. Clean them thoroughly with soapy water and set the color by soaking them in white vinegar. The garment that uses these custom buttons should be washed in cool or lukewarm water to prevent the buttons from fading.

Create a Removable Button Band

—LUCILLE STUTSMAN,
LINCOLN, CA

It's easy to make a closure on a reversible jacket so the jacket can be buttoned right over left when it's worn either side out. Just make a removable button band. Place buttonholes down both sides of the jacket front. Sew a row of shank buttons on a 1-in.-wide lined fabric band the length of the buttonholes, plus 1½ in. Button the band through the buttonholes on the left side of the jacket. The buttons are now in place to be buttoned traditionally.

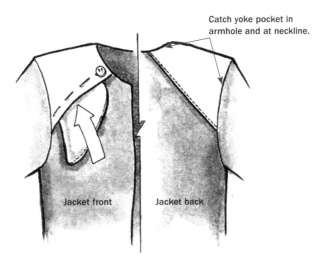

Catch yoke pocket in armhole and at neckline.

Jacket front   Jacket back

HOW TO MAKE FELT BUTTONS

Felt buttons are lightweight even when they're large; they can be used for decoration, as well as for closures. To make them, have felt, scissors, and two small bowls—one with very hot water and the other with ice water—ready.

Cut the felt into squares the approximate size desired for the buttons. Dunk a square of felt into the hot water, then into the ice water, and then into the hot water again. Between dunkings, squeeze the water out of the felted square and form it into a ball. Roll the ball between your palms with increasing pressure as it becomes round.

Set the balls aside to dry. One side may be slightly uneven; use it for stitching through the felt.

—HELEN VON AMMON, SAN FRANCISCO, CA

Sew in Extra Buttons

—PEG PENNELL, OMAHA, NE

Have you ever made a garment with several beautiful buttons, only to lose one? When you make a blouse or skirt, sew one or two extra buttons inside the garment at a seam near the hem, like they do in ready-to-wear. If a button gets lost, it's easy to snip one free and replace the lost one. For vests, jackets, coats, or pants, sew the extra buttons in an inconspicuous place, like inside a waistband or even a pocket.

Secure a Button with a Bead

—GAIL ABRAMS, CORDLANDT MANOR, NY

When the stitches securing a button must go through to the reverse side of a facing or placket, the stitches need to be perfect. Here's an elegant trick; it works on tailored, couture, or artsy garments, particularly vests, jackets, or tunics when the front is worn open. Sew a button in place as normal. For the last two passes of the needle, sew a small bead (about $1/16$ in. to $1/4$ in. in diameter) over the stitches on the inside of the garment. Match the bead to the fashion fabric or use a wildly different color as an accent.

Make Expandable Buttonholes

—LAVADA NORKO,
ELLICOTT CITY, MD

Interested in an easy way to create a comfortable, expandable closure for a waistband on a garment? Just use hidden elastic loops instead of buttonholes. Here's how: On the end of a completed waistband, sew one or two small buttons. Cut two pieces of ¼-in. elastic into 1½-in. lengths, and fold each in half to make a loop. Stitch the loop to the underside of the top band. This also works on cuffs and certain neckline styles.

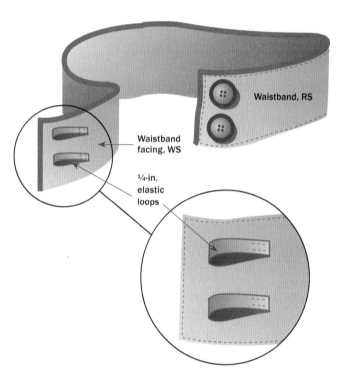

Waistband, RS

Waistband facing, WS

¼-in. elastic loops

Make a Looped Button Closure

—DONNA CHRISTOPHER,
DENVER, CO

To make an interesting button closure, start with a small standard buttonhole (about ⅜ in. long), one for each closure. Tie a 3-in. to 5-in. piece of decorative ribbon, rope, or thin bias tubing in a circle. Slip one end of the circle through the buttonhole, then slide it over the other end to form a loop, keeping the knot close to the buttonhole on the inside. The length of loop can be adjusted for the size of the button—even large or irregular buttons—and can be adapted to make a tight or loose closure.

Use Buttons as Handbag Closures

—NANCY MCKENZIE,
WAVERLEY, NOVA SCOTIA, CANADA

To make button handbag closures, you could make thread shanks, but they aren't particularly durable. To solve this problem, stack one or more plain, small (⅝ in. or smaller) buttons underneath the large button of choice. Line up the buttonholes and sew through all the buttons for a raised, shank-like button. To add even more whimsy, stack another smaller, colorful button on top.

Make Covered Buttons with No Show-Through

—ANDREA L. MOORE,
SPOKANE, WA

Covered buttons can look great, but not if the base-button material gleams through the fashion fabric. To prevent this without having to fiddle with two layers of covering material, simply fuse a circle of lightweight tricot fusible to the inside of the cover material. To reduce bulk, mark the interfacing piece by tracing around the button onto the interfacing, cutting out just enough to cover the top of the button. Center and fuse this piece on the inside of the fashion fabric cover, which should be big enough to wrap around the button and catch in the backing, following the directions that came with the button.

SNAPS

Make Buttons Out of Snaps

—V. HECKENTHALER, DORTMUND, GERMANY

To enjoy the convenience of snaps with the look of buttons, try combining the two on casual garments. Insert ring-style snaps, with the "female" side of the snap positioned on the front facing beneath the spots where buttonholes would normally go, and install the "male" side in place of buttons on the other front. Then, on the garment's right side, sew a button over each snap, directing the thread through the center of the female ring on the facing. If you use buttons that lie very flat against the fabric, the snaps virtually disappear.

Use Snaps to Help Hang Dresses

—CAROLYN BULLOCK,
CAPE CORAL, FL

Keep a dress with a wide neckline on a hanger, without having to wear pesky garment loops in your dress, by sewing the loops to snaps sewn into the dress. When the garment hangs, the garment loops ensure it stays on the hanger. When it's worn, simply unsnap the loops and put them aside for when it's time to rehang the garment.

ZIPPERS

Combine Zipper and Buttons
—JEAN LINTON, ADELL, WI

How can you have a row of half-ball shank buttons with fabric loops down the back of a dress requiring a back zipper? Here's a solution: Make 2-in. lengths of narrow tubing for the ½-in. buttons and baste the loops on the right side of the fabric, along the center-back seam of the right bodice back. Machine-stitch the seam closed using a basting stitch. Next, insert the lapped zipper, as recommended by pattern instructions, topstitching the overlap on the left-hand side. Open the seam, remove the basting, and sew the buttons in the center of the loops. With the zipper closed, the loops and buttons look convincing.

1. Baste loops to underlap.

Center back

2. Insert lap zipper. Sew buttons to right side.

Make Any Zipper Invisible
—DEE DUMONT, BAINBRIDGE ISLAND, WA

If an invisible zipper doesn't come in the color of choice, just paint the zipper pull (only the part that actually shows). Model paints, available in hobby stores, as well as cheap nail polish easily overcoat the original color. Some experimentation may need to be done to create a color to match the fabric. A pale pink over a pale blue makes a light lilac, deep green over black makes forest green, and blue over pink makes grape. Color the pull prior to installing the zipper in the garment. Cut a protective cover out of aluminum foil for the zipper and pull the tab through a small slit in the foil. Apply one layer of color at a time and allow it to dry before checking the match.

Use an Underlay to Create an Elegant Zipper
—PATRICIA BEECHER, HORSEHEADS, NY

When applying a zipper, do as the top designers do—add a zipper underlay. Protect lacy undergarments and oh-so-delicate skin by attaching grosgrain ribbon behind the zipper along one length of the seam allowance. Attach the lower edge below the end stop of the zipper. Use a tiny snap to hold the top edge of the ribbon over the zipper.

SHOULDER PADS & STRAPS

SHOULDER PADS

Prevent Shoulder-Pad Show-Through

—ELISHEVA BUSH,
JERUSALEM, ISRAEL

Shoulder pads can be real eyesores if their outlines show through light-colored clothing. Cover them with flesh-colored lining matched to your skin tone, and the outlines disappear. Cut a square with a bias length slightly longer than the outer edge of the pad. Lay the pad on the cloth with the long edge on the bias, and fold the cloth over the pad. Pin it in place, zigzag or overcast along the curved edge of the pad, and trim off the excess fabric.

Use Velcro for Shoulder Pads

—RUTH NEITZEL,
MERRILLVILLE, IN

Handknitted sweaters can improve in appearance with the use of shoulder pads. Foam pads ("no straps or fasteners needed") do the trick nicely. To make sure they don't shift or fall out, secure them to the shoulders with small pieces of hook-and-loop tape (like Velcro). Fasten the hook portion of the tape to the center of the pads with fabric glue and sew pieces of the loop tape to corresponding places in the sweaters. Sweaters will fold and store more easily without permanent pads, and one set of pads can be used for all your sweaters.

Create Shoulder-Pad Pockets for Reversible Jackets

—MELISSA ENNIS,
ARLINGTON, VA

Add shoulder pads to reversible jackets by creating a shoulder-yoke pocket with a button closure to hold the pads, which solves the problem and also adds a nice design detail. Cut a yoke pocket in one piece that fits the shoulder of the jacket with enough ease to hold the shoulder pad being used. A pattern can easily be made by joining the front and back jacket pattern pieces to create one. Topstitch the back edge of the pocket to the jacket back. Sew buttonholes to the yoke pocket edge and flat, shankless buttons to the jacket. When the jacket is reversed, switch the shoulder pads.

STRAPS

Make Quick Spaghetti Straps

—JEAN GOOD,
EAST EARL, PA

Here's an easy way to make spaghetti straps and trims out of tricot knits. Cut a strip of tricot ¾ in. wide on the lengthwise grain of the fabric. Pull the strip taut (raw edges do not fray) until it rolls into a cord. Then run the cord through a sewing machine, set on a wide zigzag stitch. It's possible to span the roll with the stitch, adding a decorative accent if the thread is a different color. Or match the thread for a more subtle effect.

Keep Bra Straps from Falling

—ANN CRISTALDI,
ATKINSON, NH

Here's an easy fix for falling bra/slip straps: Sew the "female" side of a small snap to the inside shoulder seam of blouses. Attach a thread chain long enough to go around the bra/slip strap. At the loose end of the chain, attach the "male" side of the snap.

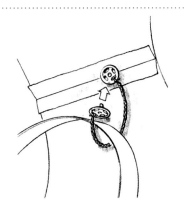

Thread Cording to Keep Straps in Place

—FAY M. DORR,
WEST PALM BEACH, FL

To keep shoulder straps from falling, insert elastic cording into the straps. Use a long double-eyed needle, or a tapestry needle with a large eye and a blunt end, to thread the cording through the strap. Even on a chiffon dress, the smooth eye end of the needle won't snag the fabric. Leave about 2 in. of the elastic extending beyond both ends of the strap. Sew one end of each strap to the dress permanently, securing the elastic. When fitting, pull the loose ends of the elastic until they're comfortably snug, then pin them in place and sew them to the garment. This method works equally well as an alteration for a ready-made dress or as a fitting fix for one being made from scratch.

TRIMS

IMPROVING LOOK AND FIT

Use Godets to Spruce Up a Skirt

—BETH WEHRMAN,
MAXWELL, IA

Transform the mood of a plain skirt by inserting a removable godet into the garment's slit. As occasions vary, so can the godets used. To make the pattern, measure the length of the slit in the skirt and add 2 in. for finishing and hemming the edges. Use that dimension to cut a bias triangle of contrasting fabric, then finish the sides and hem the bottom. Sew corresponding snaps to the inner edges of the skirt's slit and the godet edges. Sew the first snap at the top of the slit and enough snaps on each side, between the top and hem, to prevent gaps. Make godets to coordinate with different tops to change your look in a snap.

Keep Waistbands Closed with Hook and Eye

—SHIRLEY KATES,
NEWTOWN, CT

It's possible to comfortably custom-fit a waistband with hooks and eyes or bar fasteners. But to ensure stability and keep the short waistband extension from showing, sew another hook and eye or fastener near the top corner of the extension, in the opposite direction of the other fasteners. This provides a stable counterpull.

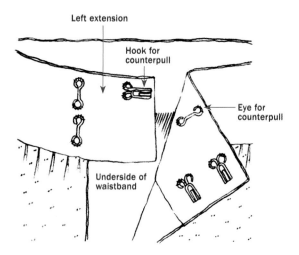

Make Pretty Belt Loops

—SHELLY SCORESBY,
HANSEN, ID

For perfectly color-matched belt loops that won't sag or droop, zigzag over a short length of elastic thread using a narrow satin stitch and construction thread. Repeat, if necessary, to cover the elastic, then tack it to the garment.

Create a Removable Jacket Placket

—MRS. M. D. WEEKS,
FORT LAUDERDALE, FL

Jackets and vests with placket fronts can only be worn closed unless the placket is detachable. To sew one that is removable, copy the placket shape off the pattern and add a seam allowance to the center front. Using clear plastic snaps, sew the snap sockets to the interfacing on the wrong side of the jacket and the snap prongs to the placket overlap. The jacket can be worn closed without a blouse and open without the placket with a shell.

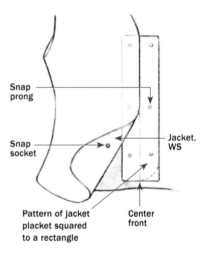

Snap prong

Snap socket

Jacket, WS

Pattern of jacket placket squared to a rectangle

Center front

Keep a Shirttail Tucked In

—BEVERLY C. STONE,
ENCINITAS, CA

Try using stretch adhesive to keep a shirttail tucked in. Apply a "wave" of glue to the waistband of pants or a skirt and let it dry overnight. Try Jones Tones 400-Plexi Glue™ (available at craft- and sewing-supply stores), which loves the washer and the dryer, and can be ironed or dry-cleaned.

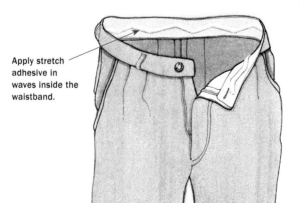

Apply stretch adhesive in waves inside the waistband.

HOW TO CREATE BUTTON EMBELLISHMENT

For some eye-catching embellishment, why not dip into that assortment of buttons you've collected over the years? Here are some ideas for button trimming your creations or spicing up ready-made garments:

• Sew buttons along the scooped or V neck of a T-shirt.

• Trim the placket and cuffs of a blouse or cardigan.

• Accentuate the hem of a skirt with buttons combined with embroidery.

• Sew a single row of buttons in a splash of colors and sizes for a random, funky look.

—GAIL MANNING, NORTH YORK, ONTARIO, CANADA

ADDING TAGS AND LABELS

Make Artistic Labels

—DIANE ERICSON,
CARMEL VALLEY, CA

Add an elegant touch to your garments with custom labels. All that's needed is a stencil and a good pen. Start with a 6-in. length of ribbon, 1 in. to 2 in. wide, either satin or grosgrain. Create an original stencil or use a commercial one (but customize it a bit). Apply the stenciled image to one end of the ribbon, allowing 1 in. to turn under at each end. Then artfully sign your name or your label's name in metallic ink (this works best on smooth ribbon). Try opaque paint markers in copper, silver, and gold made by Pigma® Micron® (check art-supply shops or catalogs).

Design Your Own Label

—DOROTHY JOHNSON,
TOPEKA, KS

Make your own garment labels using small scraps of Ultrasuede. You will need three oval layers of suede 1½ in. wide by 3½ in. long. Hold the three pieces together with a small spot of glue. With a washable marker, trace the design of your initials onto the top layer of the suede. Follow the marker with machine stitching through all three layers using a short stitch length and contrasting thread. Pull the thread ends to the back and tie them off. Cut away the first and second layers of suede. It is best to practice on scraps to perfect your design and scissoring techniques. Attach your label to the garment lining with a feather stitch.

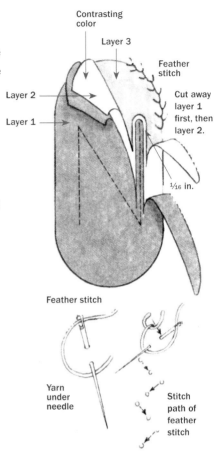

Create a Care Tag

—DOLLY NORMAN,
LONG ISLAND, NY

Why not insert a small square of nonwoven interfacing into the center back of garments created where a ready-to-wear tag would be? Write the pattern company's name, pattern number, fabric fiber content, and washing instructions on the tag using a fine waterproof marker. This will keep clothes safe while doing the laundry and help you find the back of a garment at a glance, just as with ready-to-wear.

Create Name Tags for School Clothes

—JULIE CHISHOLM,
GUELPH, ONTARIO, CANADA

Iron-on name tags are a must for sweaters and outerwear for school-age children and seniors in communal care. There are companies that process custom orders, but if you only need a dozen or so, why not use the computer? Inkjet-printable, iron-on cotton is available in sheets that are designed for adding things like photographs to tote bags and sweatshirts, but it can just as easily be used for name tags in any size or font and cut to the appropriate size. The fusible backing makes them easy to attach and prevents the fabric from fraying.

EMBELLISHING

Finish Cording and Tassels

—LUCILLE REWICK, MILLINGTON, NJ

Here's an old Girl Scout lashing method that can be used to bind covered cording and to finish off tassels on wool scarves. Make a 1-in.-long loop of the lashing thread along the end of the cording with the loop extending slightly beyond the cording's end. Now wrap the thread from the spool around both loop and cording, wrapping toward the loop end. When you've made as many wraps as you desire, cut the thread from the spool and slip the end through the loop. Finally, pull on the end of the thread opposite the loop to pull both loop and thread end under the wraps. Then trim the ends.

Create Pretty Fleece Edging

—NANCY JUNG, SAN FRANCISCO, CA

Fleece garments usually need an edging with some give, so here's how to vary the finish on the edges from the standard ribbing or bias binding: Using a serger and woolly, texturized nylon thread, overlock-stitch a length of ¼-in.-wide clear elastic (available by mail order or from most fabric retailers) around vest armholes and the lower edges of sleeves and jackets. You can use a three-thread serger and thread the elastic through the slot on the regular foot, but an elastic applicator foot does the same job. Pull the elastic slightly while serging to give a hint of shape to the fabric and provide adequate stretch. For a great look, the stitch length should be very short (0.5 mm to 1 mm), similar to a satin stitch, making the stitch as wide as possible.

Sew Better Fringe

—DEB SHARPEE, DEFOREST, WI

When making fringe on woven fabric, cross outside warp thread, and tie with next group of threads.

Crossed threads lock in place.

Twist and/or knot this group.

How to make fringed edges stronger and neater? When selecting warp threads for tying or twisting into fringe, cross the outside warp threads in each group and combine them with the neighboring group. The textile edges will become more even, since, if the threads are not crossed, they'll pull into a group, giving the edge a series of V shapes. Crossing the threads is no more time-consuming, and gives a good-looking, stable edge.

HOW TO MAKE EASY THREE-STEP TASSELS

1. Buy two matching skeins of embroidery floss, remove the labels, and cut 12-in. and 24-in. pieces.

2. Knot together the ends of the 24-in. piece to make a loop, then double the loop, slide it over the floss skeins, and fold the floss in half over the knot. Tie a slip knot in the loop and tighten it down around the skeins.

3. Fold the 12-in. floss in half and knot it securely ½ in. below the top of the tassel to make the neck. Let the ends blend into the tassel; trim as needed. You can make the tassel fatter or thinner by using more or less floss.

—MARY ANNE HIRSCHFELD, ST. MARYS, OH

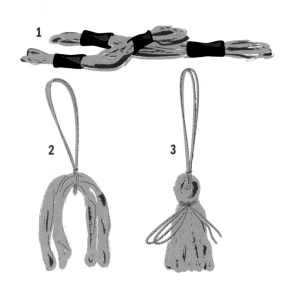

Apply Cupped Sequins

—BILL JONES,
SAN FRANCISCO, CA

Here's a great trick for applying cupped sequins. First, lay the fabric on a surface protected with a plastic dry-cleaning bag (any polyethylene plastic bag or sheet works) and pin the fabric to the bag. Next, scatter the sequins on a paper plate to make it easy to see the cupped side, which should always be up. Apply small dots of Sobo® glue to the fabric, in a dozen places you want sequins. Next, apply a small amount of glue to a pencil tip, making it tacky, and then touch it to a sequin, lifting it and carrying it to a dot of glue on your fabric. Press the sequin lightly so a bit of the glue oozes up through the hole and "rivets" it to the fabric. Then pick up another sequin and repeat the process. Clean the glue off the pencil tip when needed, and let the sequins dry before moving the fabric. (Start at first by applying six glue dots so the glue doesn't dry before all the sequins are placed.) Sobo glue works better than other glues that dry too fast or are brittle, which makes the sequins pop off. For an extra-perfect close-up finish, put a tiny dot of Tulip® craft paint (glitter or pearl varieties work best) on each sequin to cover the hole after the sequins are applied. This makes it look beaded.

HOW TO MAKE THREAD EYES

In fine dressmaking, thread eyes are usually used where fasteners might show. You can make thread eyes (or belt loops) by finger-crocheting or doing the buttonhole stitch over several threads. To finger-crochet a simple chain stitch: Use a double thread about 20 in. long (for a 1½ in. chain) with a knot at the end. Make a tiny stitch to secure the thread. Make another stitch, ending with the needle on the right side of the garment, and leave about a 3-in. loop (a).

Transfer the needle to your left hand (if you're right-handed). Hold the needle and garment firmly. With your other hand, catch the long end of the thread and pull it through the loop to form a second loop (b). Pull the thread until the first loop is tight (c).

Continue until the chain is long enough to suit your purpose. Then bring the needle through the last loop and pull it tight to lock the stitch (d). Put the needle through the garment where needed, making a few small stitches to fasten the chain securely.

—SHIRLEY KATES, NEWTOWN, CT

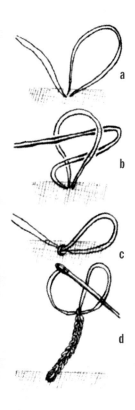

Add Piping with a Decorative Stitch

—BETH WEHRMAN, MAXWELL, IA

Adding piping is a great way to accent the lines of a garment, but it can have extra visual punch if you apply a decorative stitch to the bias fabric before insertion. Once you've selected a stitch and thread combination, stitch it down the center of the piping fabric and then insert the piping as you typically would. The stitch pattern becomes a decorative touch along the edge of the piping. Sew it down the middle—or slightly to one side for a totally different look.

Make Couched Cord Look Like Piping

—SUSAN HEIDENTHAL, PENN RUN, PA

I love the look of piping on fashions and home décor. When I was creating a new duvet cover for my bedroom, I wanted to insert piping into the seams that join the center panel with the side panels. I knew it would be difficult to match the fabric's large print if I sewed the piping into the seam the traditional way. Instead, I pressed under a seam allowance on each side panel, creating a finished fold, and laid them right side up onto the right side of the duvet seamline, matching the print. I attached the side panels by edgestitching through all layers. To make my "piping," I laid satin cording along the seamline on the right side and used matching embroidery thread to attach the cording, sewing with a zigzag stitch exactly as wide as the cording. The cording fell nicely into the groove created by the seam. The result was beautiful and easy.

Make a Ribbon Cord

—LEONA BUTCHART, LAC DU BONNET, MANITOBA, CANADA

You can make ribbon cord from a variety of narrow ribbons and/or crochet and embroidery threads using your machine's bobbin winder. The cords are perfect for making bag handles, button loops, and necklaces.

Begin by attaching 1 yd. or more of ribbon to the hole in your sewing-machine bobbin (a small crochet hook makes this easier). Place the bobbin onto the machine's bobbin winder (or use a stand-alone winder) with the tied end facing out. Hold the ribbon end taut in one hand, and engage the winder until the strand twists tightly. Stop the winder, and fold the strand in half. It will twist itself into a tight cord. One yard of ribbon produces about 18 in. of cord—shorter if it's tightly wound; longer if it's loosely wound. Tie a knot close to the bobbin before removing the strand, and use the finished cord to embellish another sewing project!

Give Garments Temporary Bling

—PENNY WIEBE, LAKEVIEW, OR

Add beads and bangles, trims and jewels, and even quilted postcards as patches to everyday jeans, jackets, dresses, and shirts with wash-away thread, and when it's time for the laundry or dry cleaner, simply spritz the back of the clothing with a bit of water and remove the embellishments. With a few easy stitches, yesterday's garments have a new look for whatever tomorrow brings, and can be replaced with new embellishments when needed.

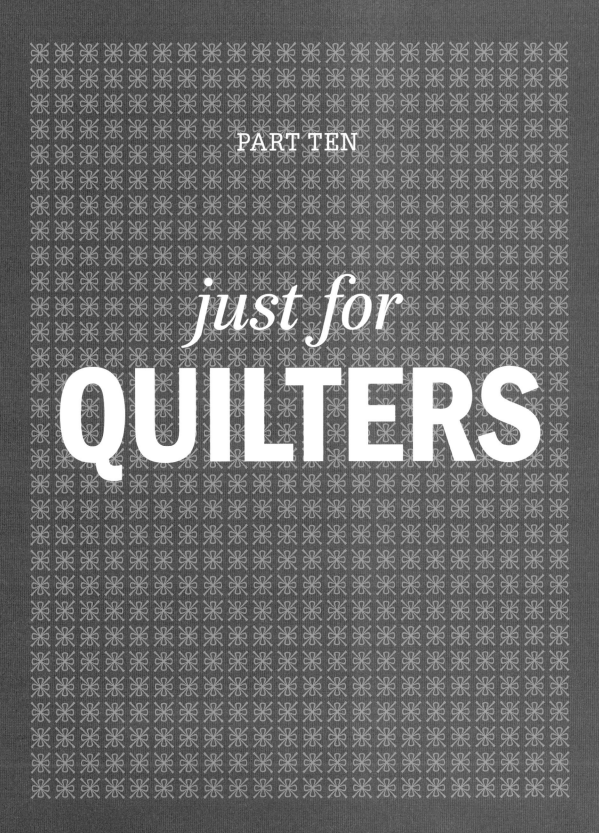

PART TEN

just for
QUILTERS

QUILTING WORKSPACE

CREATING A WORKSURFACE

Raise a Dining Table

—CAROL SUMRALL,
SUGAR LAND, TX

Many sewers use a dining-room table for cutting, pinning, and so forth, but some find the worksurface tends to be too low, which can be hard on the back, even for cutting one pattern. To resolve this issue, try placing 7-in. bed risers under the legs of the table. With it raised it to the perfect height, there will be more comfortable access to cutting board, rotary cutting mat, tabletop ironing board, and so forth, and it will be easier to cut out patterns, cut and piece quilt blocks, lay out pieces to pin, and iron oversize items without a backache. Bed risers are easy to set up and take down, and are reasonably priced. This new "elevated" workspace can also be a wonderful place to wrap gifts and work on other projects.

HOW TO MAKE A HUGE SEWING SURFACE

For those who sew large projects (like quilts), cutting, sewing, and pressing are easier and more accurate on a large sewing surface that supports the entire project. Fabrics don't stretch from hanging over the edge of a small table, and stitches are more even without the weight of the fabric tugging on the feed dogs. Chances are you don't have a surface that large waiting for you and your quilts. Here's how to create a large surface when needed.

Place a rectangular, banquet-type folding table next to a counter or island surface in your kitchen. If these surfaces have different heights, create "sleeves" from PVC pipe (the length equal to the difference in height between the counter or island and folding table), and place one over each leg to raise the table's height. The worksurface is doubled. PVC pipe is available fairly inexpensively in plumbing-supply stores or hardware stores. Specify the "schedule 40" variety to get the strongest pipe. Measure from the right-angle bend on the table leg to the floor or wherever the sleeve would "catch." Cut the plastic to size with a hacksaw blade.

To store the pipe, thread a bungee cord through the finished sleeves and hook them under the folded table. Consider also creating and storing other lengths of pipe to correspond to the heights of other surfaces or your sewing machine. In addition to being helpful and useful, these PVC pipe leg extenders are also quite stable.

—VALERIE REINHOLD TABER, ORANGE PARK, FL

ORGANIZING AND STORING MATERIALS

Use Manila Folders to Organize Fabric
—JOANNE M. SPENCER, BROOKFIELD, CT

To make it easier to put away leftover fabric after a quilting session and also to prevent neatly stored fabric stacks from becoming messy in the process of putting loose fabric away, place an unfolded manila file folder on top of a fabric stack and easily and efficiently slide the extra loose fabrics on top. This won't disturb the fabric below the file folder, and the file folder can be easily removed when it's time to access the excess scraps.

Make a Homemade Magnetic Pincushion
—LARA DILG, ISSAQUAH, WA

A strong, flat magnet works perfectly to pick up, remove, and store quilting pins. When cleaning up your workspace, run the magnet "pincushion" an inch or two above your sewing surface and floor to collect any stray pins. Always remember: Do not store magnets near any computerized product, which it will damage. Also, the magnet will not pick up fine dressmaker's pins, which are made out of brass.

Strengthen Curtain Rod Quilt Hangers
—M. PARFITT, SACRAMENTO, CA

Adjustable, telescoping curtain rods can be bent by hanging heavy quilts over them, creating a bow in the center. All that's needed to stabilize a drooping quilt rod is a 1-in.-diameter inexpensive PVC pipe (the kind used for lawn sprinkler systems), cut to the length of the quilt's rod pocket. Slide the pipe through the pocket, then feed the curtain rod through the pipe. Most hardware stores will trim the pipe to your specifications at no charge.

Make a Pin Wall
—STEPHANIE SANTMYERS, GREENSBORO, NC

Create a pin wall using two sheets of Armstrong 2000 board (a 4-ft. by 8-ft. sheet available at most lumberyards). The soft white surface accepts pins better than most boards. Cut around wall outlets with a blade and cover them with childproof caps to avoid pinning in the wrong place. Attach the boards to the wall with screws, adding a 1½-in. washer at each to prevent buckling. Tighten the screws every year or so. To keep your designs in line, draw in a 6-in. grid with a pen.

HOW TO CREATE WALL STORAGE FOR ROLLS & TUBES

Many quilting materials can be stored by rolling them up: interfacings, stabilizers, fabric scraps, even patterns. Here's how to create a handy storage unit to keep them on the wall out of the way.

1. Get a 12-in.-wide scrap of fabric or canvas, a dowel or metal rod also about 12 in. wide, and a few empty cardboard tubes from paper towels.

2. Make a list of the items you need to store, adding to the count to allow for future items.

3. Multiply the number of items by 6 in. to determine the length of fabric you need.

4. Staystitch the edges of your fabric strip, serge them, or leave them raw. Fold the short ends of the strip together, measure 1½ in. down from the fold, and stitch across, creating a casing for the dowel that will hold the unit to the wall.

5. Mark off from that stitching 3-in. divisions along the remaining length and stitch across at each mark, making casings for the tubes. (If using any wrapping paper tubes, mark off 3½-in. divisions for each, and more for any casings for larger rolls.) The tubes will make it easy to slip your rolled items into and out of storage once the roll holder is hung on the wall.

6. Finish the raw edges at the ends of the strip with simple rolled or folded hems.

—DOROTHY FUSSELMAN, CHAGRIN FALLS, OH

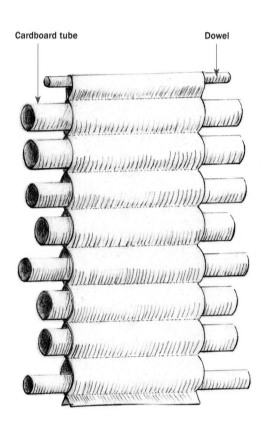

Cardboard tube

Dowel

QUILTING MATERIALS & TOOLS

FABRIC

Test Fabric for Colorfastness
—SOLANGE HAWKINS, MARIETTA, GA

Even if quilt fabrics are run through a wash cycle once before using them, it may not be certain whether dark- or red-toned fabrics will bleed color later. To test them further, stitch a scrap of dark and light fabric together and place the stitched swatch in a microwave-safe bowl of hot water. Microwave on high until the water boils. In a matter of minutes, whether the fabric will bleed or shrink will become obvious.

Crisp Fabric for Increased Precision
—JILL CARY, FRIDAY HARBOR, WA

For pressing quilting projects, dilute concentrated liquid starch according to label directions and use a spray bottle to moisten each seam before pressing it. This liquid "spritz" gives a crisp finish and makes for precision in subsequent seams.

THREAD AND NEEDLES

Make Your Own Thread Dispenser
—JEAN CROSS, CHANUTE, KS

Here's a great way to simplify cutting lengths of thread. Find a pill bottle large enough to hold a spool of thread. Next, remove the thread cutter from a dental-floss dispenser. Cut slots in the bottle cap to fit the cutter, and melt a hole in the side of the cap with a hot ice pick for thread to pass through. The spool will stay neatly in a bottle, and the thread is readily available to cut.

Prevent Metallic Thread Breakage
—ROXANNE MCELROY, ROSWELL, GA

Metallic thread tends to fray and break easily when hand quilting. To prevent this, use short lengths of thread, no more than 12 in. long. The thread has a nap; sew with, not against it. Knot the end cut from the spool. A little Fray Check squirted on fingers and rubbed along the thread helps to keep it from fraying.

Use Water to Stiffen Thread
—KATHIE HOLLAND, MORRIS PLAINS, NJ

Hand-quilting thread dipped in water and left to dry stiffens, which makes sewing through quilt layers easier. Use the extra-strong, cotton-wrapped polyester thread found in most sewing and craft-supply stores.

Use a Crochet Hook to Conceal Thread Ends

—EDITH FRANKEL, HANNAWA FALLS, NY

When an unexpected thread end shows up on a quilt project and is too short to thread through a needle in the usual way, first put the needle in, and then thread it. If the stray thread is too short even for this, use a very fine steel crochet hook (size 13 or 14) to pull it inside. The hook is so thin that it will go between the threads of the fabric without breaking them, and it won't leave a hole.

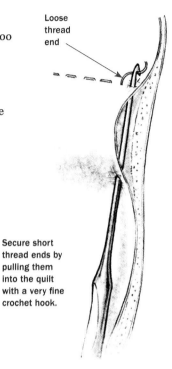

Loose thread end

Secure short thread ends by pulling them into the quilt with a very fine crochet hook.

....

Thread Needles in Advance to Speed Quilting

—LOUISE OWENS, OLD HICKORY, TN

When quilting or doing a lot of hand sewing, thread several packages of needles onto the spool of thread, wrap the tail a few times around the spool, and catch the end in the notch. When a new needle and length of thread is needed, unwind the thread and slide all the other needles down. After the thread is rewrapped and caught in the notch, cut off the already-threaded length.

....

Use a Rubber Shelf Liner to Grasp Needles

—DEBRA ARCH, KEWANEE, IL

Try using a small square of rubber shelf liner to pull sewing needles through heavy, difficult fabrics. The texture of the shelf liner is great for grasping smooth sewing needles and works especially well when hand-sewing leather or denim, or pulling a needle through the multiple layers of a quilt when tying it. Always keep a piece close at hand when quilting.

....

Pull Needles with Surgical Gloves

—SANDRA TEBBS, TREMONTON, UT

Instead of reaching for a little rubber "grabber" disk to pull a needle through stiff fabric or quilting, snip one or two fingers from a pair of snug, lightweight surgical gloves, and slip these on the fingers used for grabbing. They won't affect dexterity, and they're quite comfortable.

Use Rubber Kitchen Gloves for Gripping

—CAROL WARDROP,
KELOWNA, BRITISH COLUMBIA, CANADA

Use yellow rubber kitchen gloves for free-motion quilting. They fit perfectly, grip wonderfully, and help push the fabric accurately under the needle.

BUTTONS

Make a "Buttoned" Quilt

—LINDA GRIGNOLO,
WELLESLEY, MA

Here's a trick for you to hold a quilt's layers together without sewing zillions of stitches. Sew tiny flat buttons through the layers in place of ties. Sew buttons on one or both sides of the quilt. Remember to use very flat buttons, especially if the quilt is meant for sitting.

Use Buttons as Purse Feet

—ARDRA M. WITHERS,
ORANGE PARK, FL

To protect the fabric on the bottom of quilted purses, sew buttons as "feet." This keeps the fabric clean longer and reduces wear and tear. Coordinate the feet to the fabric in the purse.

TOOLS

Keep Leather Thimbles from Slipping

—ALICE MARIE WAY,
ALTA LOMA, CA

Stop a leather thimble from flying off when the needle or thread catches it by inserting a loop of $\frac{1}{4}$-in. quilter's tape, sticky side out, inside the tip of the thimble. This will tack the thimble to your fingernail for the duration of the quilting session.

Use a Quilt Ruler

—LAURA SABBAN,
WEST ORANGE, NJ

To use a clear quilt ruler to position pattern pieces quickly along grainlines, place the pattern on the fabric and the quilter's ruler on top of it, lining up one edge of the ruler with the selvage or edge of the fabric. All that's needed then is to wiggle the pattern until the grainline arrow matches or is parallel to one of the lines on the ruler—no measuring or repinning required.

Use a Ruler with a Rotary Cutter

—DARCY FALK,
FLAGSTAFF, AZ

To use a ruler as a cutting edge with a rotary cutter, measure along the straight grain of fabric, then use the ruler to position the sturdy acrylic cutting edge. When satisfied with the placement, slide out the ruler and make the cut.

QUILTING TECHNIQUES
& methods

MARKING

Use Post-it Notes to Mark the Spot

—MERRILIE BROWN,
CHAPEL HILL, NC

Put Post-it Notes to mark measurements for cutting perfectly sized quilt-block pieces. The Post-its leave no residue and are easier to manipulate than masking tape. This method can help avoid mistakes, especially while cutting in the midst of interruptions and distractions.

Mark Quilt Tops with Tracing Paper

—DAWN LESLEY STEWART,
HOLLISTON, MA

Pencil or chalk quilting lines, drawn directly on quilt tops, have a way of rubbing off before the quilting is finished. Try tracing the quilting design onto tracing paper and pin the paper to the quilt so it doesn't shift. Quilt through both the paper and the quilt layers, pulling the quilting thread just enough so that it breaks through the paper. When finished, unpin the paper and easily pull it free. This method is especially helpful for quilting on fabric on which drawn lines are hard to see.

HOW TO MARK A WHOLE-CLOTH QUILT

• To mark a quilting design, draw the pattern full size on paper and outline it with black magic marker. Use a water-erasable pen to trace onto the quilt top by pinning the cloth over the pattern. If the top is light colored, the black outlines make a light table unnecessary.

• Lay the top, batting, and back on a table and smooth out wrinkles. Pin the edges together every 4 in. with small safety pins. Reach under and pin at 10-in. to 12-in. intervals all over the quilt.

• Start quilting in the middle, using a 10-in. wooden hoop with screw tension. Each time you reposition the hoop, check to see that there are no wrinkles. Remove the safety pins from inside the hoop area.

• To remove the pen marks from the quilt, agitate it in the machine on the gentle cycle with cold water for a few minutes. Then place it in the dryer for a short time to fluff it, and finish drying it by laying it flat on a table overnight. Or, hang the quilt on a clothesline and spray it with cold, clear water until the marks are gone. Let it hang till dry.

• At the edge, cut rounded corners and set eyelets in from the edge of the top with just enough excess to finish off the fell line on the back.

—PAULINE BROWN, FREDONIA, KS

Keep Quilt Lines Straight

—DESIREE DOUCET,
ROSWELL, GA

Frustrated by trying to accurately mark long quilting lines before sewing them? Try spreading the fabric out on the floor. Then use a chalkline to mark the lines on the fabric. The chalk will wash right out (but always test fabric before beginning).

Mark the Seamline Only to Save Time

—BARBARA CONTE GAUGEL,
NORTH SYRACUSE, NY

The process of marking every $\frac{1}{4}$-in. stitching line can be tedious, and sometimes inaccurate due to the instability of some fabrics. Solve this problem by marking the seamline on only the more stable of the two pieces to be joined. This is especially useful when joining a bias piece with one cut on the straight of the grain, since the bias piece tends to stretch and can cause distortion in the final product. In addition to allowing for more precise measurement, this method cuts marking time in half.

BASTING

Use a Bed for Quilt Basting

—KATHLEEN VINCENT,
STAUNTON, VA

Here's a satisfactory way to fasten the back of a quilt down while sandwiching the back, batting, and top. Strip the sheets from your bed and use T-shaped upholstery pins to secure the back layer against the mattress at the top and sides. Pinning the batting and top to a sturdy backing is then very easy. When it's time to baste the layers together, you'll feel the needle hit the mattress surface, since it's much more densely woven than the project. The result is a basted quilt in record time, and no worry about catching extraneous fabric in stitching.

Maximize Margins

—HALLIE WALKER,
MATTHEWS, NC

While pin-basting your quilt, add extra batting to the margins and pin scraps of quilting fabrics there to have the same fabric, batting, and backing readily available to test stitches or design before starting on the actual quilting. After all quilting is complete, simply cut off the excess margins and finish the edges.

PIECING

Tear Fabric Instead of Cutting

—MARCY TILTON,
CAVE JUNCTION, OR

I recently designed and sewed a pieced duvet cover with several large expanses of fabric. Of course, I wanted the grain to be perfectly straight, so I tore the fabric into the proper sizes whenever possible, which is much easier than pulling a thread across the fabric and cutting. However, pulls and tugs along a torn edge often show beyond the seam, so I've learned to tear the fabric about $\frac{1}{2}$ in. larger than needed. Later I trim away $\frac{1}{4}$ in. from each edge using a rotary cutter and a clear 24-in.-long quilter's ruler.

Press for Better Piecing

—STEPHANIE SANTMYERS,
GREENSBORO, NC

Quilters strengthen seams by folding them to one side rather than opening them, but the added bulk makes one-sided seams hard to press flat. Seminole piecing requires flat seams to ensure accurate cutting and assembly, so here are some ways to press seams flat. Soft or thick fabrics should have the stitching pressed in before the fabric is opened out. Work on the face of the piecing with the seamed side down and use the iron's long edge to "strike" against the folded seam as the iron passes sideways across the seamline. Use an iron with the sharpest edge on its soleplate (the less expensive models usually have the sharpest edges). Avoid stretching the work by reserving steam pressing until all the piecing has been completed.

Arrange Unpieced Pieces

—MARY BETH BELLAH,
CHARLOTTESVILLE, VA

Once all your fabrics are in place when designing a quilt top, here's how to keep them arranged while you piece them together. Lay a length of clear contact paper, sticky side down, over the faceup arranged pieces, patting it gently to make sure they're all attached. The pieces are held securely but lightly until peeled off, there's no residue or fraying, and it's easy to replace or rearrange the pieces later. Best of all, the contact paper rolls up or folds without disturbing the pieces, so it can be taken on the go, as well as help to store quilts-in-progress securely in very little space.

Keep Your Layers Straight When Safety-Pin Basting

—CHRIS HUDSON,
DOWNERS GROVE, IL

When safety-pin basting a quilt, it is often the closing of the safety pins that disturbs the layers of the quilt and causes them to misalign. Here's how to avoid this. Tape the quilt backing, pulled taut, to the floor. Layer on the batting and quilt top. Start at the center of the quilt and pin out to the four corners, but do not close any of the safety pins till they are all in place and you are satisfied with their placement. Now when closed, the layers will remain undisturbed.

BINDING

Bind Quickly with Nylon Fleece

—JEANNE HARMON,
SEBEC, ME

Instead of binding quilts in the traditional way, speed up the process and keep the edges soft by cutting 1-in. strips from colorful nylon fleece. Since fleece does not ravel, simply fold the strip over the edge and attach it with a zigzag stitch around the border. It looks great and is much quicker to do than traditional binding.

HOW TO TIE A QUILT INVISIBLY

Antique crazy quilts rarely have ties that are visible from the front, since the ties would conflict with the intricate feather-stitch embroidery characteristic of this type of quilting. The backs of these quilts sometimes feature simple double-thread tacks tying the quilt together. Here's a method for tying a crazy quilt without any visible knots on the quilt top.

Crazy quilting is usually pieced by the foundation method, in which the patchwork is sewn first to an inner foundation fabric. Stitch the ties from the back, catching the foundation fabric only. It's possible to get the same effect on a regular pieced quilt by catching the ties in just the seam allowances.

Assemble the layers of the quilt. (Crazy quilts usually have no batting, but this will work even if you use batting.) Using a sharp or a crewel needle, poke the needle tip from the quilt back all the way through to the top at the spot where you want the tie. Slowly withdraw the needle, allowing only the quilt top to slip off the point. The needle is now inside the quilt layers.

Now, turn the needle back toward the bottom of the quilt, catching the foundation fabric and coming out the back. At this point, either tie the ends, or take another short stitch catching the foundation fabric again and then tie.

—CINDY ZLOTNIK ORAVECZ, CORTLAND, OH

Position for Yarn-Tied Quilts

—NANCY CAMPERUD,
WATSONVILLE, CA

Here's an accurate method to position quilt ties from the top when knots on the back are desired. Align and baste the quilt layers together. Then, work all yarn ties before pulling the tails to the back. After checking their placement, knot the tails.

Quilt top

Quilt back

Pull tails
to back.

Tails ready to
be tied.

Tie tails
together

MACHINE QUILTING

Make Machine-Embroidered Crazy Quilts

—LORI BOSINOFF,
SAN JOSE, CA

Machine-embellished quilts are strong and sturdy. They can be used daily and with abandon. A modern way to topstitch Victorian-style crazy quilt tops is to use a machine's decorative stitches. To achieve the best results, experiment with a sample patch or two. After patches are shaped, add the sewn embellishments along the seam edges that form the patches. Try mixing utility stitches and decorative stitches, and using fancy threads (such as Sulky rayon thread). When the right combinations are found, keep the stitches in proportion to the patch sizes. To be fancy, add pictograms (an image-embroidery process found on some electronic multistitch machines) to the center of the patches.

Uncover the Dogs When Machine Quilting

—SHARON SAUSER,
EUGENE, OR

Free-motion machine quilting calls for lowering the feed dogs to allow the quilt to move in any direction while stitching. If the feed dogs on your machine don't lower, the usual solution is to cover them so they won't catch on the fabric. If the cover leaves little room for the quilt layers under the presser foot, try leaving the cover off, then set the stitch length to zero so the dogs still go up and down with every stitch but don't interfere with the movement of the quilt.

HOW TO USE ZIGZAG STITCH TO STAY OUT OF THE DITCH

I've been trying for years to master the "stitch-in-the-ditch" method for binding my machine-sewn quilts and garments.

After sewing the binding on one side of the quilt, wrapping it around the raw edges to the back, the challenge is to stitch on the top side exactly at the seamline (in the ditch) to anchor the folded-under binding on the wrong side. Ideally, the ditch-stitching catches the underside's binding with a neat line of stitches, but that's easier said than done.

Even after meticulously basting the binding, my understitching wanders out of place here and there. The solution makes lemonade from a lemon: Instead of using a straight stitch-in-the-ditch, I now sew with a multistep-zigzag or wavy stitch, and use the ditch only as a guide. With decorative thread in the machine's needle and bobbin, the results look intentional.

—MARY BAJCZ, MILFORD, MI

Replace a straight stitch-in-the-ditch with a wavy or multistep-zigzag machine stitch, and the binding will look good on both sides.

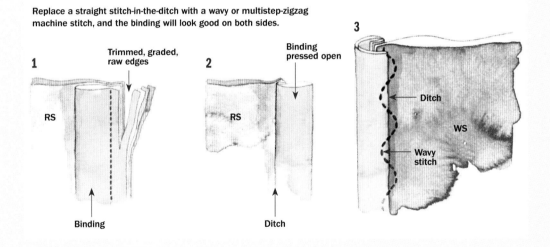

USING TEMPLATES

Isometric Orthographic Paper for Quilters
—ART SALEMME, RIVERDALE, MD

It is possible to make 30-degree or 60-degree angles for diamond, hexagon, and triangle templates without using a compass or drafter's triangles to divide a circle into six equal segments. Buy isometric orthographic paper at a drafting- or engineering-supply store to draw templates of any size easily. Try drawing the templates small and enlarging them on a copying machine.

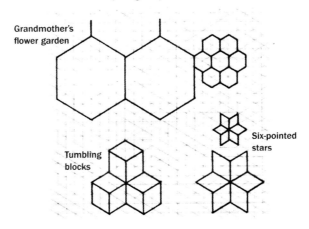

Quilting templates

Grandmother's flower garden

Six-pointed stars

Tumbling blocks

Make Multiple Templates
—BARBARA DIEGES, SOUTH PASADENA, CA

To generate lots of identical paper appliqué templates, try this quick trick: Draw the template shapes needed on one sheet and stack this atop three to six layers of template paper. For multiples of six, draw each shape more than once on the top sheet. Before cutting, staple once through each shape. This keeps the layers from shifting as you cut, and keeps the templates organized until it's time to use them. Separate with a staple remover for best results.

Manage Bulky Templates
—EDITH FRANKEL, HANNAWA FALLS, NY

To keep bulky cardboard quilt templates from slipping during marking, use double-sided sticky tape on the back of the template. Put a small piece of the tape on each corner and one in the center. Position the template on the fabric as usual. After cutting the fabric, the template will easily peel away from the fabric. The tape remains on the template so the template can be reused. To store sticky templates, place them on polyester film (Mylar) or waxed paper.

Keep Mylar Templates from Slipping

—SUE ANN SULZER, SYOSSET, NY

A thin coating of rubber cement can prevent Mylar quilting templates from slipping. Allow the cement to dry thoroughly before using the template. To remove the cement, rub a finger over the surface, rolling the cement into a ball, and lift it off.

Use Sandpaper Templates

—MRS. O. W. OLSON, MILL BAY, BRITISH COLUMBIA, CANADA

Quilting templates cut from sandpaper, placed rough side down on the fabric, stay in place while being traced or cut. For added adhesion, coat the template back with a temporary adhesive. Put the adhesive on all the corners and sharp projections, allowing the adhesive to dry thoroughly. The template will stay put for marking or cutting, but will easily pull away from the fabric. To avoid damaging the fabric, never leave a coated template on the fabric overnight.

Try Templar as a Template Material

—PAT ANDREATTA, WARREN, OH

Templar is an appliqué template material that can take the heat of irons and the moisture of spray starch without curling up, wearing out, or conducting heat like copper does. Available in quilt stores, it's transparent, easy to cut and write on, and unlike with other template plastics, shapes can be printed on it with a laser printer, great for those with computer quilt-design software.

Rebind Books for Easier Tracing

—JANET PIETRYKOWSKI, TOLEDO, OH

To copy quilt templates printed in softcover books when the binding is too tight for the book to lie flat for easy tracing, take the book to a full-service office supply store and have the bound edge replaced with a comb binding. The open book will then lay flat, and the new binding will recapture pages that have come loose.

QUILTING CARE, PREVENTION & REPAIR

CARING FOR THE QUILTER

Protect Your Knees

—PAT DICKINSON,
ESCONDIDO, CA

Some quilters protect their knees from hard floors with gardening knee pads. Another innovative way is to strap on a pair of carpet and floor tile individual knee pads with Velcro straps, which can be purchased inexpensively at local home-builders stores. Comfortable and highly portable!

Prevent Safety-Pin
Calluses

—DEBRA ARCH,
KEWANEE, IL

When pin-basting a quilt, use a 2-in. screw to easily close the safety pins. Simply insert the safety pin, bring the point up through the top of the quilt, and use the threaded shaft of the screw to lift the pin point. Then grasp the locking end of the pin and bend it down to lock over the pin tip. The screw saves a lot of wear and tear on fingers, especially when basting a large quilt.

PREVENTING TEARS

Make Quilt Ties
That Don't Tear

—LORI M. GRAHAM,
SAULT STE. MARIE, MI

Try backing each quilt tie with a small button. For a softer and less visible solution, stitch through a small piece of fabric that's been backed with a medium-weight fusible interfacing. Either way, ties will stay put.

REPAIRING QUILTS

Repairing Nicks in Quilt Pieces

—EDITH FRANKEL,
HANNAWA FALLS, NY

To repair rotary cutter overcuts and slip-ups that go into the seam allowances of still-usable quilt pieces, try taping over the nicked area with a "magic" transparent tape such as Scotch, staying clear of the seamline, and cutting again correctly. This way the seam allowance edge can still be used to align the piece accurately when you're stitching it to another piece. Don't forget to remove the tape before pressing the piece.

Use a Dry Sponge as a "Thread Eraser"

—JEANNE HARMON,
SEBEC, ME

After quilting, if the pieces are covered with loose threads and lint, brushing a dry sponge over the surface does a great pick-up job. It also works on your clothes.

Mark Removal for Quilters and Embroiderers

—SHARON SPRADLIN-BARRETT,
RICHMOND, VA

A kneaded rubber eraser (available in any art-supply store) doesn't leave eraser marks. Pull the eraser apart and knead it to soften it before rubbing out marks on canvas or fabric. Do the same afterward to clean it. Another way to remove pencil marks left on quilted areas is by dabbing glycerin on them and rubbing gently.

Clean Quilts with Automotive Gunk

—ELIZABETH A. MORIARTY,
ROCKY POINT, NC

It is possible to remove stubborn pencil lines from quilt tops (or any washable fabric) with waterless hand cleaner from the automotive section of a discount store. Just rub a small amount along the pencil line and wash as normal. This works better than most soaps because hand cleaner is specifically designed to remove grease, the culprit in troublesome pencil marks.

CONTRIBUTORS

The tips in this book have been pulled from past *Threads* issues. Special thanks go to our editors, contributors, and readers for sharing them.

A

Tia Abell, Vancouver, British Columbia, Canada
Gail Abrams, Cordlandt Manor, NY
Tenley Alaimo, Binghamton, NY
Louise Allen, Durham, NC
Martha Allen, Hamilton, Ontario, Canada
Meg Allen, Rochester, VT
Sophie P. Allen, Charlotte, NC
Mary Allenspach, Winchester, WI
Brandy Anders, Biggs, CA
Barbara L. Anderson, Urbana, IL
Lenore Anderson, Rochester, NY
Mimi Anderson, Tacoma, WA
Pat Andreatta, Warren, OH
Charlotte Andrews, Haverford, PA
Mary Applegate, Belchertown, MA
Debra Arch, Kewanee, IL
JoAnn Armor, Goodrich, MI
Patricia Armstrong, Prescott, AZ
Carol Ashendorf, Norton Shores, MI
Zany Aslam, Newark, DE
Carolyn Aurand, Dixon, IL

B

Mary Bajcz, Milford, MI
Anna Maria Balzarini, Brewster, MA
Val Barbaro, Pittsfield, MA
Marilyn Barksdale, Rehoboth Beach, DE
Peggy Barnes, El Paso, TX
Nancy Barr, Auke Bay, AK
Sheilah Barrett-Sandler, Northampton, MA
Belva Barrick, Glendale, AZ
Yelena Yantovskaya Barth, Centerville, VA
Mrs. John Bates, Clearwater, FL
Pamela Beach, Dearborn, MI
Eleanor Bearden, Granite Bay, CA
Wylie Beckert, Santa Barbara, CA
Patricia Beecher, Horseheads, NY
Joy Beeson, Voorheesville, NY
Mary Beth Bellah, Charlottesville, VA
Shirley W. Belleranti, Mesa, AZ

Cathy Bennett, Okemos, MI
Joan T. Benson, Midland, MI
Jeanette Bernstein, Cranston, RI
Mary-Ann Bielec, Niagara Falls, NY
Georgiane L. Bishop, San Francisco, CA
Carrie Black, Henderson, NV
Brenda Blackwood, Burlington, Ontario, Canada
Evelyn Blake, Roanoke, VA
Mary Blakeslee, Burlington, VT
Kathy Blinco, Doylestown, OH
Elizabeth Blodgett, Morristown, NJ
Dianne Boate, San Francisco, CA
Sue Bogan, Springfield, VA
Betty Bolden, Bolton, CT
Brenda Bolin-Sandage, Batesville, AK
George A. Bolton, Norwalk, CT
Nancy Borger, Washington, DC
Bee Borssuck, Scottsdale, AZ
Lori Bosinoff, San Jose, CA
Linda Boston, *Threads* contributor
Carolyn Bottomly, Fort Meade, MD
Brenda Boudreau, Halifax, Nova Scotia, Canada
Rosemary Bowditch, Ann Arbor, MI
Mildred Bowles, Framingham, MA
Jo Boyd, Fort Collins, CO
Julie Brady, Chandler, AZ
Michele Brakewood, Van Nuys, CA
Judith Brandau, Butler, PA
Eva Braswell, Bloomington, IL
Mary Anne Bredemann, Kansas City, MO
Anne K. Brenz, Cadillac, MI
Dolores Broberg, Shelton, WA
Nancy Brockland, St. Louis, MO
Catherine Broman, Inverness, FL
C. Emma Brown, St. John's, Newfoundland, Canada
JoAnn Brown, Harrisburg, PA
Karen Minturn Brown, Livonia, MI
Merrilie Brown, Chapel Hill, NC
Pauline Brown, Fredonia, KS
Sherri Brown, Brooksville, FL
Norma Bucko, *Threads* contributor
Carolyn Bullock, Cape Coral, FL
Samantha Burgin, Warwick, RI
Barbara Burnett, Fort Worth, TX
Elisheva Bush, Jerusalem, Israel

Louise Bushell, Cheshire, CT
Leona Butchart, Lac du Bonnet, Manitoba, Canada
Karin Buus, Ellington, CT

C

Virginia Caine, Tuscaloosa, AL
Stacey Callahan, Toulouse, France
Tonya Campbell, St. Joseph, MO
Nancy Camperud, Watsonville, CA
Dorothy Cardi, Commack, NY
Sheila Carnegie, Victoria, British Columbia, Canada
Lois Carroll, Parma, OH
Jill Cary, Friday Harbor, WA
Claudie Chan, Green Valley, AZ
Patricia Chapman, Doylestown, PA
Donna Kaye Childress, Carencro, LA
Julie Chisholm, Guelph, Ontario, Canada
Corrie Chorba, Urbana, IL
Donna Christopher, Denver, CO
Sharon Cirrito, Niagara Falls, NY
Edith Clark, Nepean, Ontario, Canada
Sheila Clark, Orinda, CA
Darleen A. Clemens, Seattle, WA
Patricia Clements, Madison, TN
Linda Cobb, Lexington, KY
Peggy Codner, Whitinsville, MA
Jane Conlon, Eugene, OR
Mae M. Conner, Daytona Beach, FL
Marguerite F. Connors, Danvers, MA
Gail Cooper, Toronto, Canada
Frances Cowan, Atlanta, GA
Ann Cristaldi, Atkinson, NH
Shirley J. Crooks, Walnut Creek, CA
Pamela Crosby, Dataw Island, SC
Roberta Crosby, Burnaby, British Columbia, Canada
Jean Cross, Chanute, KS
Audrey Cummins, Hayesville, NC
Patricia Cunningham, Ballwin, MO
Michelle Cureton, Hackett, AZ
Carol Curtis, Bellflower, IL
Juliette Curtis, Leeming, Western Australia

D

Esther D'Abate, Painesville, OH
Karen D'Alessandri, Pomona, NY
Elisa Dalrymple, Austin, TX
Lynette Damian, Milford, MI
Donna Davio2s, Steubenville, OH
Phyllis Davis, Lakewood, CO
Juanita Dean, Nashville, TN
Mrs. Nat Dean, Santa Fe, NM
Carol S. DeBaets, Charlotte, NC
Marjorie DeBenedictis, Tamuning, Guam
Christianne DeHart, Chico, CA
Joyce Deloca, Medfield, MA
Jamie DeMumbrum, Loveland, OH
Elisa J. Denaburg, Aiken, SC
Marjorie Dequincy, Sacramento, CA
Helen De Roo, Silver Spring, MD
Nellie Dery, Van Wert, OH
Pat Dickinson, Escondido, CA
Barbara Dieges, South Pasadena, CA
Mariahne Dietrich, Chatham, Ontario,
    Canada
Lara Dilg, Issaquah, WA
Katy Dill, Jacksonville, FL
Trudy Dixon, Platte Woods, MO
Kristine Donohue, Carmichael, CA
Daphne Dooling, Burlington, Ontario,
    Canada
Linda Doran, Greendale, WI
David Doren, Minneapolis, MN
Betty Dorfan, Houston, TX
Fay M. Dorr, West Palm Beach, FL
Desiree Doucet, Roswell, GA
Cheri Dowd, Aiken, SC
Hélène Muriel Doyle, Valcartier Village,
    Quebec, Canada
Dee DuMont, Bainbridge Island, WA
Elaine Duncan, Purdin, MO
Cynthia Dunn, Nederland, CO
Patty Dunn, Corpus Christi, TX
Donna Dunann, Canyon Lake, CA
Jean Dunning, Cromwell, CT

E

Janet Earnhardt, Utica, PA
Desiree Eckert, Levittown, NY
Jan Ede, Pender Island,
    British Columbia, Canada
Tess Edwards, St. Clair Park, Dunedin,
    New Zealand
Ann Ehrlich, North Collins, NY
Patricia C. Elkovitch, Skaneateles, NY
Suzie Elliott, New York, NY
Corinne Elworth, Orrtanna, PA
Janice Engle, Aurora, IL
Claude English, Sebastopol, CA
Melissa Ennis, Arlington, VA
Diane Ericson, Carmel Valley, CA
Ann Estey, Boulder, CO

F

Holly Rowe Faber, Williamsburg, VA
Darcy Falk, Flagstaff, AZ
Adeline D. Farmer, Superior, WI
Keith Farmer, Newark, NJ
Carol Farrant, San Francisco, CA
Martha Fee, Centerport, NY
Sondra Feldstein, Bondurant, IA
Jean Fengler, Sheboygan, WI
Elizabeth Ferguson, Canal Winchester,
    OH
Patricia "T. C." Ferrito, Angola, NY
Bernice Yutan Firestone, Winnetka, IL
Judith Flatley, Sterling, VA
Theresa Flynn, Longueuil, Quebec,
    Canada
Arlene Fox, Burnaby, British Columbia,
    Canada
Edith Frankel, Hannawa Falls, NY
Carol Fresia, Danbury, CT
Ann Marie Froehle, St. Paul, MN
E'Anne Frye, Topeka, KS
Bonnie Bledsoe Fuchs, Chapel Hill, NC
Dorothy Fusselman, Chagrin Falls, OH

G

Stephanie Gajewski, St. Thomas, Ontario,
    Canada
Ruth Galpin, Southport, CT
Gayla Gardner, Houston, TX
Natalie Garrity, Baltimore, MD
Barbara Conte Gaugel, North Syracuse, NY
Sally Gelbaugh, Georgetown, TX
Mary Gibbins, Glenburnie, Ottawa,
    Canada
Aleta Giddings, Surrey, British Columbia,
    Canada
Mrs. Carol Gilfillan, Bethel Park, PA
Stephanie Corina Goddard, Easton, MD
Jean Good, East Earl, PA
Judy Gordon, Elk Grove, CA
Nancy L. Gould, Hockwold, Thetford,
    United Kingdom
Lori M. Graham, Sault Ste. Marie, MI
Terry Grant, Ashland, OR
Doris Gray, Blythewood, SC
Mary E. Green, Toledo, OH
Druann Greer-Cisneros, Costa Mesa, CA
Crystal Griffiths, Baker, FL
Linda Grignolo, Wellesley, MA
Ginny Groat, Watkinsville, GA
Jan Grover, St. Paul, MN
Jean Gunnells, Dover, DE

H

Joyce A. Hall, Horizon City, TX
Heather Hamilton, Ottawa, Ontario,
    Canada
Christine Hammill, Manchester, WA
Louise Hampton, Lithonia, GA
Lois Hannula, Hillsboro, OR
Mary Hardenbrook, Huntington Beach,
    CA
Josephine Harkness, Topeka, KS
Jeanne Harmon, Dover-Foxcroft, ME
Jeanne Harmon, Sebec, ME
Doris Harris, Searcy, AR
Shirley Hastings, Kamloops,
    British Columbia, Canada
Frederika Hausman, Naples, FL
Solange Hawkins, Marietta, GA
Beth Hayes, Rhinebeck, NY
Chris Haynes, Seattle, WA
V. Heckenthaler, Dortmund, Germany
Susan Heidenthal, Penn Run, PA
Ann Henry, North Highlands, CA
Linda Henry, Fair Oaks, CA
Teresa Hering, Tukwila, WA
Susan Herrmann, Damascus, OH
Mary Ann Hickey, Chicago, IL
Cheryl Hilbrands, George, IA
Jane E. Hill, Longmont, CO
Dianne Hillemeyer, Anchorage, AK
Diana Hilliard, Oakville, Ontario, Canada
Beverly Hilton, Pembroke Pines, FL

Debra Hiraki, Burien, WA
Mary Anne Hirschfeld, St. Marys, OH
Pam Hobson, Anacortes, WA
Kathie Holland, Morris Plains, NJ
Janet Homec, Hudson, WY
Jolee Nail Horn, Charlottesville, VA
Stanley Hostek, Seattle, WA
Fredericka Housman, Naples, FL
Chris Hudson, Downers Grove, IL
Paula Hudson, Green Valley, AZ
Lauren Hunt, East Lansing, MI
Ginetta Huntress, Novato, CA
Karen A. Hurst, Altadena, CA
Dianne Huston, Morton, IL
Susan Hutchins, Sagamore Beach, MA
Alison Hyde, St. Louis, MO

I

Susan Infante, Lisle, IL
Edna Isaac, Tulsa, OK

J

Nancy Jackson, Shalimar, FL
Jacquelyn Jacobi, Victoria,
    British Columbia, Canada
Rita Jacobson, Fountain Valley, CA
Margaret James, Kingswood,
    South Australia
Mrs. Mary Ann James, Owego, NY
Dawn A. Jardine, Red Hook, NY
Jann Jasper, New York, NY
Marilyn A. Jensen, Fremont, CA
Dale Jenssen, Taos, NM
Tomasa Jimenez, Lyndhurst, NJ
Patricia Jinkens, Oxford, OH
Becky Johnson, Chilliwack,
    British Columbia, Canada
Carla H. Johnson, Baltimore, MD
Dorothy Johnson, Topeka, KS
Sue Johnson, Valdosta, GA
Lois Johnston, Calgary, Alberta, Canada
Pamela Johnston, McMinnville, OR
B. Randy Johnstone, La Luz, NM
Bill Jones, San Francisco, CA
Gwen Jones, Niagara Falls, Ontario,
    Canada
Jannaford Jones, Altadena, CA
Sarah Colley Jones, Carthage, TX

Sonya Jones, Berwick, Nova Scotia,
    Canada
Nancy Jung, San Francisco, CA
Lois Jungas, Canton, CT
Gerri Jurisson, Sun City, AZ

K

Kristine Kadlec, Los Angeles, CA
Louise Kammer, Pleasant Hill, CA
Marianne Kantor, Bondville, VT
Jean Kaplan, Phoenix, AZ
Beth Karjala, Munice, IN
Shirley Kates, Newtown, CT
Frecia Kelly, Renton, WA
Martha Kelly, Brooklyn, NY
Barbara Kelsey, Valley Village, CA
Rochelle P. Kenny, New York, NY
Manal Khalife, Windsor, Ontario, Canada
Susan Khalje, Glenarm, MD
Juliette Kimes, Dripping Springs, TX
Edna Kish, Epworth, GA
Marsha M. Kitt, Two Hills, Alberta,
    Canada
Tricia Klem, San Luis Obispo, CA
Susan Klement, Tucson, AZ
Susan Knight, Bay Village, OH
Mary Louise Kobe, Middletown, DE
Mrs. Leo Koellner, San Bruno, CA
Robbin Koller, Patterson, NY
Margaret Komives, Milwaukee, WI
Nannette Konstant, Flourtown, PA
Donna C. Kornfeld, Denver, CO
Marty Korwin-Powlowski,
    West Chester, PA
Tatiana Kosova, Montreal, Quebec,
    Canada
Virginia Kotecki, Scotts Valley, CA
Doris Kourt, Bartlesville, OK
na Krajewska, Beverly Hills, CA
Jessica Krakow, San Francisco, CA
Lauren Kramar, East Lansing, MI
Linda Kuras, Portland, OR

L

Susan Lafo, Spring Valley, CA
K. M. Laing, Capitola, CA
Julienne Lambre, Rome, Italy
Kay Lancaster, via *Creative Machine
    Newsletter*

Heather Langemann, Lethbridge,
    Alberta, Canada
Catherine Laplante, Montreal, Quebec,
    Canada
Jennifer Larson, Frederick, MD
Audrey Lear, Comox, British Columbia,
    Canada
Judy Leathley, Toowoomba, Queensland,
    Australia
Judy Lee, Shreveport, LA
Carla Leinbach, Charlotte, NC
Monty S. Leitch, Pilot, VA
Gwendolyn LeLacheur, Harsen's Island,
    MI
Pam Leland, Jamestown, CO
Barbara Lenz, Seattle, WA
Gail Leone, Cedar, MI
Judy Leslie, Coquitlam,
    British Columbia, Canada
Frankie Leverett, Atlanta, GA
Gita Levin, Cinnaminson, NJ
Jenny Lewis, Portsmouth, NH
Cheryl Licht, Palmer, AK
Barbara E. Lies, Riverside, IL
Jean Linton, Adell, WI
Deborah C. Little, Alva, FL
Jennifer Lobb, Nanaimo, British
    Columbia, Canada
Judith Long, Cranberry Township, PA
Mary Longren, Holton, KS
Kyria LoScalzo, Hemlock Shores, CT
Rebecca Lowell, Santa Rosa, CA
Pat Lowther, Augusta, ME
Marvis Lutz, Portland, OR

M

Nancy Macaulay, Micanopy, FL
Tindy MacBain, Ann Arbor, MI
Annemarie Macfadyen, Chester,
    United Kingdom
M. Elaine MacKay, Thamesford, Ontario,
    Canada
Susan Mackenzie, Grants Pass, OR
Alida Macor, Martinsville, NJ
Dorothy Madias, Hampton, SC
Effat Maher, Victoria, British Columbia,
    Canada
Jan Mahusky, Painesville, OH

Lynn Mally, Irvine, CA
Grace Maloney, Oakville, Ontario, Canada
David Mangels, Woodinville, WA
John Mangiapane, Naugatuck, CT
Gail Manning, North York, Ontario, Canada
Liv Manzer, Victoria, British Columbia, Canada
Safeyyah Mar, Saint Paul, MN
Cathie Marano, Lake Hopatcong, NJ
Jean Margolis, Sebastopol, CA
Aileen Margulis, Jericho, NY
Margaret Marinucci, Langhorne, PA
Dorothy R. Martin, Rockville, MD
Elizabeth Martin, Seattle, WA
Joy Masters, Fairfax, VA
Elizabeth Mattfield, Long Beach, WA
Ellen Maurer, Boulder, CO
Anna Mazur, Avon, CT
Robin Mazzola, *Threads* art director
Jane McCartin, Brush Prairie, WA
Mary Jane McClelland, Diamond Bar, CA
Karen McCormic, Many, LA
Linda McCoy, Oostburg, WI
Darlene McDonald, Black Creek, British Columbia, Canada
Roxanne McElroy, Roswell, GA
Myra Mae McFarland, Fort Wayne, IN
Janet McGlynn, Neenah, WI
Mary McGuire, Houston, TX
Nancy McKenzie, Waverley, Nova Scotia, Canada
Martha McKeon, Sandy Hook, CT
Shirley McKeown, Adelphi, MD
Emily McNamara, Goodhue, MN
Carol McNeal, New Orleans, LA
Diane McNevich, Newark, DE
Susan Delaney Mech, Plano, TX
Patricia Meeks, White Salmon, WA
Retha Meneghini, Escondido, CA
Elizabeth Merritt, Saint Paul, MN
Julia Mesnikoff, Colorado Springs, CO
Joan Meyer, Brunswick, GA
Maureen Tayse Miller, New Carlisle, OH
Nancy Miller, Atwood, KS
Patricia Miller, Dallas, OR
Phillida B. Mirk, Islesboro, ME
Samina Mirza, Katy, TX

Sandy Moeckel, Los Gatos, CA
April Mohr, *Threads* contributor
J. W. Monko, St. Louis, MO
Mary Mooney, New York, NY
Andrea L. Moore, Spokane, WA
Betty J. Moore, North Bay, Ontario, Canada
Susan Morgan, Salt Lake City, UT
Elizabeth A. Moriarty, Rocky Point, NC
Janice Morrill, Waterford, MI
Kathleen Morris, Augusta, GA
Patricia Morrow, Erie, PA
Martha Moser, Evanston, IL
Grace Mullins, Putnam Valley, NY
Teresa Murders, Salem, OR
Colleen Murphy, Louisville, KY

N

Debbie Nacewicz, Wilbraham, MA
Barbara Nachtigall, Roslindale, MA
Laurie Nauss, Sauquoit, NY
Catherine Neff, Muscoda, WI
Ruth Neitzel, Merrillville, IN
Erin Nesmith, Enid, OK
Eve Ness, Saxtons River, VT
Judith Neukam, *Threads* contributor
Michelle Newcome, Atlanta, GA
Sarah Nock, Marietta, GA
Karen Noe, Cedar Rapids, IA
Shirley A. Nooyen, Elk Grove, CA
Lavada Norko, Ellicott City, MD
Dolly Norman, Long Island, NY
Heidi Normandin, Madison, WI
F. Novarra, Tualatin, OR
Barbara Nowich, Kansas City, MO
Susan Nunn, Raleigh, NC

O

Eileen Olmstead, Madera, CA
Mrs. O. W. Olson, Mill Bay, British Columbia, Canada
Cindy Zlotnik Oravecz, Cortland, OH
Julie Ormsby, Memphis, TN
Evelyn Owens, Roanoke, VA
Louise Owens, Old Hickory, TN

P

L. D. Pace, Toledo, OR
Jennifer Pakula, Croydon Park, Australia

Marina Rodriguez Palacios, Buenos Aires, Argentina
M. Parfitt, Sacramento, CA
Bernadette Parrish, Cockeysville, MD
Antonio Patterson, Brooklyn, NY
Yvonne Paul, Winter Springs, FL
Charlene Pawluck, Charlottetown, Prince Edward Island, Canada
Robin Peabody, Naperville, IL
Mrs. Lee Pecora, Massapequa Park, NY
Leslie Pelecovich, Stamford, CT
Peg Pennell, Omaha, NE
Ilya Sandra Perlingieri, San Diego, CA
Zee Perry, Escondido, CA
Cindy Peterson, Myrtle Point, OR
Rachel Pfaffendorf, Clear Lake, SD
Marge Pfeil, Arroyo Grande, CA
Julia Pickett, Houston, TX
Charlene Pierce, Marshall, Saskatchewan, Canada
Janet Pietrykowski, Toledo, OH
T. J. Pike, Hurst, TX
Lonnie Piposzar, Pittsburgh, PA
Lois Pitcher, Ithaca, NY
Julie Plotniko, Parksville, British Columbia, Canada
Marli Popple, Armadale, Victoria, Australia
Susan Pottage, Colorado Springs, CO
Susanna Prentiss, Head of Chezzetcook, Nova Scotia, Canada
Anna Presland, Seattle, WA
Ann M. Prochowicz, Trempealeau, WI
Myra C. Propst, Shelby, NC
Laura Proudfoot, Palos Heights, IL
Linda Przbyszewski, Charlottesville, VA

Q

Connie Quarré, Bellevue, WA

R

Terri Ragot, Groton, MA
Paula Rak, Wrangell, AK
Judy Rand, Coconut Creek, FL
Sheri Rand, Eugene, OR
Kathryn Ray, Richmond, VA
Marie Rebello, Mississauga, Ontario, Canada

Nan Reber, El Segundo, CA
Luanne B. Redwood, Chicago, IL
Carolyn Rehbaum, Altamonte Springs, FL
Blanche Rehling, Millstadt, IL
Anna Victoria Reich, Albuquerque, NM
Phyllis Rettke, Bellevue, WA
Lucille Rewick, Millington, NJ
Julie Rhodes, Cedar, MI
Wanda Rice, Lyons, CO
Dorothy Richards, Escondido, CA
Elizabeth Lee Richter, Huntington, CT
Ellen J. Riggan, Gloucester, VA
Susan Riley, Sudbury, MA
Mary Rino, Bountiful, UT
Nora Roark, Fortuna, CA
Jennifer Robison, Ravenna, OH
Linda Rock, Winnipeg, Manitoba, Canada
Michelle Rodman, Amarillo, TX
Janet Rogers, Dorset, Ontario, Canada
Luisa Rojas, Washington, DC
Lynn Roosevelt, Greenville, SC
Debra Rose, Crystal Beach, Ontario, Canada
Ellen Rose, Dallas, TX
Phyllis Rosen, Aiken, SC
Anne Ruby, Brookline, MA
Elaine Rutledge, Chunchula, AL
Elizabeth Rydman-Harris, Santa Fe, NM
Jim Ryerson, Victoria, British Columbia, Canada
Elizabeth Rymer, Hurricane Mills, TN

S

Laura Sabban, West Orange, NJ
Betty Sager, Spring Valley, CA
Art Salemme, Riverdale, MD
Suzanna Sandoval, Bellevue, WA
Stephanie Santmyers, Greensboro, NC
Angélique Sarolea, Vista, CA
Sharon Sauser, Eugene, OR
K. C. Saxe, Sioux City, IA
Lynn M. Schelitzche, Burnsville, MN
Jeanne F. Schimmel, Hobe Sound, FL
Cecelia Schmeider, Pelham, MA
Helen M. Schmidt, Brooks, Alberta, Canada

Sandi Schmitt, Gaston, OR
Shirley Schoen, San Francisco, CA
Jan Scholl, State College, PA
Diane Schultz, St. Paul, MN
Candy Schwartz, Greenfield, WI
Shelly Scoresby, Hansen, ID
Merrilyn Scott, Jacksonville, FL
Alis M. Wintle Sefick, Baldwinsville, NY
D. Self, Aurora, CO
Aries Selwood, Columbia, SC
Jane Seright, Coldstream, British Columbia, Canada
Claire Shaeffer, Palm Springs, CA
Judith R. Shamp, Indianapolis, IN
Deb Sharpee, DeForest, WI
Dottie Sheldon, Winter Park, FL
Elizabeth (Betty) Shelton, Cedar Rapids, IA
Nancy Sherba, Pittsburgh, PA
Eleanor L. Shields, Santa Rosa, CA
Jocelyn Short, Arvada, CO
Corinne Shoulders, Madison, MS
Nancy Shriber, Springfield, VA
Fred Shultz, Burtonsville, MD
Lorelee Sienkowski, Packwaukee, WI
Rene Simpson, Brighton, South Australia
Teresa Simpson, Knoxville, TN
Lorraine Sintetos, Felton, CA
Dorothy Small, Poughkeepsie, NY
Shelby Smarte, Midway, KY
Jean Smiling Coyote, Chicago, IL
Jill Smith, Lincoln, NE
Judith E. Smith, Fanwood, NJ
Parker Smith, Chicago, IL
Patty Smith, Merion, PA
Susan Smith, Delphi, IN
Alyce Julien Smith-Robinson, Donaldsonville, LA
Anne Smock, East Noriton, PA
Jean C. Smolens, Wilmington, DE
Margaret Smrke-Glover, Etobicoke, Ontario, Canada
Barbara Snyder, Sebastopol, CA
Linda Soeder, Kitchener, Ontario, Canada
Linda Sommer, Whitby, Ontario, Canada
Joanne M. Spencer, Brookfield, CT
Jean K. Spero, Columbus, OH

Sharon Spradlin-Barrett, Richmond, VA
Johanna St. Clair, Port Jefferson, NY
Vicki Tatum Stammer, Arlington, TX
Diane Starkey, Cedar Rapids, IA
Ann Steeves, Burlington, MA
Marsha Stein, Waterbury, CT
Teri Stern, Chapel Hill, NC
Carol Claire Stevens, Jackson, MI
Dawn Lesley Stewart, Holliston, MA
Phyllis Stillwell, El Cajon, CA
Sherry Stockton, Kitchener, Ontario, Canada
Beverly C. Stone, Encinitas, CA
Susan Stone, Amelia Island, FL
Carol Stoner, Denver, CO
Emmy Storholm, Heron, MT
Pat Storla, Moscow, IN
Margaret C. Story, Goodrich, MI
Cindi Stowell, Round Rock, TX
Susan Strange, Glencoe, IL
Lucille Stutsman, Lincoln, CA
Darlene A. Suchyta, Dearborn, MI
Mary Sullivan, Framingham, MA
Sue Ann Sulzer, Syosset, NY
Carol Sumrall, Sugar Land, TX
Christine Sutherland, Perth, Western Australia, Australia
Arlene Swain, Kissimmee, FL
Jane Swanson, Lucca, Italy
Karen Sweeney, Hartwell, GA
Susan Sweet, Richmond, CA

T

Valerie Reinhold Taber, Orange Park, FL
Ann Taecker, Watertown, SD
Pamela Tallman, Huntington Beach, CA
Claudette Taylor, Ellsworth, IA
Norma Taylor, Oro Valley, AZ
Sandra A. Tebbs, Tremonton, UT
Lynn Teichman, Lewisburg, PA
Susan Terry, Norfolk, VA
Lucy Thompson, Livingston, TX
Helen Thorkelsen, Bonnylake, WA
Tisha Thorne, Washington, DC
Sandra Thwaites, Oakville, Ontario, Canada
Marcy Tilton, Cave Junction, OR
Toni Toomey, Woodbury, CT

Heather Torgenrud, St. Ignatius, MT

Alice Townsend, Vero Beach, FL

Stephanie Trelick, Pittsburgh, PA

Susan Trousdale, Hartington, Ontario, Canada

Katia Tsvetkova, San Francisco, CA

Mrs. Gerald Tubbs, Penn Yan, NY

Lesley Tucker, Sarnia, Ontario, Canada

Jane Tutton, Vero Beach, FL

V

Victoria Valdes-Dapena-Hiltebeitel, Collegeville, PA

Antoinnette Valla, Dix Hills, NY

Jane VanBemden, Oviedo, FL

Marie Van Bockern, Spokane, WA

Diana Van Der Sluys, Calgary, Alberta, Canada

Sheryl VanDusen, Kamloops, British Columbia, Canada

Patricia Ann Van Maanen, Friday Harbor, WA

Sandra Vassallo, Rozelle, New South Wales, Australia

Viola Clara Vaughan, Indianapolis, IN

Sarah Veblen, Sparks, MD

Linda Velsor, Catawba, NC

Lisha Vidler, Cordova, TN

Linda Vielhaber, Sterling Heights, MI

Kathleen Vincent, Staunton, VA

Liz Violante, Marco Island, FL

Linda Lee Vivian, Lennon, MI

F. William Voetberg, Grand Rapids, MI

Helen von Ammon, San Francisco, CA

W

Jean Wachs, Anderson, SC

Kathy Wagner, Seattle, WA

Kay Wagner, Ph.D., Golden Valley, MN

Muriel Waits, Mt. Orab, OH

Hallie Walker, Matthews, NC

Kathy Walkowski, Pewaukee, WI

Carol Wallace, Waldorf, MD

Caroline Wallace, Barstow, CA

Carol Wallis, Beverly, MA

Robin Ward, Poulsbo, WA

Lena M. Wardell, Burlington, Ontario, Canada

Carol Wardrop, Kelowna, British Columbia, Canada

Alice Marie Way, Alta Loma, CA

Lisa Weatherall, Bloomington, IN

Mary E. Weaver, Savannah, GA

Teena Wedemeyer, Dawson Creek, British Columbia, Canada

Mrs. M. D. Weeks, Fort Lauderdale, FL

Beth Wehrman, Maxwell, IA

Grace B. Weinstein, Los Angeles, CA

Mattie Welch, Alna, ME

Jenny Wesner, Indianapolis, IN

Diane J. Whippie, Kent, WA

Beverly White, Longmont, CO

Peggy White, Springfield, MO

Stephanie White, Schaumburg, IL

Sylvia Whitesides, Lafayette, IN

Nancy Whiting, Lancaster, PA

Barbara Wickham, Carmichael, CA

Penny Wiebe, Lakeview, OR

Suzan L. Wiener, Spring Hill, FL

Laurie Wilcox, Palm Desert, CA

Candice E. Williams, Rocky Mount, NC

Susan Williams, Lakewood, CO

Lisa Willis, Huntsville, AL

AnnMarie Wilson, Garland, TX

Joanna Wilson, Dover, DE

Sharon Wilson, Wavell Heights, Queensland, Australia

Stephen Wisner, Maplewood, NJ

Ardra M. Withers, Orange Park, FL

Wendy Witter, Peace River, Alberta, Canada

Chris Wojdak, La Mesa, CA

Gayle Wolfe, Victoria, British Columbia, Canada

Karen Roth Wolff, Aliso Viejo, CA

Karen Wolff, Laguna Hills, CA

Karen Wong, Round Rock, TX

Louise Wonnocott, Rockhampton, Queensland, Australia

Sandra Lee Woods, El Paso, TX

Barbara Worden, Mechanicsburg, PA

John J. Wordin, Shelley, ID

Louise Worman, Deposit, NY

Meryl S. Wynne, Victoria, British Columbia, Canada

Y

Peggy D. Yackel, Plymouth, MN

Jean Yaeger, Novato, CA

Amy T. Yanagi, Millersville, MD

Gail Yano, Potomac, MD

Lily Yost, Des Moines, IA

Cynthia Young, Fresham, OR

Philippa Young, Busbridge, Godalming, Surrey, England

Z

Kathy Zachry, Springdale, AR

Arlene Zajicek, Memphis, TN

Shirley Zak, Montara, CA

Dorothy Zaleski, Southington, CT

Anna Zapffel, Key West, FL

Dana Zaruba, Cobble Hill, British Columbia, Canada

Laura Ziemer, Portland, OR

Judy Zifka, Bend, OR

Caroline Zimmermann, Lancaster, CA

Chana Zweig, Philadelphia, PA

ILLUSTRATION CREDITS

Part 1
p. 22: Clarke Barre

Part 2
pp. 32, 53, 93: Karen Meyer

pp. 33, 40, 57, 68, 77, 79, 81, 84, 89, 95, 96, 101, 109, 110: Clarke Barre

pp. 37, 44, 59, 78: © The Taunton Press, Inc.

p. 42: Frank Habbas

pp. 46, 85: Carol Ruzicka

pp. 54, 58, 75: Threads Staff

pp. 61, 74, 98: Robert LaPointe

p. 66: Kathy Bray

p. 82: Linda Boston

Part 3
pp. 115, 128, 130: Clarke Barre

p. 116: Robert LaPointe

p. 23: David Page Coffin

Part 4
pp. 139, 146: Christine Erikson

pp. 139, 152: Clarke Barre

Part 5
p. 178: Karen Meyer

p. 180: © The Taunton Press, Inc.

p. 186: Carol Ruzicka

pp. 187, 200: Robert LaPointe

pp. 190, 198: Clarke Barre

p. 201: Linda Boston

Part 6
p. 206: Robert LaPointe

pp. 210, 215: © The Taunton Press, Inc.

p. 214: Carol Ruzicka

p. 217: Threads Staff

p. 218: Karen Meyer

p. 220: Michael Gellatly

p. 222: Linda Boston

Part 7
p. 229: Mariah Graham

p. 230: Karen Meyer

pp. 231, 234: Clarke Barre

p. 233: Carol Ruzicka

p. 235: Robert LaPointe

Part 8
p. 244: Karen Meyer

p. 245: Carol Ruzicka

Part 9
pp. 277, 281, 285, 288, 291, 293: Clarke Barre

p. 278: Threads Staff

pp. 283, 295: Carol Ruzicka

p. 284: Lainé Roundy

pp. 290, 296: © The Taunton Press, Inc.

p. 291, 294: Frank Habbas

p. 294: Christine Erikson

Part 10
p. 303: © The Taunton Press, Inc.

pp. 306, 313, 315: Clarke Barre

p. 314: Christine Erikson

METRIC EQUIVALENTS

One inch equals approximately 2.54 centimeters. To convert inches to centimeters, multiply the figure in inches by 2.54 and round off to the nearest half centimeter, or use the chart below, whose figures are rounded off (one centimeter equals ten millimeters).

⅛ in. = 3 mm	9 in. = 23 cm
¼ in. = 6 mm	10 in. = 25.5 cm
⅜ in. = 1 cm	12 in. = 30.5 cm
½ in. = 1.3 cm	14 in. = 35.5 cm
⅝ in. = 1.5 cm	15 in. = 38 cm
¾ in. = 2 cm	16 in. = 40.5 cm
⅞ in. = 2.2 cm	18 in. = 45.5 cm
1 in. = 2.5 cm	20 in. = 51 cm
2 in. = 5 cm	21 in. = 53.5 cm
3 in. = 7.5 cm	22 in. = 56 cm
4 in. = 10 cm	24 in. = 61 cm
5 in. = 12.5 cm	25 in. = 63.5 cm
6 in. = 15 cm	36 in. = 92 cm
7 in. = 18 cm	45 in. = 114.5 cm
8 in. = 20.5 cm	60 in. = 152 cm

INDEX